Shadow Child

An Apprenticeship in
Love and Loss

Beth Powning

VIKING

VIKING
Published by the Penguin Group
Penguin Books Canada Ltd, 10 Alcorn Avenue, Toronto, Ontario,
Canada M4V 3B2
Penguin Books Ltd, 27 Wrights Lane, London W8 5TZ, England
Penguin Putnam Inc., 375 Hudson Street, New York, New York 10014, U.S.A.
Penguin Books Australia Ltd, Ringwood, Victoria, Australia
Penguin Books (NZ) Ltd, cnr Rosedale and Airborne Roads, Albany,
Auckland 1310, New Zealand

Penguin Books Ltd, Registered Offices: Harmondsworth, Middlesex, England

First published 1999
1 3 5 7 9 10 8 6 4 2

Printed and bound in Canada on acid-free paper ♾

CANADIAN CATALOGUING IN PUBLICATION DATA

Powning, Beth
Shadow Child

ISBN 0-670-87798-0

1. Powning, Beth. 2. Miscarriage – Patients – Canada – Biography. I. Title.

RG648.P68 1999   362.1'98392'0092   C98-932258-0
Visit Penguin Canada's website at www.penguin.ca

To Tate Powning
son, brother, grandchild, nephew, cousin
with love

And to my parents—
patient, wise and endlessly loving

"No other child can take his place, but he has perhaps made a place—a union more complete—for their environment."
—Ann Morrow Lindbergh, *Hour of Gold, Hour of Lead*

"In many cases . . . the patient who comes to us has a story which is *not told*, and which as a rule no one knows of. It is the patient's secret, the rock against which [s]he is shattered."
—C. G. Jung

". . . and after a while it rises and becomes a creature like her, but much smaller.

So now there are two. And they walk together like a dream under the trees."
—Mary Oliver, from "A Meeting"

Acknowledgements

To those people who appear, unwittingly, in this book: Barbara Kolsun, Mark Davis, Bob and Kathy Osborne, Bronwen Martin, Erin Osborne, Akou Connell-Delaney, Russell and Mary Wilkins, Mark Connell, David Powning, Lee Danisch, Bear Legère, Mary Johnson, Claude Bénévente-Loven, Greg McLeod, Dr. Len Higgins and Dr. Mendell Robinson.

To the aunts, uncles and cousins who share some of these memories.

To the Arts Branch of the New Brunswick Department of Municipalities, Culture and Tourism; thanks for the creation grant that helped during the time I was sifting memories, searching for this book.

For technical advice, Ann Swift and Barb McMillan.

To those people who called, wrote, listened and shared during hard times: Peg and Pat Powning, Arnie Becker, Lee Whitney, Bethany Powning, Kathy Hooper, Sue Hooper, Yeti Agnew, Susan

Glickman, Andy Powning, John Crawford, Rachel Connell and Judith Williams.

To those who have opened their hearts and shared their grief: Sue McKay, Lee Saunders, Sonja Carhart, and most especially, Karl Dennis and Cathy Scanlan. To the memory of their beautiful children.

To Aaron Bailey, my friend.

To Dr. W. E. Smith, who helped me sift through the debris.

To Dr. S. Khedheri, most especially, who has stood with me through so many storms. Your caring has helped me heal.

To the people who have helped in the making of this book: Aaron Milrad, my agent; Janice Weaver, the copy editor; and all the people at Penguin who have given their energy and creativity to this project, especially Cathy McLean, Laura Brady and Susan James.

To my editor, Jackie Kaiser, the primary catalyst for *Shadow Child* and the person without whose encouragement I would not have written this book, without whose unfailing support, wise critique of the first draft and insightful editing I could not have made it the book it eventually became.

To my parents, Wendell and Alison Davis, who have listened, endured, laughed, cried, waited, loved.

To my husband, Peter, my best friend—who made this journey with me, whose heart aches in the same measure as mine, whose love has shaped me like a fire—more love and thanks than can ever be expressed.

To my son Jacob—who gave me the courage to write this book, convinced me of its necessity, loved its creation, listened with calm strength as I read parts of the manuscript to him—my deepest love and thanks.

And to all parents, everywhere, whose lost children live in their hearts.

Shadow Child

Contents

Shadow Child

Prologue

As I *surface from sleep*, sounds clarify and become simple. Peter lies on his side with his back to me; I can hear his slow, deep sleep-breathing. The window is cracked open just far enough to bring the April night into our slope-ceilinged bedroom. The brook is swollen with snow-melt; it breaks loose from the forested hills, coils with a breath of ice through the greening pasture, splits around our house and barns, islanding us on high ground, and is gathered by the Hammond River, whose headwaters are in our valley. The rush of waters, darker than wind and steadier, is the sound of northern spring, when what has been stilled runs free.

Something else, though, has awakened me. I lift my head from the pillow. The sound is regular and insistent, like a child calling. A mother instinct sharpens me.

It's an owl. I wait, listening for its deep, wild voice, but I hear only the brook waters. The owl calls again, and then there's an answering call. It comes from the copse in the hill pasture, on the west side of the brook. The answering call is higher. I think of it as a female voice, tough, smaller, more remote. The deep voice calls again, and then their voices overlap, and they call at the same time, continuously.

I listen, propped on one elbow. I think how the owls are like me and Peter. We lie in bed, back to back, and talk to one another in the darkness without seeing each other's faces. We need to know only that the other one is there; that the other one wants to listen, wants to respond. After thirty years of marriage, we need only the brush of a finger on smooth skin to feel less alone, reassured of our primacy in someone else's heart. Although we've each disentangled ourselves, bit by bit, from the thicket of couplehood, and have emerged, scarred, after plucking out thorns of need, resentment, jealousy, competition, compliance, assumption, smothering; although we feel equal, and distinct, and secure in ourselves; still, or increasingly, we realize that it's our love for one another that feeds our separate strengths.

The maple bed we're lying in belonged to my grandparents, who in turn inherited it from my great-grandparents. Its four posts are shaped like pawns in a chess set, pear shapes set on thick, penny-round discs, ending in fluted legs and topped by knobs worn smooth by sleepy hands; the glossy footboard curls at its lip, like a wave. Sometimes I imagine the bed as a ship carrying us through the night, keeping us safe, especially when the winds of February blizzards are so strong that we can feel the house shuddering as if it's alive, its mute timbers expanding like a ribcage.

I love thinking of Granny and Poppy sleeping in this bed, since we're alone here. When we came to this place, in 1972, we never thought about whether we would miss the people we were leaving behind; we were like hawks, circling on the buoyant updrafts of our imaginations. We didn't think about how we would change, or be changed. Rather, we filled notebooks with plans; we made lists; we determined what we would do, and how. We imagined ourselves doing everything we wanted to do, saw ourselves as the people we thought we would make ourselves become.

I slide down onto my side and lie facing the window with my palms pressed together and propped beneath my cheek so my best ear will be able to hear the owls. The notes of their conversation are like amber beads: round, full, complete. Around me, the house, even in its shadowed stillness, feels alive and vital, like the heart of a lily.

We've always slept in this little north-facing room; it doesn't get the morning sun, but from its window we can keep an eye on the barn, with its changing cast of animals (horse, pony, sometimes chickens, once ducks, cow, goats), and on Peter's studio. I can see my gardens, perennial flowers, rows of raspberry canes, raised beds for vegetables. The things in this room that I brought from Connecticut—the bed, a mirror with a blue eagle clutching arrows in its feathered talons, the table with a hole for a wash bowl, an arrow-backed chair—have no intrinsic power, do not keep me moored to the past as I thought they would when I brought them here. I saw them, the morning after we immigrated, strewn randomly on the driveway—chairs tipped with their legs in snow patches, mirrors leaning against the house's peeling paint—and I felt as I did when, as a child, I saw my parents in some strange place and was shocked by their rumpled familiarity, and wanted to put them back where they belonged. I sensed, that morning, that these things, like me and Peter, could never be put back; that they, like us, were patches on a quilt, and that time would fade them, soften their edges, make them part of the fabric until only close scrutiny could identify their careful stitches. Now these things surround me and Peter in the intimate familiarity of our bedroom. The furniture is exactly the same as it was the morning we arrived; the mirrors hang in the same places on the walls, the bed hasn't moved for years. The rungs on the chair are still worn in the same places, from children's feet. These things are no longer part of my past, but have become part of my present. They have their place within this fragile and fleeting composition that I call my life. But they are less changed than I am.

It's me who has changed. I see these things differently. I don't see my granny when I look at the bedpost dimly outlined against the wall, but I hear the sound of weeping as Peter and I cried in this room; or I picture our son, Jacob, when he was two, industriously climbing over the headboard; or I remember how I couldn't fit between the bed and the wall when I was pregnant, but had to go sideways.

Time folds me into its bewildering layers.

Soon I'll be fifty. I'm a mother, a daughter, a wife, a writer. I can state all of these things now without ambivalence. I can see myself almost clearly. I feel my own resignation, my own humility. Oddly, what I've learned is that the making of self is more a matter of yielding than of forcing; it is like a gradual clarifying, and the slow, surprising emergence of an unexpected shape.

In the night, I'm like the mouse that the owls seek. The soft wings of death rise on either side of me and my heart fills with a dread that sunlight dispels. Jacob is leaving for England tomorrow. He's taking himself, like a crudely defined sword, to the forge. He wants to be sharpened, honed; he wants his innate qualities to be tempered. He wants to return with a shape that he himself can see. Or so I imagine. For I can never truly know my son's soul, or my husband's; all I know, absolutely, is that when I embrace them, I can hear their hearts beating and then my own heart swells like a seed in warm soil.

Jacob will make his own mistakes that are nothing like mine. I think he knows more about some things than I did at his age. Do all parents feel this way? Does every generation feel that the succeeding one has come slightly farther, is slightly improved? Yet every parent must watch with pride and anguish, and remember

Shadow Child

how they, at such an age, had no understanding of how the bright, sharp life that they honed with such passion would so soon become blunted, nicked, scarred, even bent or broken.

But I won't tell my son that he can't shape his life. That's not quite true, anyway. I've shaped mine; Peter and I, rather, have shaped ours. It's the extent to which I've been shaped that makes me cry quietly in the night, and the shaping still to come, which I can't anticipate, can't control, can't prevent.

I, too, left home the summer I was seventeen; for a while, I had stern and extravagant plans, and my goals, strong as an icebreaker's prow, defined my path. I couldn't possibly have lived then as I do now, looking back rather than ahead. Now I wear a necklace of stories; I'm not in a hurry to make more. My granny crossed her legs at the ankles, neatly, as she sat knitting, and she tipped her head to one side and watched the stitches gathering on her needles. She'd smile, a lovely, loving smile, although her face was sad. I feel like her. I'm not broken, but I'm nicked and scarred. Sometimes I feel blunted and am surprised at how my passions have shifted, been reassigned. My life is like a dream that I'm trying to understand. Bits float up, come into focus. Details loom. Colours become significant, and strange events seem inevitable. I begin to understand myself. I know, for example, why my son's leaving, which during the day I find exciting, makes me cry at night. I know why I hate to say goodbye to people I love. I understand why I've learned to wait, to yield, to listen, to let events unfold.

In this night, when I'm lying awake and listening to the owls and the lilting waters, when I'm hearing the night come alive with its whisperings, stretchings, soil-stirrings, and I know that in its darkness the daffodils have speared the leaf-matt, the rhubarb licks the soil with its red tongue and frog eggs sway in the pondweeds; in this night, I'm a mother. I'm a mother tossed in the wave of my love; helpless, vulnerable. I'm a mother, whether my son is here or not, whether my son is alive or dead. In this night, I'm also someone's life partner. I know, and am known, in a way that is increasingly irreplaceable. I imagine how differently I would feel if I lay here alone, without Peter. I wonder if I would move through the rooms of the house with an anguished heart, seeking its life and finding only silent space, empty chairs. I wonder how much of myself would be gone if I were without him. I'm a child, too, for my parents are like small gods or angels who travel with me. They are sweet and patient; they forgive even the unforgivable. They've been all the places I have, and arrived there first. They wait for me to understand. And I'm a writer. Without the mirror-life of my words, I'm hollow. I find my life's spirit behind my hands clasped over my face, as I wait for words that will reflect the world and release its beauty. I listen to the owls and I think, "I will write about them," and I feel strong. Then I think of my son alone, on the road, and my heart twists with helpless fear, and yet even so, I feel serious, purposeful. I am both the owls and the mice they hunt. Like the owls, I'll keep calling in the night; like the mice, I'll gather my grasses.

Sometimes I shape; sometimes I let myself be shaped. What I've had to learn is when to do one and when to do the other. Controlling, allowing, they're the plies of strength, they twist around one another like the wool with which I make our winter's mittens. Sometimes we are not meant to choose. Sometimes we are meant to let ourselves drift, be tossed, lie bereft, like driftwood that has no power of navigation. In old age, restlessness is replaced by patience. I feel it coming, and I know its strength.

I lie curved around my soft belly, which is dappled with blue-silver marks. My body still waxes and wanes, continuing its dark workings, as blood, like the moon, makes a regular and somehow comforting appearance. This small, sturdy body has taken me to places I never imagined, places where Peter couldn't follow. My soul has been driftwood in its sea. I've carried life in my womb, and I've carried death. I've given birth to both.

There's always another child. He's the child we never knew. He's the son we never held. He's the shadow child who went ahead of us, from one mystery to another.

I'm not humble. My parents said I had to learn everything the hard way.

I never thought that the most important path I would walk would be the one that taught me how to love; or that I had to lose the chance to love in order to find my way, stumbling, tear-blind, onto it.

I

1959–1974

Chapter One

Life wraps around me like strong arms. I'm being carried, lost in the dark feathers of sleep. I rise and fall like a bird as someone's legs swing, steady as breath. I'm part of their rhythm, chest-clung, marsupial. I sleep, and yet know that I'm going somewhere. There are lovely dips and glides, voices at the edge of awareness like muttering thunder. Light burns coal-red on the insides of my eyelids. Creak of wooden stairs. My bed comes rising to receive me, a blanket grows up over my shoulders. Some sweet lips press my cheek, and then I'm falling, gliding, into the pillow and beyond, twirling headlong into my own darkness.

The sun keeps track of me. Winter trees shatter its rays into diamonds and they fall in shimmering facets directly onto my bed. I surface from sleep like a fish; one swift tail-flick and then an easy drift upward towards the light. The sun is with me all day, like a friend; it warms my dented spoon, shines in the steam curling from my oatmeal, silvers the red petals of my mother's geraniums. It slants across the floor, where I sit combing the mane of my stuffed pony; the blue shadow-lines of small-paned windows enclose squares of light that shift across the floorboards and bend up the plaster walls when the smell of tomato soup and toast comes from the kitchen. At naptime, I take Golden Books to bed with me; I sleepily absorb pictures of white houses with round shrubs and straight, paved walkways. Mothers in frilly aprons wave at fathers in suits. A robin sits on its nest, its sharp beak wide open and its head thrown back; the bird, like the little girl playing hopscotch beneath its nest, is happy. The book drops from my hand. The sun on its textured page is edged with decline; later, after our naps, my brother and I stumble downstairs into the bonfire light of winter sunset. There's ice on the fields. Lights click on in the neighbour's cow barn; the evening star steps forward in the sky like a ballerina. Our noses are pressed to the window as our daddy comes over the lawn, looking for our faces. He passes into the cold shadow of the back porch, where the cats are milling. I kneel on the couch; I can make black spots with my fingertips on the frost ferns.

We sit in the same places at the table. Our parents sit at either end; I sit across from Mark, who is two years older. The big fireplace is behind me, and I can see my reflection in the windows. When we bow our heads to say grace, I peek at the candle flames and think about how I'll stick my fingers in the hot wax when I blow them out after dessert, which is chocolate pudding tonight. Before supper, my mother put a chair by the electric stove so I could reach the pudding and stir it. "Make a circle and draw a line through it," she told me. She looped back my braid just before it fell into the saucepan.

I don't think I can get up the stairs later. I'm too sleepy. My mother tells me that her father told her, "You can always do one more thing." My grandfather wears rimless, octagonal glasses and takes sunbaths with black plastic eyegoggles that Mark and I try to balance on our noses. His arms are lean, their skin as tough as a turtle's neck and as brown and wrinkly. His fingers lift and settle like butterfly's wings, nervously tapping the back of books when he's reading poetry out loud. The stair treads feel too high to climb. I put my hands on each one.

The sheets are cold when I slide my bare feet between them. My bedroom is unheated. I make myself into a snail, pull my flannel nightgown over my toes. My bedroom has pink-and-white striped wallpaper and a brown stain on the plaster ceiling. The room is tiny and is where my life begins. It's my first place beyond the womb, beyond my own body. All the elements that will shape my life ebb and flow in the shadows as I hear my mother's steps going down the creaky stairs; in the shadows are my father's red-and-black-checked jacket, my granny's knitting basket, wild grapes on stone walls, the smell of cows, the sounds of rippling bathwater and footsteps in church. All these things become the dream from which I will awaken, and the rest of my life will be like the day that follows, wreathed with spirits.

My brother came first. I'm always aware of the fact that he is older. I feel less powerful than him, less important. He and my father tease me. Usually, they don't realize that my rage is not funny to me, although once my father snatches me up and exuberantly tips me upside down when I have a mouthful of saltines. When he realizes that I have fat tears spilling from my eyes and crumbs spraying helplessly from my lips, he is as shocked and remorseful as if he'd stepped on a kitten, and I cry harder because I see how much he loves me.

My mother told me that I was the little girl she'd always dreamed of having. There's a black-and-white photograph of me kneeling on a bench in a loose nightie, looking out a window. My blonde hair, like thistledown, is translucent in the spring light. The little girl looks grave, as if she's contemplating something that she can't quite understand. I look at this picture of myself and remember the confusion of childhood. Children see exactly what they are looking at, and are told that it's something else.

I'm surrounded by people whose deepest feelings are never directly expressed. No adult cries; no voice is ever raised in anger. Mark and I are aware there is a layer of our lives that we have no access to. Conversations stop when we come into rooms; our mother's crossness or our father's silences are bewildering, like strange coats hanging on hooks when there are no visitors.

I strive to overcome the feelings that my grandmother brings into the house with her. She's my mother's mother; her husband, my grandfather, teaches Victorian literature at Brown University in Providence, Rhode Island. They've chosen to be called Mère and Père, from their summers spent in Quebec. Mère is like a bus or a car; something large, with momentum, that won't be able to stop itself if you get in its way. She seems top-heavy, she has a "bust" rather than breasts; she wears a full-body corset that makes her fatness solid, rather than jelly-like. Her cheeks are slab-like, heavy, and carry her mouth down slightly at the corners. Her spectacles glint, like some instrument made to magnify her intense, evaluating stare. Her mind is restless, darts like a fish. She has a university degree, but no position in the academic world. She teaches English to foreign students; they come to tea. She's written, and had published, a children's book. She is delighted by beauty, whether an orange butterfly on red bergamot or a well-proportioned house, and calls these things to our attention, sharing her keen eye, her ready enthusiasm. She's an avid traveller, despite her ailments, and a voracious reader. She has strongly held opinions on world events, which belie, or counteract, her own insecurities, fears, jealousies, passions, expectations, frustrations. She rocks from side to side as she walks and carries a corduroy cushion to sit on. She tells me her feet have been too small to carry her weight ever since she was a child, but she walks with a force that sweeps Père along behind, as if he's her lifeboat, obediently bobbing in her wake. My grandfather laughs frequently, as if its carefree sound will be like oil on water, and he lets his hand drift elegantly on his wrist, like a feather stroking the air. Whenever they arrive at our house, Mère is suffering from the drive and comes through the door needing immediate attention: tea, water, pills. She can hardly greet me and Mark until she's been settled and cared for. My own lack of pain makes me feel unimportant. I evaluate them both, these grandparents, to see why they seem to take my brother more seriously than me.

No one in my family acknowledges the way my grandmother's presence threatens to sweep us from the shore and carry us helplessly out to sea. My father becomes grim. My mother worries about my behaviour, becomes tense and controlled. I'm aware of the change in the atmosphere without knowing why, the way my father and I can step out the back door and swear we smell snow on the air. We don't discuss any of this, ever. Once, Mère says to me, "We're not one of these families who say terrible things about one another." We are one of the nice families. It seems to me that we are supposed to be the people in the Golden Book.

Children don't grow up, but rather grow away. We have different acuities when we're very young, which we lose and then, if we're lucky, rediscover. When I'm little, everything in my world has a name except this dark, atmospheric turbulence. Everyone pretends it isn't there, but I am afraid of it. It's like the place in our dirt-floored cellar that is so frightening that I've never been there: the cobwebby darkness behind the dusty stones of the central chimney.

The men in my father's family are doctors and lawyers. His parents, Granny and Poppy, live in Windsor, Connecticut, in the winter, but spend every spring, summer and fall in the family home in our village. Our house isn't in the village, but lies four miles north.

It's an old farmhouse, mouse-ridden, creaky-floored, painted red. It is surrounded by the cornfields, pastures and hayfields of three dairy farms. Mark and I make treehouses in the woods, wade in rootbeer-coloured rivers. At six o'clock, the suppertime train blows its whistle when it crosses the road; I can't see the train, but the diminishing, steady racheting of its wheels leaves a reverberant and poignant quietness that's taken up, in spring, by the peepers down at the Lewis Pond. Between our house and the village, the road dips into valleys and climbs hills; it passes pine forests and cow pastures that are raggedy, by late summer, with thistles and goldenrod; it skirts ponds where mockingbirds ride cattails and lily pads quilt turtle-infested black waters. The village is one street, which runs along a hilltop; the white spire of the Congregational church rises above the maple trees. Most of the houses were built in the late 1700s; they're large, white-clapboarded, with small-paned windows, and are set back from the street by lawns and stone walls. My grandparents' place has been in our family since it was built. Nothing is ever taken away from it, it seems, only added. The attic is filled with spinning wheels, flatirons, hat boxes. There's a Civil War uniform in a closet, and a sword in a scabbard. There are pince-nez, rock collections, a mahjong set, a side saddle and so much crockery in the pantry that we play store with tiny hand-painted bowls from China and knives with ivory handles. The lawn is terraced; there are three levels, separated by stone walls. Poppy, who is allergic to honey bees and must be heavily veiled, keeps an apiary up behind the compost heap. The grape arbour winds, like a green tunnel, between the stone wall of the upper lawn and the pine trees. Beyond the gardens and lawns, a hayfield runs up to the Catholic church, and beside it is an apple orchard. A windmill rises over the barns, where Poppy keeps a cider press, bushel baskets and his Farmall Cub tractor. Poppy wears khaki pants and a khaki shirt. He wears oiled leather boots and carries a gold pocket watch with a chain.

Shadow Child

His hair is silvery white and he has a big belly. He seldom laughs, but has a grave, sweet smile, especially for me. I love to sit on his lap and tell him stories; he listens as if my capriciousness is a glass of wine, leavening his seriousness. Granny is so small I can lean against her with my head on her shoulder. She is like a glass jar filled with light. There's nothing inside her but love. She makes me feel as if I am her whole world, as if I am the reason she patiently continues to limp through her days, stirring oatmeal, basting turkeys, folding sheets, weeding gardens, planting bulbs, washing dishes. Her little eyebrows, like a terrier's, rise in delight when I come into her kitchen; she limps towards me with her arms wide. Her walls are covered with letters and drawings that Mark and I and our cousins have sent her; she is like a child herself, and we have to keep her from whispering to us what she got us for Christmas. I want to protect her. I treat her like someone who is slightly deaf (as she is) and who neither needs to, nor should, hear everything. I protect her unconsciously, as I am myself protected. I want to believe that I am as wonderful as she thinks I am.

No one in my father's family complains about illness the way Mère does. This is seen as a virtue. I hear my mother use the word "stoic" when describing her in-laws, and I make one of my aunts laugh immoderately when I repeat this observation. I don't know why she finds this so funny, but learn, years later, that she, who married into the family, felt oppressed by their dogged work ethic, their emotional repression. What is buried in my mother's family frightens me, because I sense its hidden anger; but what is unspoken in my father's seems noble, because I sense no pain, only a kind of placid acceptance of tradition, and its preeminence and our subservience to it, so that the place itself, my grandparents' house and barns and gardens and attics, shapes our rituals and dominates our concerns. I learn, from both sides of my inheritance, that feelings are either irrelevant or dangerous. The world of my childhood teaches me to foster harmony, to slide like an egg into my place in the box.

I have secret places. I have a secret life. When I'm very young, and for several years, a voice runs in my head continuously. It is like an omniscient narrator who comments on everything I do. Up on the hilltop, across the stone wall and beyond the pasture where our horses and ponies graze, are our woods. When I go there, I step across a threshold in my head. Groups of trees become a neighbourhood of stone houses; I stoop, entering their low doors, gathering my imaginary hooded cloak around me. I squat by my make-believe fire, stir invisible rabbit stews, talk out loud to whichever character is involved, at that moment, in my unending story. Later, running down the field in winter dusk, I murmur to myself, "It was getting late, so she started home." I spend hours by myself, with myself. Mark and I go to school in the village, travel on the schoolbus. My mother's vision of our life, at that time, is like a kind of spell that she's woven. It's like an iridescent bubble on whose surface slide and blend *The Wind in the Willows*, Beatrix Potter, Tasha Tudor, poetry, health food, Quaker meetings, home-made maple syrup, kittens, puppets and wildflowers. It's fragile, subject to shattering. I'm not sure which world is real, this one or the one that's outside us, the stormy air that our bubble navigates. I'm protected; much besides emotion is hidden. I absorb the fact that pain is not something to share. I sense that the world beyond our home is like a vicious dog that I might pass safely if I walk with my head down, not looking at it, wrapped in myself, disallowing its existence. Our home is not like anyone else's. I'm not quite sure whether I want friends to come visit. I want to protect my home's innocence, which I know I cherish, and yet, obscurely, I sense its frailty; I'm afraid my schoolmates might expose my home to the searing light of their incomprehension, or to ridicule.

Shadow Child

When I'm eight, I have no idea that there's such a thing as my real self, but I do know that I shed my school clothes with relief. I drop them on the floor and let them lie there, my plaid wool skirts with small plastic belts, my round-collared white blouses, my headband with teeth to hold it in place, my Hush Puppies and ankle socks, and I re-dress in clothes that really fit me and make me feel most myself. Like my mother, I, too, have an interior life, a visionary world. Only mine has no outward manifestation as yet; it goes on in my head while I'm riding bareback on my pony, Willie, trotting up the winding lane by the pond and pretending that I'm an English child in Devonshire, going home to tea; or being National Velvet, carrying my china horses up to the woods; or carrying a book (*The Borrowers, A Lemon and a Star, Five Children and It, Fell Farm Holiday*) to the Indian Rock in the hollow of the hill, a giant boulder where Nipmuck women once ground corn, and where I put my feet in the oval hollow worn by their pounding-stones in the rock's surface and prop myself against the young and supple swamp maples, which hide me from the cars and tractors that travel the nearby road.

No one can come between me and the words I'm reading. No one can change them. The worlds I enter are always there, and are always exactly the same. I read some books so many times that I can quote pages from memory. They add a dimension to my own life; when I'm sitting at the supper table, I'm holding something inside me, some sense of possibility, of breadth, of mystery. These places are my own, these moated castles where I play with ghost-children, these nights in which a magic cat turns me into a pigeon, or I fly with my brothers and sisters on a magic bed. I begin to write stories. My grandfather Père is delighted, although he reads them far too fast and without real comprehension. When I'm ten, I have tea, frequently, with Essie Bates, who is a children's author. She lives in the village. I realize that she's just like me, even though she has white hair and smells like dried rose petals.

She spends her life, just as I do, writing down the places she wants to go, creating safe places where nothing changes.

I decide I'm going to be a writer when I grow up.

My recurrent childhood nightmare is about my father. An evil monkey crouches in a corner of my sandbox, which fills the frame of my dream-movie, huge as a beach; up in the right-hand corner, a train hurtles towards my father. My terror of the monkey immobilizes me, and I know I can't move to save my father from the train.

Few children on our school playground in the 1950s talk about what their mothers "do." It's fathers who take risks, whose worth can be measured and compared. All of our fathers belong to the volunteer fire department. I'm awakened in the night by the searing, dispassionate wail of the town fire siren; my father's feet thud to the floor, he hurries past my door wrestling with a shirt. Mark stands in his pyjamas at his own door. We run downstairs and watch as the tail lights of Daddy's pick-up truck recede into the night. He comes home hours later, grim with fatigue, smelling of smoke. Once, his eyelashes are singed to half their length and the hairs of his eyebrows are stubbly, curl at the ends, and stink. I sniff them while my mother watches, her hand making a fist on her mouth.

My father teaches mechanical engineering at the state university. I can't imagine what he really does. When he comes home at the end of the day, he's still stuffed inside the person he's been wearing all day like a suit. I'm shy of this person when I'm little, just as I'm shy of the navy uniform that hangs in the closet. My mother never becomes someone else, and I sense that she is not quite pleased with my father when he first comes home, that she, too, is waiting for him to reappear in his jeans that smell of pine boards and paint. He makes furniture in his shop in the old barn, which is attached to our house by a breezeway. I love to stand by his lathe, feeling sawdust knuckling into my socks, watching golden wood chips spray from his chisel as he makes it bite into the spinning block of wood. The muscles of his forearms bunch like branches. His body is hard. He's tense, he never stops being busy, and when he sits down for supper, his fingers drum the table until my mother's glance warns him to stop, to bow his head, to say grace.

He's the town prosecutor and the first selectman; he rides his horse in the Memorial Day parade, his shoulders squared by his navy uniform. He pounds fenceposts, holds nails in his mouth, helps our neighbours bale hay, can wear dimes in the smile lines beside his cheeks, tells me stories about when he was the lion-tamer in the circus and Mummy was a tightrope walker, elicits squeals by making the blood veins on the backs of his hands wriggle like blue worms.

At the town garage, where I sit on the swivel chair in the office yearning for peanuts from the dispenser, which I can never have, my father and the mechanic bend over the truck's engine, wiping their hands on rags. I make the chair swivel by putting my toes on its rungs, and I stare at the calendars. At the bottom of the month are the names of spark-plug or motor-oil companies in large letters. At the top of the month are large, full-colour photographs of women. They are wearing bikinis and high heels, or they are completely naked except for a garter belt trimmed with lace. They kneel so their rear ends stick up and their breasts are compressed between their arms. Their hair is blonde, flipped up at the ends; they hold their heads back, faces raised, scarlet lips pushed out disdainfully. These are women that are for men. They are like the women in magazines who hold apple pies with lattice crusts or balance immaculate towels on one arm, the other saucily on a hip.

I don't know about Amelia Earhart, Rachel Carson, Ella Fitzgerald, Isak Dinesen. I take it for granted that men do almost everything that's really important. Women have babies and raise families, nurse, teach elementary school, sit behind telephones, typewriters and sales counters. Or pose naked.

When my brother and I pretend to be the Hardy Boys, I'm Joe. When we watch television at our friends' houses, I don't identify with the women in beehive hairdos who sway their hips and serve food to men. I'm the sheriff or the cowboy riding the rearing horse, one hand on my pistol; I'm the lawyer, the doctor, the judge, the boy with the dog. I'm tough and strong, silent and cold. My mother tells me that she named me Beth for the gentle soul in *Little Women*; yet when I read the book, I want to be Jo, the tomboy. My mind sees the shape of my character and makes up a body to match: lean, hipless, muscular. I want to run as fast as the boys can, to swing so high that I make the chains buckle. I want to wear hockey skates and scrap with boys on farm ponds. I'll jump off the roof if my brother dares me to. I'll pick up the dead snake and carry it home. When we ride with the 4-H horse club, my pony, like me, can't bear to be anywhere other than at the front. He's in a full gallop to outpace the larger horses, and I fall and am hurt frequently.

I decide that I am someone who will be, like men, in control. I need to push myself, as if I'm in secret training for a race that I'm not sure, in the end, I'll be allowed to run. I become competitive; I have to be the best; I have to get the grades, win the ribbons, win praise for what I do rather than for who I am. Who I am is a puzzle and a conundrum, not something I'm proud of. I'm still a compliant girl when I have to be. I feel myself change when my feet are encased in slippery dress shoes and I'm wearing white gloves on my hands at Easter. I feel myself becoming someone else; I'm told how pretty I look. I feel that the adults think this

proper and polite girl is who I really am. My sense of falseness
becomes second nature.

I remember my mother less clearly than my father because she is
closer to me, both physically and emotionally. She doesn't go
away and come back. She's like the knothole in my door, which
I can fit my fingertip into, or the sound of willow branches
squeaking against the bathroom window. She's like my surround-
ings; I expect her never to change. When I'm four, I'm distraught
when she gets new eyeglass frames; I cry and am angry. How dare
she be anything other than what I want her to be? Once, when
I'm older, I go into her dressing room and find her, unusually,
naked. She's embarrassed and reaches for her bathrobe. I'm fascinated by her luminosity, the expanse of her pearly flesh, her bottom like a peeled pear. She wraps her privacy away from me, but
giggles; she has a mole between her brown eyes and furrows in
her forehead that she calls worry lines. Her thick hair is short and
flips up around her face, rolls back from her forehead like a cresting wave. She wears rimless glasses whose nose-pads leave pink
dents on either side of her nose; without them, she looks innocent and helpless.

My mother talks to me about selflessness. She tells me that it is
a good quality to have, that I should always put other people's
needs before my own. And yet she's still, herself, trying to come
to some accommodation with this ideal. She does more than keep
house; she does more than fold sheets, ball socks, hang clothes on
the line. She keeps geraniums on the sills of the east windows; sun
shimmers through their red, white and salmon-pink shell-shaped
petals, throws trapezoids of sash-shadow across the blue wainscot
and white plaster walls, gleams on the copper warming pan that
hangs beside the granite fireplace, a fireplace so large that I can

23

stand in it. Across from the hearth is the dining table that my father made; at the end of the room, separated by a counter, is the kitchen where, every morning of my childhood, my mother moves quickly, light-footed, her hands describing the symphony of eggs and bacon, oatmeal and pancakes. Home is a fabric and she weaves it, sliding her shuttle back and forth, making a design that she chooses, thread by thread: the smell of molasses cookies, blue delphiniums against the grey-walled barn, dotted Swiss curtains on the canopy bed, silent grace before meals, poetry read aloud on Christmas Eve, tiny pots of pansies at our places on Easter morning. She calls her mother every morning, says, "Hello, Mother, how are you?" and then, for hours, it seems, talks reasonably about dosages, ointments, prescriptions, heating pads, all the while making sympathetic sounds. She tends other old ladies, in trailers, nursing homes, mental institutions. She takes soup to them, homemade cookies, bouquets of forsythia and pussywillows. She wears a head scarf when she goes out, and carries her gifts in a basket. On Christmas Eve day, our family makes a ritual of visiting all the old people in town who might otherwise be alone. She tells me that home and community go together. She goes to PTA meetings, Ladies Aid, Couples Club, Grange. She runs for the school board and, once, for the state legislature. She starts groups when she perceives the need for them.

But she's doing all these things for someone else. She's doing them for us, or for the old ladies, or for the town, or for the world at large. I want to do something for me. I don't want to be one of the flowers in a bed. I want to do something in my life that's singular. I imagine myself playing a piano on a concert stage; riding a show horse in Madison Square Garden; skating in the Ice Capades; being a movie star.

Perhaps I sense that my mother is not entirely sure she's made the right choices; maybe I sense her frustration, and her jealousy of my father, who is climbing the academic ladder; or maybe I'm confused by the fact that she worships her aunt Bernice, who made the choice to have a career, rather than a family.

My mother tells me I could go to Radcliffe College someday, since Aunt Bernice is the dean. I absorb two messages: I'm supposed to be selfless, do things for other people, put my own needs aside; and yet my parents won't be pleased with me unless I, like Bernice, go to the one of the best colleges in the United States, have a career like those of the brilliant young women whom Auntie describes in her polished, modulated voice. These are the messages I'm receiving, whether or not they are really sent. These are the choices that I feel inside myself, and that seem irreconcilable.

Bernice was born in Calais, Maine; her mother grew up across the river, in St. Stephen, New Brunswick, where Bernice's grandfather owned an axe-handle factory. These are my Canadian relatives, whose world was contained, like a story, within a single phrase—Old Oaks, the name of their house. Bernice speaks of this world as if it holds a magic that she's left behind and yet wants to keep alive by naming its elements: fragrant sweet peas, the raspberry patch and the "shrub" that her aunts made, the tea set and netsuke her missionary aunt brought from Japan. I absorb, without wondering why, the fact that Bernice mourns this place. It's like the mother she never knew, who lived her short life tending its gardens, seeing the river from its windows; who married Bernice's physician father and died of appendicitis when Bernice was five. I sense the shadow of this childhood grief; it wraps around my great-aunt like an invisible cloak. Her eyes, deep-set, hooded with drooping lids beneath strong eyebrows, are complex, seem engaged in inner dialogue, their kindness edged with sadness. I hear sorrow in her frequent, gracious laugh. She's tall and walks slowly, like the queen; she wears suits from Paris in shades of red or pink; she wears heavy rings and brooches rimmed with sapphires. Her white hair is swept into a French twist.

She never had children, although at the age of forty she married a man with a grown family. She doesn't know about children. At Aunt Bernice and Uncle Leonard's summer home in the Berkshires, the treehouse is carpenter-built and has a stair winding round the tree's trunk; it has a perfect tea set inside it. It makes me feel as if my own ideas aren't good enough; as if my own imagination is inferior. I feel like Alice in Wonderland when she sips from the little bottle labelled Drink Me and gets stuck inside the rabbit's house, inhibited by her sudden new size. My usual appearance doesn't belong here; muddy corduroy pants and manure-stained sneakers, my braids flattened, twisted and twig-clung. Mark and I sit with our feet side by side on the white carpet and lift our tea cups while the adults talk about the United Nations, Fulbright scholarships, international law, fellowships. I'm learning the art of concealment, the art of the divided self. I'm accommodating feelings of self-betrayal and self-doubt. I'm acting the role of the child whom my aunt Bernice will approve of, whom my parents can be proud of, as if the other, hidden one isn't suitable

The knowledge of children is different from the knowledge of adults. It's not on the surface, where it can be retrieved and made useful. It lurks, as true and valuable, as deep and forceful, as a dream. I know that my mother loves her aunt Bernice better than she loves her own mother. I know that Mère, my mother's mother, also knows this and keeps it inside her like one of her many lacerating pains. I know that Mère is jealous of her husband's love of Bernice, his beloved younger sister. I know that both my mother and my grandmother feel Bernice has attained some place that they will never reach. I know that they both wish they had achieved this same kind of respect, of recognition. I know that I am supposed to achieve what they did not. I know that if I don't, they will feel I've failed them.

I don't worship my aunt Bernice, although she is one of the only women I know whose value, like a man's, can be added up on a piece of paper. Her name, eventually, will be engraved on a building. What she does has a name, gives her power. What she does affects every lift of her finger, every step of her foot, is as palpable as my grandmother's pain.

I know these things, but I have no idea that I know them. I absorb them the way a child learns language. I let these pieces of information gather in the place where I'm storing the materials for the building of my self.

The walls of my bedroom are covered with pictures of horses cut out of magazines. I pore over a catalogue from an equestrian supply company, just as my brother pores over his hot-rod magazines. I'm in love with English saddles, Pelham bits, braided reins, martingales, black-leather riding boots, jodhpurs and hacking jackets. I own none of these things, but I spend hours brushing my pony's thick mane and weaving red yarn into the braids I make in his forelock. I have one doll, whom I name Kevin for my young boy cousin; he's a baby doll, with a sweet face whose eyes slide open when he's sitting and close when he lies down. The plastic eyelids are timmed with soft lashes. I never play with my doll; I keep him in my closet, tucked under a blanket in a doll's crib that my father made for me. I soon realize that it's unusual for girls not to play with dolls, so I take what comes naturally—a disinclination—as a virtue, as something I've chosen and am proud of. It's a choice I can make that no one can do anything about.

I don't realize that Willie, my pony, is my baby. I take care of him with more real devotion than I'd ever give to a doll. I have to give him hay and water every night from the time I'm seven years old. I love our cats. I love our border collie dog. I love the Johnny-jump-ups that I plant in a section of my mother's perennial garden. I love the pale, thread-stemmed bluets that thrust up through the warm winter grass. I love the beds of purple violets

27

that spread down from the woods and thrive in the cool soil by the spring. I love the venerable oak tree whose massive branches overhang our pond. Love is something that I never name; it's the reverse of those other, dark feelings that also have no name. My own love, and my own ability to love, is not something I can separate from the things and people and animals that I cherish; I know, only, that I want nothing to change, ever; I want nothing, and no one, to leave me. I can't bear the thought of my oak tree dying, or of Willie being hit by a car, or of a bulldozer tearing into the field of bluets. I can't imagine that my grandparents will die, or that our house might burn down, or that our dog could be shot by our neighbour. Love is so much a part of who I am that I know it only as something that shakes my heart with fear. It's like the dream of my father and the train. It's my own helplessness. It's what makes me vulnerable.

I never think about love as something that I will need, in my life, either to give or to receive. I grew up with love, just as I grew up without poverty. Love and money are not goals, since I never lacked them. What I want is not to be someone's little sister or someone's pretty little girl. I don't even want to be someone's mother. I want to be me, separate, distinct, known and respected for what is absolutely my own.

I don't know what fulfilment my mother gets from having children. I don't know who she would be if she didn't have me and Mark. I look at pictures of her in a scrapbook. There she is at work camp in New Hampshire with my father; they're standing on a log dam and she has a corn-cob pipe in her mouth and is sliding her eyes sideways, impishly. She's a teenage girl, not even my father's girlfriend; she's still flirting. But I can hardly believe that's really her, because I know her as mine, although I have to share her with Mark. She's someone I see in pieces, like a jigsaw puzzle. First I lean against her sturdy, warm legs; maybe I pat one with my small hand. I know the hem of her skirt and the stripy, cloth-covered cord of the iron; I hear its gurgling, thumping hiss over my head. I see the reflection of my bedside lamp in her glasses, and sleepily watch her hands turning the pages of a book. We're walking together across the wet grass and she shows me how to pick my feet straight up, carefully, and set them straight down. We're "the girls," like a team; we're the ones wearing white gloves and hats, and when I'm little, I'm proud to be dressed just like her. I hear her wedding ring nicking the edges of cake pans as she turns them like tambourines, tapping flour from their buttered bottoms. She makes a ritual of Christmas cookies, of advent calendars that she draws herself; she takes us into the woods to gather moss for the crèche. I'm unaware that it's she who creates the magic of Christmas. She brushes my hair, which is so long that I can sit on it. Hers are the only hands that gently unpick snarls; that softly gather strands of my hair and fold them, over and across, making my two braids. Hers are the hands that lay warm washcloths across my eyes when I'm sick. She loves being my mother. I, too, am hers; I make her who she is, and yet she can see only pieces of me. We're puzzles to one another, and our lives will be spent watching the pieces come together, seeing the pictures that we hold in our minds gradually coalescing into something different and new; raw and painful until we get used to them.

I don't know, as my aunt Bernice does, what it is to be without a mother.

I think of a mother as something that I have, but I never think of a mother as something that I'll be. I think of being a mother as a kind of trap, since I have no idea of how it has enriched my own mother, or what it really means to her. I see my mother hunched on her chair, doodling with a pencil, listening to her mother's complaint, while time spins in the moted sunlight. I hear about how the childless Bernice travels to Paris, Copenhagen, Tokyo; I hear that she's had lunch with Freud's daughter or the secretary-general of the United Nations. I sense that women who do "nothing" but keep house (as almost all of my friends' mothers do) are shallow, trivial and inferior to men: I absorb this from tone of voice, jokes, male body language, popular songs, boys' comments, the books I read, television, advertisements, playground taunts; from magazines in the dentist's office, where I see women dressed in high heels and gingham aprons, wearing lipstick, where I flip past articles on meringue, bathroom decor, teething, "dressing for hubby" and feel as if I'm reading about prisoners who either don't know they are in jail, or else have done something to deserve to be there. Or perhaps they are there because they can't do anything else. I don't realize how I take my own mother's lovely home-spinning for granted; how I have no true idea of its value, of what it has given me, of who it has made me or of how much of my mother's energy and creativity has gone into its shaping. I have no idea that I'm beginning to absorb the propaganda, to think that the concerns of women are silly, embarrassing, without value. Somehow, I deny the fact that I am going to be a woman.

I don't see the blooming of my body as the miracle that it is. There are no ceremonies to celebrate my fertility, to help me understand that I'm graced with power, that I am like all women now. No one interpets the spill of blood from my body, or tells me that I am as beautiful as the moon, which waxes and wanes, or that I can be serene and majestic now that I have kinship with the tides of the sea, the hidden dens of tigers, the sheaths of apple blossoms.

No one helps me understand my privilege. No one points out to me the expression in a mother's eyes, which someday will be mine. No one tells me I'm the bearer of miracles.

Shadow Child

My mother does the best she can. She tells me the "facts of life." We giggle together, furtively, when she shows me how to wrap my tampon tube in toilet paper and bury it at the very bottom of the wastebasket. I lie on my bed, curled in a fetal crunch, racked with menstrual cramps so severe that I'm in a chill, I'm sweating. My father passes my open door, stops, begins to speak, and then goes away quickly. Our culture doesn't have a special hut for me to hide in until my period is past; but my father isn't allowed to comfort me, can't embrace my female pain, has to pretend he doesn't see it. My blooming shatters my precariously assembled sense of self, and the fairy-like, wispy-haired child I was is long gone; so is the sturdy little tomboy. I develop a belly, I become pudgy. I wear a full set of braces on my teeth and plastic glasses that are called flesh-coloured. I begin to compare myself with my best friend, who becomes tall and slender, who is attractive to older men and knows it. A new kind of competition creeps between us, one I know I can't win. I sit on the toilet and gather the roll of fat on my stomach, and I want to cut it off with a pair of scissors. I can't bear to look at myself in the harsh light of dressing-room mirrors. I have my long hair cut off and get a permanent. I come home with a mass of tight curls; I know my family is trying very hard not to laugh. I'm beginning to despise myself. I embark, fiercely, on my first diet of celery and Metrecal when I'm twelve.

No one names what is happening to me. There's neither frank acknowledgement of biological facts, nor metaphorical language to shape the power of my womanhood. Instead there is shame, furtiveness, guilt and confusion. Blood, vulva, vagina, menses, labia, clitoris: my friends and I, when I'm in high school, carry these words around with us like chicken guts in a bag, which we can withdraw in bloody handfuls and throw in the faces of boys. We're not sure what to do with our womanhood. It makes us second-class citizens. It gives us rage.

The cicadas build the heat into buzzy spears of sound that cease, abruptly, in the lush languor of the maple leaves. I'm eight years old, and Mark and I are playing softball with village kids. We're on Granny and Poppy's terraced lawn.

Mark's at bat and I'm in the outfield, punching my fist into the palm of my glove, when he puts his bat down and turns towards me. He says he won't play until I put on a shirt.

I'm neither shocked nor angry. I simply don't understand what he's saying. What is most amazing to me is that my normally placid brother stands obdurate, with a clouded face, and will not lift the end of his bat until he sees me turn away, until he's sure that I'm going obediently over to the cool shade beside the barn, until he sees that I'm squatting by a pile of T-shirts, lifting and dropping them until I find my own.

Chapter Two

During my last year of high school, I pore over college catalogues and discover one that seems exuberantly different.
Sarah Lawrence College believes in learning as an end in itself.
Projects and papers replace exams, reports are given in lieu of
grades. I study black-and-white photographs of young women
wearing leotards, leg warmers and ponytails; they sit cross-legged
on wide stone walls, books propped in front of them. I sense the
threshold that they sit on and want to be there, too, pausing for
a brief time while I consider the branching, beckoning paths of
the world, which begin on the other side.

I like the college's emphasis on self-motivation; I send for an
application form and spend two weeks completing its essay questions. I savour the fact that no one in my family has ever been
there, no one has any connection to it or even knows much about
it; no one's influence or reputation will precede me.

The campus is in the wealthy suburbs north of Manhattan. Its
lawns, wisteria arbour, performing arts centre and brick buildings

are discreetly fenced and gated, separating the college from the surrounding streets, where huge stone houses, like racehorses, stand docile and groomed behind their lawns and are set within bowers of azaleas, lilacs, rhododendrons. But I can hear, like the rumour of war, the distant and endless whine of highways; I can smell the greasy city air that wreathes languorously beneath the sharp scents of mown grass, chrysanthemums, leaf piles. When I say goodbye to my brother and mother, who deliver me to my dorm, I hug them and then stride away feeling exhilarated, as if for a long time my arms have been lugging burdens that I'm finally allowed to drop and leave behind. I feel weightless. I never look back to see the expression on my mother's face.

No one is watching when I tear off the double-breasted navy suit jacket that my mother and I bought together and try on my roommate's Salvation Army wardrobe, complete with beads and high boots, while Janis Joplin wrings our hearts. No one watches, or judges me, as I embark on a new journey; the words that I once read to myself, alone in the secret places of my childhood, surround me here like leaping flames. Teachers toss words like dry tinder onto bonfires. Words spark darkness, shoot sideways like errant firecrackers. I study acting; my lines possess me, repeat endlessly in my mind, keep me awake at night. I erupt into character for my friends—on buses, in Grand Central Station, striding through the winter dusk of the cloistered campus. I read philosophy, legs curled around a wooden chair in the religious hush of the library; head in hands, I feel the muscular power of an idea whose meaning I can only barely grasp. Cross-legged on my bed, I underline my paperback Tolstoy, scribble notes in the margins. I'm exposed to the voices of Faulkner, Schopenhauer, Virginia Woolf, Jung, T.S. Eliot, Dickinson, Karl Marx. Each voice is distinct, complex, laced with veins of pain and confusion, clarity and revelation. I lose my virginity, without pleasure, with relief. I buy a fur coat for fifty cents and wear it inside out. I learn how to make people laugh. I sense my own seriousness, I glimpse my own abilities. I'm pushed and encouraged by teachers. I write passionately in my notebook.

I spend the summer working with an international youth group in a remote mountain village in Mexico. I've been trying to fracture the shell of silence that has surrounded subjects of pain in my childhood; if pain is so dangerous that I need to be sheltered from it, then it's something I'll actively seek. I want my parents to understand that I'm strong enough to confront harsh things. Over the summer three babies die, and I attend the funerals in the village. We gringos are given seats in the kitchen, close to the table, where I discover, at the first funeral, that the wax doll surrounded with flowers is a real dead child; I understand this, with shock, when the mother waves her hand over the fly that is crawling up the baby's nostril. We're handed small mugs of sweet tea. The dead child's aunt offers us cookies from a plate. Later, on a misty evening smelling of pine trees and the smoke of burning cedar, the funeral procession straggles up a rock-strewn track between the potato fields. I'm holding the hand of a little girl named Rosa who has become my shadow. Her face seems dusty with dried mucous and dirt. She's barefoot and her faded red dress hangs from one thin shoulder. I see her mother up ahead, with a baby cocooned in her woven shawl. No one is wailing or weeping. Our skin is burnished in the mountain light, and the priest leads the procession, wearing a white robe trimmed with lace. He came from Tlaxcala. After he buries the child, a couple steps forward shyly. They've been waiting a year for him to come and consecrate their marriage.

When I return to the United States in late August, I'm astounded by its affluence, and by how no one seems aware of it. My eyes see the world differently. My childhood seems small and remote, like a painting hung too high in a guest-room, and my family slides into the background. Right now, I need, most of all, not to need them.

In early October, my friend tells me that the date she arranged for a boy from her home town has fallen through. He's coming to the college for the weekend; would I stand in? I refuse. I've just broken up with someone, I'm not interested, I have too much work. She pleads with me, and reluctantly I concede. The first time I hear Peter's voice is when I call her dorm just before supper on Saturday. She's telling me that she's taking us to a party in Harlem and he's arguing with her, telling her it's a bad idea. They sound like quarrelling siblings; she tells me that he's scared. I think about this as I scuff under the wisteria arbour on my way to meet him. I'm scared, too, but didn't dare say so.

I have a cigarette in my hand the first time I see Peter. He's wearing jeans, a black T-shirt, a string of tiny coloured beads and aviator glasses. His light brown hair is shoulder-length and very clean. I can't see his eyes; they seem hidden by the glasses, and he keeps his arms crossed over his chest. He and Barbara have been waiting for me in the science library, where she has a campus job. I feel reckless. I'm wearing a baggy blue sweater and woven leather Mexican sandals. I've knotted a scarf around my neck and my long hair is loose down my back. Barbara and I met in theatre class, and we exaggerate ourselves to one another and love our outrageousness. I greet Peter. Barbara hisses at me to put out my cigarette and I push the lever on a sand-filled pedestal ash stand. The egg-shaped aluminum cups part and I drop the burning cigarette in.

"No, you're supposed to butt it out first," Barbara says.

I push the lever again and spit, repeatedly, down into the sand. I can tell that Peter thinks this is wonderful.

At supper, I incite a minor food fight in the cafeteria by throwing a very small piece of bread at an old boyfriend, who retaliates instantly with a handful of green jello.

Shadow Child

Peter and I sit side by side in the lighted train heading down to 125th Street, where we are going, not to a party, as Barbara, in typically hyperbolic fashion, has indicated, but to the home of her current boyfriend, who lives in Harlem. Peter sprawls in the seat next to me, his long legs stretched out; he talks simply and easily. He tells me the names of his two younger brothers and of his sister, who has the same name as me. He tells me the name of the family dog. We talk about our parents. He seems to be solidly and comfortably connected to his own past, and he brings it with him into this moment. He asks me about my family. He and Barbara toss their shared memories back and forth like a bright ball that falls into my lap, too.

Barbara's boyfriend, Billy, meets us at the station so he can escort us through the streets. He seems to know everyone, slaps palms, keeps an invisible protective net around us. No one acknowledges us. The pretenses we might use on the cloistered campus have no place here.

Billy's parents and younger siblings stay in the kitchen of their fifth-floor apartment so Billy and his friends can have the living-room. We peek in and they wave at us, but don't come out. We smoke a joint; Billy brings beer, puts a stack of records on the record player. He and Barbara disappear into the hall. Peter and I go to the window. Manhattan spreads its phosphorescence across the sea of darkness, but just below, boys are karate-fighting under the streetlights, kicking, whirling, elbows high, hands chopping. Peter and I watch, mesmerized, and the sides of our hands slide close and touch. Barbara and Billy come back from the hall, flushed and laughing, and Billy changes the record, drops the needle onto Smokey Robinson and the Miracles singing "My Girl." The living-room is just big enough for two couples to hold tight to one another and revolve slowly, like the shimmering lights on the horizon. Peter takes my hand and leads me gently away from the window. After a while, I feel his arm lift and hear a clicking sound. He's taken off his glasses, and he leans down and kisses me, once.

At the end of that year, another student tells me that we are her favourite couple. She says it's because Peter's love for me is so obvious.

I'm startled to realize that Peter loves me the way my granny does. At first, he doesn't know anything about me beyond what he's felt, sensed, intuited. Yet he loves me instantly, and without reservation; by nature he's impulsive, and he's as reckless with his love as he is with his money, which he spends unstintingly on the second weekend we're together, when we go to the Village Gate and hear Thelonious Monk, and then he takes me out to dinner. He wants me from the moment he meets me, and for the rest of his life.

He's the first boyfriend I'm not on guard against. I'm not afraid to hold him, to be held by him. I love the feeling of his springy athletic body; I love the smell of his clothes, the way we press our legs together when we walk so we become a three-legged person. I love the way he's frank, steady, at home with himself. He loves my outrageousness. He respects me, he's a bit in awe of me. He tells me he's never gone out with a girl like me before. I've never encountered his kind of love. He's fond, he's openly and easily affectionate, he loves to hold me, he's gentle, he's tender. He'll tell me anything; he'll do anything for me. I understand that I am the most important thing in his life.

I'm overwhelmed by his love, and somehow afraid of it, as if I can't believe either that I'm as wonderful as he thinks, or that I will ever be able to return his love as fully, as generously. I feel like someone who walks into a house she didn't plan on buying and realizes, suddenly, that it's going to become her home. It's not that Peter completes me, or fulfils me, or augments me; rather, together we're safe. We're as soft as puppies in bed at night; my shoulder slides beneath his arm, his legs scissor between mine, my ear's on his chest, his palm cups my head. We sleep encased in one another, drifting into oblivion on the dark surf of each other's heartbeats.

And yet, when I meet Peter, I've only just begun to glimpse my own separateness, the singularity that I've been seeking; and then it's swept into another current, like two rivers joining and continuing as one. I'm just flinging my arms wide to begin my own experience of the world when I become part of a couple. I feel a slight reluctance that I'm afraid to admit to, or to reveal, in the face of Peter's passion. I'm still determined to be me. There's some part of me that I hold, unconsciously, in reserve, like a special flower that I'm growing in secret. It won't be part of our couplehood. It won't be part of being a daughter or a friend. It will belong to no one but me as it grows; I won't share it until it's fully formed, until I myself can see its shape.

When Peter asks me to marry him, I say yes, but I feel as if we're playing a game. I do my best to assure him that I love him, too; but when I imagine my future, I see brightly coloured fragments, like several jigsaw puzzles strewn together. I don't know which pieces belong to the puzzle that's my life. I'm not sure how to start making my selection.

All of our parents disapprove of our living together, or travelling together, without being married. In the spring, we begin looking for an old van; we've decided to spend the summer in Mexico. I want to take Peter to the mountain village where I worked. Instead, I find myself, one morning in June, standing in front of the bathroom mirror at my parents' house. It's the morning of my wedding; it's eight months after Peter and I met; I'm nineteen years old.

I feel a familiar set of emotions; I sense that I'm really doing all this to please someone else, but I hide this feeling from everyone, even, finally, from myself. I accept what's happening. Peter and I become husband and wife, and I trust that I'm doing the right thing, I try to believe that I want to do everything I'm doing; I put on a face of happiness and gratitude. My own negative feelings seem so inappropriate that I can't even admit them to myself, and yet I feel as if my wings have been clipped. I'm angry with myself for not believing in my own goals strongly enough to insist on their value. Obscurely, I feel that I'm really not good enough, or of enough value, or strong enough, to have continued on the paths I'd been striding, heading towards various imagined lives: an actress, a writer, a professor of English literature. I'm shocked to encounter new assumptions about my capabilities now that I'm married. Men assume that my husband will be making decisions for both of us; all our bills come to Peter Powning; the bank teller speaks to me condescendingly and wants my husband's signature, and I detect the subtle shift in authority, as people direct questions to Peter first and then slant their eyes, briefly, towards me.

I had planned to spend my third year of college in England, where I'd been accepted at a university for my junior year abroad. Peter had been made wretched by this plan ever since he heard of it, and when we marry I abandon it. I don't understand the degree to which I will regret this decision later, or the way in which this feeling of acquiescence, which I think is agreement, becomes familiar and a pattern that's hard to break. I know that there's a warped feeling left, once I've made the decision to abandon my plan. I'm like a child who knew she shouldn't let go of her balloon string, but thought it was the right thing to do.

I decide to apply to theatre school in Boston instead, but arrive for my audition on the wrong day—the theatre door is locked, and I kick it in a rage. Finally, I drop out of school for a semester and work in a bookstore. We rent a cottage from my great-aunt in my home town; it's in the village, across from Granny and Poppy's house, which, for the first time in its long history, is no longer owned by our family. Peter is studying ceramics, impatient to leave university and set up his own studio. But for him, as for all the young men we know, college is the only alternative to being sent to the Vietnam War. Although I am bereft without classes, papers, research, projects, he feels imprisoned by school. Many of his classes have no relevance to his future; he wants to begin making a life where he can be with me, make his own choices, be his own boss.

I make the mistake of reading *Jude the Obscure*, which fosters both black feelings and a grim vision of irony. I have a dream that I'm locked in a giant birdcage; I'm wearing a cheerleader's red skirt and I'm waving crepe-paper pompoms. I try to believe that I've either made my own choices, or, like Jude, been thwarted by twists of fate; but my dreams tell me what I really feel: that I've been manipulated, and that I've betrayed myself. Dreams, however, are like a set of directions written in a foreign language. They only confuse and frustrate me; they poison my daytime life, so I crumple them up and tuck them to the bottom of my soul's rubbish heap.

Eventually I return to Sarah Lawrence as an off-campus student; I commute to New York for two days of classes a week. I identify my major field of study as creative writing. We have two tiger cats and we put up a small chicken pen in the jungly undergrowth behind the cottage. We love being together, make a Happy Solstice card of ourselves naked, only our heads showing above a pile of pumpkins, gourds, squash and ivy vines. Peter puts his energy into creative means of avoiding the draft; he applies for conscientious objector status, which he doesn't receive, then is called up for a physical, which he tries to fail but doesn't. We hear of young men we knew in high school who have died in the war. Peter punches me one night when we're both asleep; he dreams that he's resisting being dragged aboard an airplane. Eventually he receives a peculiar classification that means his file has been shelved; the army sees him as more trouble than he's worth. We become more engaged, however, in the environmental movement than in the anti-war movement. We discuss ways in which we could live so that we will not harm the earth. We raise two pigs at my parents' place and have them professionally butchered; I learn how to cook pork chops, ham, bacon, ribs. We take aluminum milk cans to a local farm and bring them back filled with hot, raw milk. We begin to collect pamphlets from the U.S. Department of Agriculture. We buy a grain mill and grind our own flour. I learn how to make bread, to preserve applesauce in glass jars, to make jam from the wild grapes that sprawl everywhere on stone walls. We meet new friends, Bob and Kathy Osborne, who married at the age of eighteen and are renting a house down in the valley. We're amazed to discover that they are doing the same things we are, and are dreaming the same dreams. We imagine, together, a life on the Peace River in Alberta; words excite us: *Canada, foothills, portage, log house, kerosene, trap lines.* We decide, the spring after we've been married for two winters and Bob and Kathy have been married for three, that we will go to Canada and look for land. None of us, however, has a car good enough to get us out West. Bob infects us with his enthusiasm for New Brunswick, where he went once as a child. We borrow my parents' Rambler and decide we'll start our search closer to home, in the maritime provinces east of Maine.

Life is like a game of chess, where one seemingly insignificant move changes the entire configuration of the board and all its possibilities; once you've made your move, the change is irrevocable. You can't reconsider. You can't go back. Nothing stays the same.

Shadow Child

It takes me a long time to learn this. I think that if I get married and don't like it, I can get unmarried. I can pick up where I left off. I think that if I move away from home, home will continue on as I left it; and if I come back, it will be waiting for me. I think, therefore, that I can take risks. I think that I can make changes, as if time and consequences will be suspended, as if I can try out life, like a dress I might return.

We buy our farm in New Brunswick in the same impulsive and random way in which we meet and marry and are thwarted from going to Alberta. Peter and Bob and I wander the back roads of New Brunswick for a week in May, when the fields are gilded with furry dandelions and earth-smelling winds ripple the rivers, dishevel the manes of grazing horses, fling and ribbon the white blossoms of serviceberry trees. We debate over whether to turn left, up a valley, or continue on down to the coast. We've just crossed a covered bridge; a cemetery by the roadside lures us, makes us feel there might be a hidden village at the end of the valley, and so we turn left. There is a church at the valley's end, and two working farms with weathered barns and white houses; there is one more farm set far back from the road. Its driveway starts at the place where the road narrows and begins a steep, winding climb up into the forested hills. The driveway is a long dirt lane that winds between a wind-rippled field of young timothy on the north and a lush, brook-laced cow pasture on the south. The fields are drifted with yellow dandelions; beds of trout lilies fill warm hollows. The house is set back from the lane by a lawn whose unmown grass dances in the wind; a row of old maples stands at the edge of the lawn. Two ancient workhorses stand drowsily in the pasture just across from the house. The house is white; its windows have red sashes and forest-green frames. The house and barns are clustered together, dwarfed, to my eyes, by fields that seem like seas, so open, so filled with light and sky, they are; so quiet, so empty.

The two-hundred-and-fifty-acre farm is for sale. It has stood untended for one winter.

Three days later, we stand in the farmhouse kitchen with a real-estate agent and sign an agreement to purchase.

We make this choice, we seek out this place. And yet for years I can't quite believe that we have really come here; I feel as if I'm a child watching, amazed, a movie about my own future. It's as if all the small decisions I myself precipitated or participated in have rippled irrevocably forward like small waves that coalesce, suddenly, into one huge one, which sweeps me off my feet and carries me to a place I never planned to go.

We immigrate at St. Stephen, New Brunswick, on April 21, 1972, when we're twenty-two years old. It's two summers after we bought the farm; we've spent the winters in New England and the summers in Canada, and now we have all our belongings in the truck: cats in the cab, piano on one side of a borrowed horse trailer and my pony on the other, everything else in the back of the pick-up. We're here for good. The imaginative cord that binds me to my parents and to the nexus of my childhood with its beloved secret places—the Nipmuck boulder, my oak tree, my spring violets—the cord begins to fray in central Maine. I'm no longer attached when we arrive on a cold spring night after a severe Canadian winter, when there's still knee-deep snow along the roads and the house is filled with such a dank chill that we rummage through our suitcases for mittens and hats and wear them while we make a fire in the kitchen stove.

That July, I stand in the barn door holding a bucket of hot milk from my Jersey cow. I think about how I belong to no one here, and to nothing. No tree carries memories of childhood climbing, no old person remembers me as a child. There's no playground on whose swings I sailed into the summer skies; no

Shadow Child

store whose counter was once higher than my head; no pond I swam in with my best friend. There are no aunts and uncles, no cousins, no grandparents. There's no door of any house I can push open without knocking, knowing my mother will be taking the light steps of her ongoing kitchen dance, knowing my father will be there to gather me in a hard-armed hug. There's only grass and sky, it seems; and within this space, Peter and I, and our friends Bob and Kathy, who have built a log cabin on fifty acres of the farm, are free to make the life we've imagined. We're like children on a deserted beach, scooping sand while seagulls mew and cry over the sun-dancing waters; we pile, smooth, industriously crenellate, gathering and shaping the sands of our dream. Meanwhile, and endlessly, swallows angle between the empty barns like swift arrows; wind creases the timothy of the fields. There's no sound but birds, running water, whishing wind. Snipes fly so high we can't see them, but the hollow, diminishing whooping of their wings as they dive down the sky on opalescent June evenings becomes the heartbeat of the farm, the life that circles and wheels far beyond our own driven, excited busyness. It's the rhythm of what we don't know and can't predict. It's the song of the wild.

Kathy wants to start a family as soon as possible. Bob is going to make furniture and wood toys; their place is up at the edge of the farm's farthest field, a half-mile due east of our house. Peter is going to make pots; I'm going to be a writer.

The northern summer light is clear and rich. We rise with the sun, start a fire in the cookstove. We can see the blue-grey spiral of Bob and Kathy's breakfast fire rising from spruce trees that float like boat's masts in the lifting, balsam-scented mists. We make tea with King Cole teabags in a brown pot that we bought at Moffett's hardware store. Milk still comes in heavy glass bottles with cardboard lids. Everything is quickened by the romance of the unfamiliar. As I pin clothes on the cord that sweeps across the

45

lawn like a fishing line, beaded with dewdrops, I'm seeing myself in the light of morning; I'm in the moment of lifting wet clothes from a basket made of split ash, I'm alive within my strong young body, I'm smelling the camping smells of spruce trees and wood smoke, I'm feeling as if time is a dimension without limits. The end of my life is so far away that I can't begin to imagine it. Everything seems possible.

My fingers are rough from gardening, hammering, throwing rocks, cutting trees; my hands ache in the night. There is so much to do, and we have all the energy we need to do it. Nothing keeps us from starting project after project until there is not enough time in a day to do them all. Peter and I love to work; we love to work together. We are motivated by the excitement and gratification of imagining something and then making it real. I buy chickens and bring them home in burlap bags, and suddenly the forlorn henhouse in the deep grass is alive again; the sun turns its dusty glass windows blood-red in the evening, when I push my way through the tall grass; the hens are making quiet crooning sounds, and I reach into the nesting boxes and my fingers discover ten eggs, which I carry into the house, wash and set in egg cartons, seeing them as soft and luminous as baby cheeks, in the dusk. We plough a piece of field and plant thirteen twenty-foot rows of potatoes; I wade waist deep in glossy leaves. We make a bridge over the brook so Bob and Kathy can get a cement truck across it; we stamp on its fresh lumber with our work boots, sit on its edge and dangle our feet over the beds of wild mint and the cold, running water. Peter splits twelve cords of wood; I watch him, naked to the waist, swinging an axe. I fill a freezer with butter, vegetables, applesauce. We strip wallpaper down to the white plaster, peel linoleum from the floors, tear down walls, knock a hole in the east wall and put a window there, so that sun falls on the kitchen table when we're making tea in our overalls at six o'clock in the morning.

Shadow Child

We've modified our original dream of being entirely self-sufficient; we decide we have to make at least one thousand dollars a year with the pots Peter will make. We convert the little granary next to the horse barn into a pottery studio. In the beginning of the summer, light lingers until ten-thirty, and we work until it's too dark to see, hammering shingles, shaving soft brick, painting floorboards. We build a catenary-arch kiln, make ware shelves and counters for wedging clay; we buy Mason jars, for glaze chemicals, at farm auctions.

Fall comes. We make it through our first winter, and then summer comes around again, only this time and forever afterwards, we don't return, like the birds, but we're here, waiting, to welcome it.

Peter becomes known as the potter. In summer, we learn to recognize curiosity-seekers by the hesitant persistance of the cars that come up the lane, past the meadow, under the row of maple trees. Everyone asks me if I make pots, too, and when I say no, they either say "Oh, you must be the helper," or else ask me if I have "family." I learn that this doesn't mean my parents or my brother, but children of my own.

I learn not to say that I'm a writer. I have nothing to show. I have no way to prove to anyone that it really is what I do. I can't bear being asked whether or not I've been published, or where my work can be read. I feel myself losing definition, standing in Peter's shadow. I realize that my contribution to this life that we've chosen is cyclical, perishable; the bread that I bake in the woodstove is eaten, my Jersey butter is spread, my vegetables are harvested, my flower gardens flourish and fade.

I make a desk in the corner of the living-room by putting boards over an old table. I set out my Smith Corona typewriter, a mug of pencils, bond paper. I want to make something that will last. I never ask myself what I'm seeking, why I am compelled to reach for the elements of time and place, gather them in fragments, reconfigure them in a shape I can hold, recognize, return to whenever I want. I know only that when I sit at my desk, I belong to myself, and that words are my religion. I think that when I'm old and have nothing, neither Peter, nor place, I will have words. My desire to shape and save the slivers of insight that come like shards split from the brittle edge of life replaces, in importance, the books that I carried to my secret places as a child. It's my faith. Writing, I believe, will always be the thing that gives my life meaning.

I begin the long journey of finding a voice that I can someday reveal to the world. I'm not discouraged, yet. I don't know how long it will take.

The past, when I'm twenty-four, is so close to me that I can see only its details. It's still attached to me, like a tail that I can lick or curl around myself, snugly. I can't see it like the plot of a novel, with one event impinging upon another, and so making a pattern that might seem predictable in hindsight. I don't see how it's both inside me, like a dream that I'll never forget, and yet how far I am travelling from it. I still think that nostalgia will nourish memory, like soft rain on soil. The future scares me because I can't imagine it. Peter and I discuss the fact that I love to remember the past, whereas his mind soars in the other direction; he loves to imagine the future. I feel insecure there. I want to proceed step by step, making my present serve the future, so I'll have some idea where I'm going and how I'm going to get there. I live my life like a student following a university syllabus. First I'll rewrite and publish the novel that I wrote as my undergraduate thesis. Then I'll write a book of short stories. Then, perhaps, we'll have children.

Neither of us really knows whether we want to have children. It's a topic we discuss endlessly, particularly once Bob and Kathy have their first child, a son; then we find that all the other young people we meet are beginning their families. Peter and I observe their lives the way an atheist might analyze a church service. When we visit their homes, there are playpens in living-rooms, piles of folded laundry on couches; we can't ever finish a conversation, and it seems to me that the lives of my women friends have no boundaries. They live within a distracting continuum; no dish is washed without another one being dirtied, there's no distinction between day and night, every quiet time is sandwiched between chaos. Babies cry; children whine, argue and wheedle; parents negotiate with one another, pass children back and forth, stuff them into snowsuits, gather toys and food and bottles, are preoccupied and speak to each other, or other parents, inclusively, as if their concerns, now that they are parents, cannot possibly be understood by those of us who are not.

My friends ease their babies into my arms, thinking that I will be delighted. I feel stiff; I hold the warm bundle carefully. My arms don't fall naturally into the shape of a cradle; I feel myself resisting the selfless tenderness that the tiny creature elicits. I'm relieved to hand the baby back, to be released from its inert dependency, which keeps me from leaning into my own dramatic expressiveness, my hands gesturing, my face alive. In November, at our pond, I watch young mothers squatting by their children, lacing tiny skates, pulling mittens onto tiny, petal-soft fingers. I'm sitting by myself, lacing up my hockey skates. I'm relieved to finish, to stand on my blades and push away, with no one needing me to wipe streams of mucus from a cold nose, no one wanting me to freeze my fingers while I fumble with their stiff laces, no one wanting me to skate backwards slowly, holding their hands as they take tiny, stumbling steps on their slippery blades. I'm free to skate hard. I'm free to walk back across the fields afterwards, hockey stick on my shoulder, standing next to Peter and waving to our friends as they strap their chattering children into car seats and drive away down the road. I'm free to go into our quiet house,

49

where the wood furnace is rumbling in the cellar and the cats come padding into the kitchen, yawning, looking for food. I'm free to sit in the rocking chair next to the wood cookstove, writing a long, descriptive letter to my parents while darkness falls and the lid on the saucepan begins to rattle as water comes to a boil.

When we've been living here for two years, we can see the results of our work. We begin to make attachments, connections. Peter belongs to the provincial craft council. We go to craft fairs. I subscribe to Canadian literary magazines. We buy a white workhorse; on winter evenings, we hitch up the two-seater sleigh and fly through the dusk to have supper with Bob and Kathy in their cabin at the edge of the forest. Snow-bursts from Tony's hoofs glitter like handfuls of sparks, prismed by the long, last fingers of winter sun. Or sometimes, after we've fired the kiln, friends come with wine. We hear the contracting glazes tinkling as we unbrick the arch; we shine flashlights into the hot darkness and glimpse glazes that are freckly; toast-brown or shiny sea-green with red blushes. The pieces of this life, which first seem isolated from one another, begin to connect; we become part of the history of place. The moose, shambling down the driveway in the morning mist, carries us into our neighbours' stories. The blueberry rake, which I take off the pantry shelf, reminds me of the previous summer, when I bought it at the auction barn and met friends. In the emptiness of a place with no memories, we cherish each one, as they accumulate like pennies in a jar. In the emptiness of a place with no history, we begin to see our own forming.

I think about getting pregnant, and I feel as if I'm sitting in the open door of an airplane with a parachute on my back. I can't imagine what will make me decide to jump. There is no return. I'll be tumbling, freefall. I have no idea what a parachute feels like when it opens. I can't imagine the bliss of floating silently down beneath its sheltering canopy. I imagine only the terror of the dark, unsupported plunge.

Shadow Child

Peter and I talk sententiously about zero population growth. We talk vaguely about adopting a baby, and I feel an easy glow of excitement about this, as of some abstract goodness we might do, someday. We imagine ourselves as a couple without children, which is easy to do because it's how we are now. I can picture us continuing, never arriving at the moment of decision, until biology deems that there is no choice left. I can't imagine how anyone can make a decision to start life, any more than I can imagine deciding when to die. It seems like something nature should determine. The fact that we're free to choose bewilders and obsesses me and Peter. It's not like any other decision. Its consequences are truly unimaginable.

Our friends think we are being ridiculous. Bob says he's going to put pinholes in my diaphragm. My father raises his eyebrows at me and says he thinks that he and Mum lived together for a while before they had children, but he can't really remember it.

Chapter Three

Ι t's February 25, 1974, and Peter and I have just returned from
Montreal, where we walked the snow-banked sidewalks carrying suitcases filled with pottery wrapped in red felt. Two galleries placed large orders, and we feel as if we're on the brink of a
new epoch. We arrive home late and fall into bed, exhausted.
We've been sleeping in hotels, so when we hear a violent pounding and yelling in the night, we're both disoriented, not knowing
where we are. I hurtle out of bed; I don't come fully awake until
I'm halfway down the stairs. I hear a confusion of noises: someone
is yelling downstairs, while Peter, out of bed now, too, is calling
me back.

I realize that someone is violently beating on the locked door
of our kitchen. It's the dead of night, yet as I run down the hall,
the house is filled with dancing shadows, and when I come into
the kitchen, it is filled with pulsing red light. I open the door and
Bob is there, frantic. The barn is on fire.

I run out the back door and stumble forward into a wall of

heat. My skin is instantly parched. There is a vast roaring, like a hurricane, with an underlying greedy crackling that comes louder as the flames leap to new fuel. My heart beats so violently I think it will burst my chest. The windows of the pottery glitter in the leaping light. I can see the skeleton of the horse barn; its timbers are still connected, making a cage within which the fire rages. The hay in the loft is white-hot. In the moonlit fields, the barn is like a giant's bonfire, lighting the sky, turning the snow blood-red, shooting sparks, cracking, splitting, hissing, roaring. The sound shuts down my brain, makes me race mindlessly back and forth. I run into the pottery, whose south wall is seeping smoke. I can't decide what is the most important thing to save. I pick up precision scales and then drop them; I snatch up a wooden stool, put it down. Peter shoves a box of his glaze recipes into my hands. The room is strangely suspended, everything orderly, and yet unnaturally lit from the outside, as if a searchlight is playing on every surface. We are yelling at each other and can't hear over the roaring crackle. I feel as if we're standing inside a cauldron. I run onto the lawn. Someone is shouting to Peter that the phone line is gone. I find one of my cats crouched, paralyzed, in the driveway and I snatch him up, put him in the house, thinking he will be safe there. Neighbours arrive, leave their trucks under the trees and come running up into the glare. No one can hear what anyone else is shouting. Someone is gesticulating, waving a fire extinguisher. No fire trucks come. Someone roars that the hundred-gallon propane tank is going to blow up. I run across the field and sit on the hill, holding my face in my hands.

There's no wind, and the wood-shingled roof of our house is glazed with ice. The fire spreads only to the pottery, whose south wall has begun to blaze. The fire lights the sky for miles; it has become an inferno. Nothing else moves; the dark forests, the unlit houses, the icy fields are motionless, as if stricken.

The barn burns like a person standing with raised arms. As if

I'm seeing its creation in reverse, I watch the outer walls burn first, while the barn's frame and its internal supports become the last things to fall. The massive timbers over the doors, the upright supports, the stairs to the hayloft, the stalls: they stand, strangely motionless, in the midst of the pulsing flames; they are golden, as incandescent as molten steel. I'm shuddering, sitting in the snow, staring through my fingers, thankful that we boarded out the animals when we went to Montreal. The barn begins to disintegrate bit by bit, one section falling inward and carrying the next, and then it becomes something else: flame, heat, ash, cinder, smoke. Most barns are claimed by time—by rot, beetles, moss and jewel-weed—but this one disappears in a matter of hours, in its prime, when the hayloft is filled with pale green sweet-smelling bales; when it's still a place where cats hide their kittens, banty hens make egg-shaped hollows in loose hay, mice scurry along beams; when its eaves are lined with the dried-mud nests of swallows and the tattered remnants of paper-wasp nests, and its dusty windows are veiled with last summer's spider webs; when its warm air is alive and peaceful with the breathing warmth of cows and horses, the placid grind of cows' jaws, the stomping of horses' hoofs. In the winter night, the barn becomes the element that destroys it. Its own dry timbers, its hoof-scarred floorboards, its hay, its dusty shelves, all burst into flame like torches, explode, shatter, fall in showers of sparks.

I watch until the barn walls collapse, folding over the heart of the fire; I watch one of the pottery walls waver and fall forward into the driveway. Miraculously, the propane tank doesn't blow up. I stumble through the field, climb the barbed-wire fence into the driveway, walk over to Russell and Mary's house. Their kitchen is filled with people. It's three in the morning, and Mary's curly grey hair is dishevelled; she's talking steadily in her Irish accent, making tea for all the neighbours who came out to help, slicing bread with her hand on the loaf as if she's steadying a

Shadow Child

child's head. I feel like a stranger as I walk in. I feel as if it is not my barn that has burned, but theirs. They're talking about events that happened in that barn fifty years ago, just as, after a person has died, people sift and sort through their memories, recounting anecdotes or recalling moments in time that they offer like beads balanced in the palm of their hand. I sit on the wood in the woodbox and Mary hands me a cup of tea; she calls me dear and pats me kindly. I see fire flickering around the edge of the stove lid and think how it is the first time I've thought of fire as a dispassionate force with two faces, one docile, one savage. Someone is standing at the window and calls out that the fire trucks have finally arrived from the nearest station, which is forty miles away.

I hear Mary explaining to someone that our horse and pony and cow weren't in the barn; that we'd only just got home and had boarded them out. I cradle my tea and sit for a while; I finally stop shuddering. I don't say anything and no one bothers me. Everyone knows how to let me be alone; how to surround me with life and unnecessary activity, tea-pouring, sandwich-making, pipe-stuffing; how to fill the air with sounds of acceptance and resignation; how to patch a rent. I don't know that I'm part of a ritual that has been enacted time and again in this valley, a ritual that I will come to know and depend upon. I'm glad I came. I get up, saying I have to find Peter. Hands pat me encouragingly. I glimpse my face in the hall mirror on my way out. My expression is open, unprotected, like the insides of the barn. I feel as if I've been scorched; a layer has been peeled away.

When I walk back home, the sky is beginning to lighten. On the eastern horizon, the spruce trees, no longer thrown into relief by the fire's glare, are standing black against the pale light that unfurls behind them. Another day begins, just as if nothing has happened. As I come up under the row of maples, I see the firemen coiling hose onto the truck. There is nothing left to do, except to resume. It's going to be a grey day, and in the bleak light, I see that all that's left of the barn is a pile of black timbers. In the smoldering ashes lie pitchfork tines, chains, loops of half-burned baling twine, a rake head. The catenary-arch kiln stands amid the blackened remains of the pottery like a shard, recognizable, but useless, separated from its function. The acrid smell of creosote mixes with the faint smell of the chickens who burned to death.

Peter comes up the driveway. He's haggard, his face streaked with ashes. He looks as if he wants to reassure me that everything's going to be all right, and yet he's stunned. His desire to fix, to comfort, to progress, is like a promise that someone else has made him break. Without speaking or touching, we stare at the smoke unfurling from the charred beams like the plume over a town dump.

After a fire, there is a hole in the landscape, as if what has gone was less substantial, all along, than the things that waited to fill its space: sky, hills, a wild cherry tree at the edge of the marsh. The most startling thing, when I step out the back door of the house, is the new view of the back field. Every night, in my mind, I reconstruct the barn and the pottery, deliberately fixing them in my memory before the details fade. I imagine the texture of the pottery's wood floor, which I painted red; I remember how Peter's wheel sat just beneath the small-paned window and how the north wall of the barn was covered with old licence plates. We try to make a list of what we lost.

A couple of days later, there's a mid-winter thaw; in the driveway, the mud is knee-deep. We spend days hauling the blackened remains of the fire to the dump in the woods. We pile it on a flat-bed wagon, which we haul with the dented, rusty Massey-Ferguson tractor. Spruce needles lash my face as the tractor lumbers over the rutted track through the trees; in a small clearing,

Shadow Child

where wild raspberries lean like brown pencil strokes, there's a great pile of trash: rotting cardboard, pulpy lumber, linoleum, plastic curtains, blue tin mugs with rust holes, swollen styrofoam coolers, apple-juice cans with faded paper labels, broken glass. Porcupines have stripped bark from all the young spruce trees and their trunks glisten, yellow, doomed.

Peter and I throw once-loved possessions onto the dump. The little English pony saddle I paid for myself, by washing windows and polishing shoes; Peter's stainless-steel gram scales; my grandfather's shovel, only the head left, warped; the potter's wheel, its sides collapsed: we hurl all these things, standing with our legs braced on the wagonbed. They curve through the misty air and make sounds when they land that disrupt the dripping quiet of the woods; the tinkle of breaking glass, the clatter of metal against wood, the hollow clank of a bucket handle.

Curious ravens fly over, so low we can hear the swish of their wings. The sleek, black birds are the only apparent life in the forest in winter. Everything else has gone to ground: bears are denned, insects are buried deep, buds are encased. The birds cruise the skies as if seeking something; they are sharp-eyed, observant. I feel as if my energy alarms and fascinates them. They land on nearby branches, and then make explosive croaks and fly away.

When we found this dump in the woods, our first thought was that we would clean it up; now I'm glad it's here. I'm alive in the cold, wet air, and Peter and I are working steadily, throwing these possessions away one by one, without pause. I feel a nimbus of danger surrounding me, like a new conception of life, a new sense of who I am. I understand how lucky we are that the house didn't catch on fire, that Peter and I didn't burn to death in our sleep. I'm willing to start again, however many times, if to do so is the price I have to pay for my own existence. These warped and scorched things are like sacrificial lambs. I'm willing to exchange them for the moment that I'm living. We give up on the list we try to make of the things that we lost; there isn't time to dwell on what can't be recovered. I understand for the first time the uselessness of nostalgia, the tyranny of things; my grandfather is not part of this shovel, my childhood is not held within the frame of this little saddle. For the first time, we understand that there's no immunity, there are no exemptions. We thought that we were fitting one plan to another like slotting a tenon into a mortise. We thought that as these plans were realized, they would exist like a frame, like a structure, solid and indestructible. But we sense that nothing really supports us. The imminence of tragedy hangs over us on black wings; it cruises, cold-eyed, omniscient and seemingly without justice.

The Saturday after the fire, twenty friends arrive. We dismantle two-thirds of one of the barns we've never used; its roof is sagging, its walls are buckling. We sort and stack its lumber, which we will use to build a new pottery studio. The next week, our fathers arrive. They unload nail pouches, hammers, rubber boots, tool boxes. They look eager, younger, vigorous with our need of them; they stay for ten days, and when they've left, we've raised the frame of a new pottery. Then Peter's brother David comes to live with us, to lend us a hand during the three months it takes to construct a new studio and rebuild what's left of the old cow barn.

One night I'm sitting cross-legged in a wicker chair in the living-room. The brothers are washing dishes, engaged in childhood reminiscence. I crouch over my journal, holding a fountain pen that stains my forefinger with ink. I'm seeking some scrap of comfort, a pebble of truth. I want to write something that I can return to, something that will continue, and gather momentum, like a river. Finally, I scratch with the metal nib, *"There are inevitable tragedies in life, and we can't avoid them. Life becomes a process of accepting what fate has in store, as well as moulding it however you can. I feel that the purely optimistic era of youth is over."*

Shadow Child

No one blames us for losing the barn. No one ever figures out why it burned, no one even hints that it could have been our fault. But we feel that something of incalculable value has slipped through our fingers, like an ancient vase that we were holding and then, inexplicably, dropped. We feel the impulse to repair the damage as quickly as possible, to put the pieces back together again. But it's not the same vase. We're not the same people. Much has been lost that can never be retrieved. Not only have elements of a community's history been destroyed, but we've been tripped in our stride, our legs knocked out from under us.

I see a new side of Peter. He gets his hair cut short, as if he can't be bothered to think about himself. He works endlessly; he doesn't walk, but runs from place to place and seems to be thinking about ten things at once. He's not working with the buoyancy of excitement, but he's driving himself, trying to get past this, to return to the place where we were on February twenty-fourth. He wants to be making pots. He becomes less boyish, more efficient and competent. He figures things out, learns new skills. He takes charge.

We work through the rest of the winter, through mud season and the softening days of spring. Peter and David and I, along with occasional helping friends, build a new studio from the ground up, on the site of the old one. We do over again what we'd done only a few years earlier: frame, lay joists and plywood, nail board-and-batten siding, stuff pink insulation between two-by-fours, run wiring and install outlets and fuse boxes. Peter builds a chimney; we lay steel roofing in a snowstorm, lashing ourselves to the ridge-pole. We bring old windows into the house to reglaze and paint before installing them in the new studio. We build counters, ware shelves; Peter buys and installs a new potter's wheel. We tear down the lovely, ruined, catenary-arch kiln and build a new square one. When the studio is done, in late April, we begin on the remaining third of the cow barn. We go into the woods to cut and bark spruce trees for beams; we hand-shovel three feet of rotten hay to make way for a cement floor; we build stalls, make a grain bin, repair the roof.

At night, my fingers go numb and the palms of my hands feel as if they're being bored with a hot poker. My wrists and shoulders ache; I have tendinitis in my elbows. I go to see our doctor. He is the father of four young children, the town's only surgeon; like us, he's a recent immigrant to Canada. The hospital is in the old army barracks, under a row of wind-ragged balsam poplars, with a view over the five valleys that funnel brooks and roads down into the vale where the town lies. He tucks a pipe in the pocket of his lab coat; its aroma precedes him as he walks down the waxed, green-floored halls. He speaks with a British accent. He is stocky, economic in both movement and emotion; his eyes glance up over repressed smiles, his eyes are ironic. He's one of the "new" doctors. Our elderly neighbours tell us that he is a man of few words.

When we immigrate, he fills out our health forms. We like him. We sense each other's instinct to absorb the present and to put our pasts, his Middle Eastern, ours American, quietly away; to let the edges of difference be worn smooth, like sea-pebbles rolling in surf. We respect this similarity, and do not speak of it. When Bob and Kathy have their first baby, he invites me and Peter into the delivery room only minutes after the birth, understanding how we and our friends are each other's only family here. I trust him.

On this day, after we've talked about my hands and he chides me for working like a man, for abusing my body, he asks me if Peter and I have been trying to have a baby.

"No," I say, surprised. "Why?"

He seems embarrassed. He looks down quickly, raising his eyebrows as he begins scrawling a lab requisition with his scratchy ink pen. "No, it's nothing," he says. "I just thought that since

Shadow Child

Kathy was pregnant again, you might be thinking about having children."

I tell him hesitantly that I'm not sure I want to be a mother. He's truly amazed, but seems slightly indignant, as if this is a preposterous concept. "You'd be a wonderful mother. Think of how much you have to offer. You and Peter. . . ."

I feel a familiar sense of self-betrayal. It's as if I don't fit inside myself, as if who I am inside warps the person I am on the outside and makes me awkward, clumsy, inadequate. I feel a familiar inability to complete my statement, to explain its underlying meaning.

No one expects Peter to stop making pots, to postpone his creative life to have children. But I don't tell anyone that I'm a writer. Nobody knows about my secret creative life, or that when my story was published in a literary magazine in April I felt like a jeweller who saw her ring being worn for the first time on someone else's hand.

I'm afraid that I might, after all, be striving for something I can never attain. I might put off having children and then never become a writer and then be too old to have children and then have lost everything.

One day, in the midst of rebuilding, during lunch, I say to Peter, "If we had a baby, could I still write?"

He considers this. He knows what I'm asking. He says, "Well, I could take the baby in the studio, mornings."

I feel it's an unfair question that I've asked. We can't know the answer; Peter's response can only be something to reassure us both. But something new enters our lives as we ponder this. It's a glimpse of immortality, a sense of our two spirits combining, and continuing.

Just before the fire, Peter and I entered a new phase of our obsession with whether we would have children. We began evaluating our friends' child-rearing techniques, discussing how we would bring up our children. The idea of being parents creeps up on us so gradually that we hardly realize that we now take it for granted that it's something we'll do someday.

But before the fire, it was only an idea. We still had no intention of starting a family. I still thought that I would be an established writer before being swept away on the current of motherhood.

Now, during the winter and spring after the fire, our words on this topic come slowly, without facility. We can't articulate to each other the way the fire has changed us, how it has both mocked and challenged us. I feel wary, as if I've been temporarily blinded and have grown accustomed to feeling my way with my hands. We find ourselves subtly rephrasing our goals. We're no longer certain that we can stride confidently down a path we've chosen ourselves. We sense that we've been arrogant, that we've been taught a lesson. We never come around the bend in the road without bracing ourselves for the sight of our house in flames, or the sight of a smouldering ruin. I can't see sunset-burnished windows without a jolt of shock, a jag of remembered terror. We don't see clearly how the impermanence of the material world makes us seek another kind of creation, but we sense that the same power that consumed the barn has another face, another form.

Spring light opens the days, makes them softer, friendlier. The hard twigs of pussy willows split their claw-like buds; fat, kitten-grey aments toss on the watery breeze. In the quiescent light of sunset, the poplars and birches on the hillsides over the farm are pink, their buds swelling; peepers begin a faint, silvery ringing. The damp air is alive with the smell of cold mud.

One morning, red-winged blackbirds drop from the sky into our maple trees. They come in a great flock, with the force of a new idea, changing the landscape. Hundreds of birds chatter at once in their burbling metallic trill. Their feathers flash in the sun, as sleek and promising as blackberries.

I step out the back door, on my way to the barn. Birdsong breaks over me like a wave. I stand listening, smelling the sharp earthy air, watching two ducks flying low over the fields. I lose my momentum. My fingers uncurl at my sides.

I imagine a child running in the spring sun, hands out as if to pluck the voices of the blackbirds from the air.

I feel a child's spirit quickening within me, stirring from rooted darkness, unfurling towards the light. I press my fists to my chest. I turn, my face alive; I think I will tell Peter, but even as I walk towards the barn, the feeling fades like the dispersing of the delicate mists of dawn.

II

1974–1975

Chapter Four

The land lives through, and beyond, its seeming death. In April, snow-melt fills the brooks, and then, in May, the tiny flowers of wild forget-me-nots cover their banks with blue mist. In the woods, violets and trilliums pierce the black mulch of snow-pressed leaves; one day, we see a young moose ambling past the new animal barn, the hair of her mantle gleaming.

David leaves; our animals return from the farm where they've been boarded since February. We sell the cow and buy Toggenburg goats. I buy a dozen red hens. The new animal barn smells of fresh lumber and tar paper. Peter begins to make pots.

Kathy stops by on her way back from town. Her little boy, Erin, is fascinated by her belly and shows it to me. It's no longer a soft swell, but has become taut. She begins to wear jeans that have an elastic front. Her blonde hair is haloed with sunlight as she sits in the rocking chair by our woodstove with her hands on her belly. She looks like a Scandinavian mother in a fairy tale. She's serene, patient, her usual sharpness entirely gone, as if absorbed; her long hair twisted into a bun and wisping around her broad forehead; smile lines creasing her red cheeks. This time, her pregnancy intrigues me. I try to disguise this from her, and from myself, but really I am as curious and fascinated as Erin is by the sense of contained mystery that she carries with her; by her body, which we watch as if it's only partly hers now, and partly someone else's.

Later, I sit at my desk with my chin in my cupped hands. The window is open, and I can smell sun-warmed earth. Sun glances off dandelions. I don't feel like writing. I feel the strange little gut-quiver that began a month ago when Peter and I talked about having a baby. I don't imagine a child with a name and a personality. It's something else, this feeling, a sexual feeling, an impulse that is not rational. It's the strange sense that within abandonment, submission, ceasing to try, lies concealed the potential for change.

I feel as if I'm resisting something that is waiting to happen. It's as if I'm standing by a garden plot that is ready to be seeded; it's been ploughed, and harrowed, its soil is rich and fertile, I'm holding a packet of seeds, and yet something keeps me from kneeling and dropping the first one. Everyone is waiting for me to do it. It seems a kind of perversity that I don't, that I won't. I begin not to understand myself; I begin to waver in my resolution.

On my desk is the manila envelope that I just brought in from the mailbox. It's addressed to me, in my own handwriting. It's another story returned. Inside I will find an impersonal rejection slip, and I'll feel the empty-handed devastation of not being good enough. It is me, I think, who has been rejected: my voice, my soul, who I am.

Sitting at my desk with warm, early summer air stirring my long hair, I glimpse the shadowy sister-self who watches me, at this moment, with the face that I saw in Mary's mirror after the fire; it's the face without a mask. Its expression is eager, scared, sweet,

Shadow Child

patient. I feel that if I get pregnant, she is the person I will become. The rational part of my mind assures me that I won't lose the rest of myself, but I'm not sure. And yet even within this uncertainty I'm still possessed by the slightly wild and reckless excitement that Peter and I both felt as we began to talk about making a baby. For me, the dangerous decision is the one that everyone expects me to make. If I make it, I know that everyone will approve, will be excited, will tell me that I've done the right thing.

I don't make a choice at this moment. Rather, I wonder if I might let life make a choice for me.

That night, we sleep with our window wide open. I make a tent over my head with the blankets so that only my nose is cold. Peepers are singing their night song, a mud-song, stalk-song, root-song, and it rises from the darkness with the sweet familiarity of unspoken love. Peter tells me there's a great horned owl making a noise like a washtub bass; I can't hear it. I roll over and put my arms around him. We're lying under a wool blanket and a heavy feather comforter. Our skin is satiny as new-laid eggs. I press my face against his cheek. I can't speak my words out loud. I whisper them so quietly that he becomes suddenly very still, and then asks me to repeat what I said. I whisper again that I'm not wearing my diaphragm. I feel his arms tighten around me. He puts his lips in my hair. We lie very still.

We make love, having made no real decision other than to let life decide. Never have we felt so naked.

My womb sheds its lining at the next full moon. I realize that even though nothing has happened, I've already changed. I feel strangely rejected, dejected; unchosen. I tell Peter that I'm not pregnant, and we are both disappointed and then laugh at ourselves, amazed. No one knows we're trying. Then we clasp each other again, in the warmer darkness, under one blanket and no quilt. During my days of digging in the soil with hot sun burning my freckled shoulders, of dipping bisqued pots in chalky pink glaze, of resting my fingers on the keys of my humming electric typewriter, I carry a feeling that's like a small golden acorn. It rests in my heart. As I stand in the raspberry patch looking at the blue-flag iris, deep-rooted in the wet soil by the brook, I press the heel of my hand to my chest. Sometimes I'm scared; sometimes I'm excited.

Life starts with giving up control. There's simply the absence of defence. There are no skills to acquire, no plan to follow. It seems strange that all we have to do to make a child is leave the diaphragm in its round plastic case, unopened. There is no striving, or was not for us, whose bodies were fertile and ripe as the frogs in the pond.

We wait, and we wait, and days go by. I think I might be pregnant, but it doesn't really mean anything to me. Peter and I have never had a face-to-face discussion, in the clear light of day, about having a baby. We've never talked about when it would be due, or discussed making the spare bedroom into a nursery, or thought about names, or analyzed any of the other changes we will have to be ready for. We've simply let our bodies follow an impulse, thinking that in all probability nothing will happen for quite a while.

The summer comes breaking over us like a cresting green wave, curling, falling, tossing us in its febrile maelstrom. Last spring, I dug up lilac bushes from an old cellar hole and planted them at the four corners of our house; they bloom for the first time, their purple blossoms languorous and fulsome as testicles. Five baby goats prance stiff-legged in the daisies, their tiny smiling lips nuzzling the palms of my hands as I kneel in their pasture under the summer clouds. As I cultivate my garden, leaning over my hoe, working between rows of young beans, I can see Peter working in his studio; I hear the hum of his wheel, see his slim back through the open door, the heels of his hands pressing a twisting column of brown clay. I'm thinking about my goat herd, the pure-bred buck I'm having shipped from Ontario; I'm thinking about the buckwheat that our neighbour Harry is helping us plant, and about my new story, which is still in the euphoric planning stages. Then I think that I might be pregnant. My mind hangs a blanket in front of this idea so I won't see it. It can't be true. We were testing our commitment to an idea, not making a baby. Faced with the possibility that somehow a choice has been made, I shy away from my part in the decision. I deny, to myself, the part I played. I decide that I really don't want to be pregnant right now, and am probably not.

Then my breasts begin to ache, and all I want to do is sleep.

Dr. Kay examines me internally, pushes gently on my belly, confirms that I am almost three months pregnant. He is delighted.

I feel bewildered. The little golden acorn has exploded within me, and it contains feelings that can't peacefully co-exist. I resent Dr. Kay's excitement. His interest in me seems to have quickened only because I'm going to have a child, as if who I was, or might be, is of little concern.

Mostly I'm afraid of the unknown. I feel as if hands clasped me and made me walk, blind, over strange ground to an unspecified destination. I have no choice. I might pluck at these hands, but they will not leave me. The way will be easiest if I close my eyes and walk steadily.

At first I resist. I've only just started taking my own steps. I've only just begun to choose my own direction. I've only just begun to glimpse myself.

I panic at night, when I'm tired. I can't remember why we did this. I forget the child-spirit that touched me in the spring light. I forget the gut quiver of excitement. I can neither understand, nor imagine, that I am no longer only me; that the fatigue I feel is only a shadow of the new burden I will carry, forever.

Mornings, I awake from uneasy dreams. I'm nauseated; I lie on my side, teeth clenched, breathing carefully through my nose. Then I sit up slowly and hold my head in my hands until the queasiness subsides. The unchanged sounds of summer seem to come from the pages of a children's book whose illusion I can't believe.

I am not joyful or serene. My mind touches and recoils from all that lies ahead. I see a list of words I have never associated with myself. They are alien, sharp with fear: labour, delivery, breast-feeding, teething. I am the girl who did not play with dolls. I am the girl who couldn't bear the sight of my body because it wasn't as lithe and straight as the tomboy-me who lived in my mind's eye. I had forgotten that the children Peter and I had tentatively begun to imagine would need me as their vessel, their bearer, the ship in whose dark cabin they would make the long passage from there to here.

My parents come to visit. We're putting in hay; it's July. Summer clouds tower over the fields. My mother does the dishes after sup-per, and Peter and my father and I take the tractor and the hay wagon up to the east meadow. In the long summer dusk, shadows stretch from the bales, making black oblongs across the stubble that gleams in the rich light like scarred gold. Swallows cut across the sky, scything the hapless insects whose wings are iridescent in the lingering light. I drive the tractor, turning the steering wheel hand over hand as we come down the hill with the final load.

We walk to the house together after the last bale is tossed into the mow. The cold air smells of spruce trees and hay; there's a pale sky-gleam over the western ridge, and pebbles in the drive are just discernible, rolling before our boots.

Shadow Child

Night suddenly becomes night, shiny-black beyond the windows, once we come inside. The kitchen is clean in a way that is not mine, but reminds me of childhood: dishtowel neatly folded over the edge of the sink, wildflowers in a pottery vase in the centre of the scrubbed wood table. My mother is on the phone when we come in. She smiles at the receiver as she sets it gently on its cradle.

"That was Aunt Bernice," she tells us, as we pause, shedding hay and the night's grace. "Uncle Len died tonight."

Death puts its finger on our chests, suspending us in its presence. No one speaks. We stand silently spinning our emotions into containable packages.

My mind wings like a swallow down over the darkness to Cambridge, where I last saw my impeccable uncle Leonard, dressed in a three-piece suit with a triangle of handkerchief where his trembling hand could easily find it. He placed his finger on a picture of himself in a scrapbook and said, "There is a gentleman who has not quite yet passed away."

Tonight, on the phone, my aunt Bernice told my mother not to come back for the funeral. She said, "You need to be there, Alison, with your daughter. You need to be there with the new life that's coming, as this life leaves.' "

Here it is again, the sense everyone else seems to have about my pregnancy, their perception of it as an event of profound significance, when I haven't yet got beyond my own anxiety about what's happening to me. Their words, their emotions, break on me like water on rock, and I want to argue with their excitement, I want to say: *I am me, I am me. See me. I was growing into myself, I haven't stopped.*

But I feel something else tonight. Death stands here with us, with its stark silence. Where there was Uncle Leonard, now there is absence. I hear my childless aunt's words; into the absence comes new life.

I feel a sudden, startled silence within myself. The clamouring voice of my self is stilled. I begin, at that moment, to listen, to realize that within the inner hush there is something new to hear.

In August, I can see my belly. I stand in front of the mirror. I'm beginning to be excited. I'm astounded by how I look like a Rubens angel; how my body is not fat but abundant, and my skin glows. People look at me knowingly, with little smiles at the corners of their mouths.

I work at my desk in the cool, early mornings, crouched over my paper with sharpened pencils and a mug of tea. I see the cows lying in the wet grass under the maple trees, chewing their cuds, staring east as the sun comes spearing through the spruce trees. I feel blessed by daybreak; I touch the mystery of emergence, I feel the stillness of those things that have embraced the night. I'm trying to make something that holds truth; I want to make beauty like the dewdrops that mirror the world on their transient surfaces. I want words to curve like chalices around feelings, ideas, memories.

I spend the days harvesting my garden.

I'm filling my freezer with plastic bags of chard, green beans, broccoli; I line the shelves of my pantry with jars of raspberry jam, and hang bunches of savory and thyme and basil behind the woodstove. I slice apples and slide the round, star-holed circles on string, which I loop, like a clothesline, from the ceiling. The kitchen doors and windows are open, so I can feel the breeze as I work over the woodstove; I smell woodsmoke and phlox, goldenrod and vegetable steam, hear clothes snapping on the line. On the floor, there are bushel baskets of onions waiting to be braided, and the counter is covered with pie shells that I'm going to fill with wild apple slices and freeze. I feel like a small animal, a squirrel or a chipmunk, not winging south but preparing to settle in for the long winter.

Shadow Child

I sit, exhausted, in the green rocking chair by the stove. I close my eyes and drop my head back. My chopping knife hangs loosely in my hand.

I feel a small tick in my belly.

My mind shuts and opens, like a door closing on one place and opening on another. I drop the knife and sit up, both hands on my belly. The water continues its rattling boil, but the sound is suddenly loud; sunlight is broad, washing over the yellow-skinned onions and the succulent green basil. My eyes fly open to a new present. I wait. I feel it again, a small urgent tick. It is not mechanical, like the twitch of a muscle. It's urgent, willed.

I sit in the sunny kitchen in the late summer, in my twenty-fifth year, and forget everything I am doing, or plan to do; I wait, amazed, listening with the palms of my hands. Then I jump up and go out to the pottery studio.

Peter washes the clay from his hands, wipes them with a towel. All the time, his blue eyes are looking at my belly. He puts his hands there, and we both watch. I feel the kick. It's like a friendly shove, a nudge. It's like a voice that we hear for the first time. My eyes fly to Peter's face as I feel it.

He is totally still, astonished, his face open with wonder. I see that he, too, has met our child.

Frost comes and my garden is finished. Everything seems higher, as if claimed by the hard blue sky. Leaves, seeds, bits of bark, geese, swallows, everything leans into the wind, is carried away.

In September, Kathy gives birth to a baby girl. Bob and Kathy and Erin bring her to see us on their way home from the hospital. We stand in the driveway, our faces burnished by afternoon light. Kathy calmly folds a piece of white blanket back from the baby's face. Each eyelash is curled by the swell of her cheek. She is like a seedling, still creased with the folds of long containment. Bob

75

tenderly lifts the blanket at the bottom, shows us the miraculous sight of tiny feet, toes neat as unshelled baby peas. They name her Bronwen.

The next morning, I walk across the fields. I cross the big hayfield, and then another field; I cross the bridge over the brook in the hollow, where I feel the chill morning air rising from the water, and come over a rise. Bob and Kathy's log cabin sits under a maple tree at the far corner of the field, smoke rising from its chimney and from the stove-pipe of the barn on the hillside, where Bob is making furniture. As I push open the back door, I can smell the fresh scent of laundry, which is hanging on a line strung between the house and a spruce tree.

The baby is in a cradle in the sun. The walls of the cabin are the colour of honeycomb; the floors are varnished pine. Erin tips over a drum-shaped container of coloured wooden blocks. On the woodstove, the kettle croons like a setting hen. Kathy makes tea; she is calm, unhurried. She seems as centred as a woman newly in love. She touches everything deliberately, lingeringly, as if she forgets that her fingertips are no longer resting on her baby's face.

I curl in a chair, cupping my tea with both hands.

The baby in the cradle stirs suddenly; her fists paw the air. Her face puckers and her mouth opens in a cry of distress. Erin bundles across the room, interested. Kathy scoops her from the cradle. She sits in a rocking chair, one hand deftly arranging blouse and breast while her eyes hold steadily on the baby's face. She speaks lightly. "It's okay, shh, here's your milk." The baby's eyes close, her expression smoothes back into its unfathomable remoteness; her lips make tiny sucking sounds, and Kathy's fingers relax on the white blanket. Erin stands on tiptoe to peer into Bronwen's face.

When the baby has finished nursing, Kathy puts her into my arms. I feel awkward, afraid to move, thinking I will make her cry. The sun is hot on my shoulders. The baby is solid and warm. She smells sweet, a baby-smell as singular and lovely as fresh-baked bread. She opens her eyes and we look at each other. She doesn't blink, but gazes at me; she's still in another world, and its peace is her only emotion. She's looking into my eyes, but she's not seeing me. She looks far beyond me and sees everything that I have forgotten.

That night, Peter and I lie side by side on the living-room floor. He presses his ear into my belly. We wait, together, for the little nudge. We look at each other, realizing there are not two of us here, but three.

"Hi, Sprout," Peter says, making a megaphone with his hands, his lips moving against my skin.

In late November, I sit in the kitchen, knitting. Next to me, the woodstove radiates heat; in the firebox, a log crumbles. Embers tumble through the grate onto the floor tiles, where they flicker and fade.

We've lost power; no phone, no electricity. The snow started quietly last night, but now wind rips the snow from the ground, chases it in furling sheets across the fields, slashes it against the windows. The blower on the furnace doesn't work; the kitchen stove is our only heat source. This morning, I brought my notebook and papers to the kitchen table; I lit a kerosene lamp to dispel the cold white light. The wheeze of the tea kettle and the hiss of burning logs were steady as heartbeat, unaffected by the moaning shudderings and convulsions of the wind as I scratched words on yellow paper with my pencil.

Now I'm making tiny blue mittens without thumbs.

I feel as if I'm in a ship. As long as it makes its way sturdily through the storm, we're safe, warm, provisioned. My fingers lift and wind the wool, and I think of potatoes and carrots in the root cellar, cords of dry wood, braids of onions, jars of preserves. Peter hauled buckets of water from the brook at lunchtime. Bread rises in a bowl.

I lift a grocery box onto the kitchen table. Inside are baby clothes that Kathy dropped off for Sprout.

I take each thing out of the box: terry-cloth jumpsuits, flannel nightgowns, receiving blankets. I hold them up, and then carefully refold them. I smooth the tiny arms before bringing them forward; I make the feet turn perfectly inwards. I shake out the blankets, fold them against my belly. I make piles of separate items. I put them back in the box.

I lift the stove lid and twist a chunk of wood onto the pulsing coals. Then I stand with my hands over the heat, looking out the east window where the landscape has vanished like my own vision of the future, replaced by shadow and light, unspecific.

The baby lies on the other side of childbirth, an event that I can't imagine. Nor do I know whether I'm carrying a boy or a girl, or what this child's life will be like.

Like the storm—which brings me to the one room where there is water and heat, clarifying my needs and reducing my options—so I am distilled as the baby grows. Past and future wing in separate directions and grow small as soaring hawks. This child, who did not share my past and will shape my future, claims all of my attention. I stand by the stove, feeling the restless manoeuvrings in my belly. The storm shrouds the house, and the house carries me; and I feel, in my increasingly careful hands and my gathering patience, how I learn, already, to protect and cherish the life that I, in turn, enfold.

I am afraid of hospitals, needles, blood, pain. I can't hide from these fears, so I decide to acknowledge them, engage them. I read, think, reason with myself. I squat, exercise, rehearse. One night, I sit for four hours without moving, reading an entire book

Shadow Child

by a British midwife. She says to think about how animals give birth: quietly, in darkness, breathing deeply, with eyes closed. I sit, when I've finished, thinking about how I'm like a bottle with a ship inside and I have no choice, the ship must emerge. My feelings plunge and soar. One minute I imagine myself curled and relaxed; the next, I'm screaming, feet trapped in stirrups. I've read too many Victorian novels. I remember, instead, what Kathy has told me in her calm, matter-of-fact way. She says it's hard work, that's all. I work now, my eyes closed, mentally battling and gaining ground.

We begin going to a Lamaze class at the public library on Thursday evenings. There are six other couples. All of our babies are due in January or February. Everyone seems edgy, and we listen to our instructor with intense concentration.

Every night, at home, we have a practice session. Peter squeezes just above my knee as hard as he can, while I close my eyes, rub my belly lightly with my fingertips and breathe in, breathe out, practising mental travel. He holds his watch and times the contractions. We begin to be proud of ourselves. We're young parents, preparing ourselves for the moment when we'll meet our child. When we've finished our exercises, we return to our endless debate about names. We love to name things. We name our tractor, our car, every animal, even the goat kids we're going to sell. We ridicule each other's choices, and then return to serious reflection.

In December, the neighbours give me a surprise baby shower. It's a cold night, and we drive down the road to their white farmhouse, where I'm amazed to see trucks and cars lining the road. Everyone is there, even Armour Black, who walks the back roads with an axe on his shoulder and has neither hair nor teeth. The men play cards in the kitchen, and I hold court with the women in the living-room, with an upside-down umbrella filled with presents. I feel blessed. I feel as if loving arms are wrapped around me.

Our child has been welcomed by the community, has been greeted by old men in suspenders, by the slap of cards, by shouted insults; our child has slept within me while around us plates are balanced on knees, women make pithy comments, family photographs gleam on the pump organ, there's the smell of tea and a babble of talk. The little house is warm and vital in the frozen black night; it sends its lights onto the snow, holds a whole village under the silent stars.

I'm losing my hearing. It is a degenerative disease, encoded in my genes. The loss has crept over me gradually, muffling, damping, eliminating entire ranges of sound. I haven't heard an owl since I was a child. I don't hear bees, the brush of wind against my ears, train whistles, cat purr. I stand close to people and watch their lips. I ask questions so I can control conversations. I know the isolating feeling of a general laugh whose origin I have missed.

My ears begin to ring. Dr. Kay sends me to an ear specialist. The specialist examines me, and then tells me that I have a bony growth on my stapes, which keeps it from vibrating. He can perform microsurgery to replace the stapes. It will restore my hearing only partially; the operation is not without risk and is not always successful. He tells me that if I get pregnant again, the disease will accelerate, even after I've had the operation. Chances are I would become completely deaf, in which case even a hearing aid wouldn't do any good. He tells me that the disease can be passed on to my children, especially to girls. He tells me that I should be content with one child and not risk a second pregnancy.

Peter and I drive home from Moncton in silence. Fear drains me of energy and loosens the sinews of resolve. I slice bread on the wooden table starkly, as if I'm a blinkered cart horse. This child I'm carrying is the only one we will ever have.

Shadow Child

I wear a pair of Peter's overalls. I can't see my toes and can barely fit between the end of the bed and the wall. My breasts are blue-veined, sweaty where they lie on the swell of belly. I look at Peter's body in amazement. I can see muscles like sand-ridges on his stomach. I put my ear on his belly and can hear only the empty gurgle of digestion. He lies on his side with his ear on my taut skin and says he can hear, just barely, a heartbeat. I can push on a slippery hard knob in my belly, and it pushes back.

I am me, and I am more. My body works independently, beyond my will. It blooms like a rare flower, astonishing me. I feel as if I, too, like the baby, am trapped inside myself, small and restless within this fecund package. We're together, separate souls inside one body. I feel hiccups, somersaults, kicks; I stagger to the toilet four times every night, and know if the baby is sleeping or awake. We are still together, but the baby is rapidly outgrowing me. It becomes less a part of me. We begin, even now, the process of separation. I feel the baby's urgent need to emerge and begin.

On Christmas morning, Peter and I unwrap presents for Sprout and are more excited than we are about anything anyone sends us for ourselves. There's a book of poetry from David; hand-knit baby mittens with strings; a pair of tiny shoes. Peter puts the shoes on his fingers and makes them walk. My father sends a wooden toy-box that he made. It's painted blue. Inside, it smells like fresh wood and varnish. We prop its lid open and arrange the toys, books and clothes inside it. I sit on the floor, leaning against the couch, my belly between my legs. The cat picks his way between a white receiving blanket and a pile of brand-new cotton diapers. Every day, now, is edged with the glitter of anticipation, even though Christmas is here.

There's a massive three-day blizzard, and then the temperature plummets and there are more storms, more snow. The pottery studio is sunk in a wind-well, surrounded by blue-lipped drifts. We cross-country ski every day, pushing through powder snow so deep we can't see our skis. I feel as if I'm carrying the baby in a papoose slung on my belly. Someone has given us a blue corduroy baby-carrier; we discuss, as we push across the blueberry barrens at sunset, the snow tumbling in glittering red bursts from our poles and skis, how Peter will know what it feels like to be pregnant when he carries the baby on his chest, spring skiing.

Every day we work on the nursery. It's a tiny room on the south side of the house, with a sloping ceiling. We strip wallpaper, patch plaster, paint the walls yellow. We rent a floor sander and return the spruce floorboards to the clear white of living heartwood. Peter spends evenings in the woodshop, making a set of shelves.

I stand in the doorway of the nursery before I go to bed at night. Daily, something new happens. The little room changes from a seldom-used unheated storage room with sagging wallpaper painted pink into the heart of our home. I can't wait for the paint to dry, the varnish to set, so I can bring in the cradle, the toy-box. I can hardly wait to spread the little white blanket, to smooth away every wrinkle.

The baby is due February fourth.

Finally, there is nothing left to do but wait. It is like the phase in a garden when the plants have reached perfection, and it is time to pick them. But I am in the hands of something greater than myself. I can only wait, endure, dream, drift.

I'm sitting in the nursery on a sunny morning at the end of January. There are frost ferns on the window; outside, the snow fractures the light, its crystals shifting in a ceaseless glitter, sparkling blue, red, gold. The room is as clean and pure as the blue-shadowed snow. Over the cradle, there's a drawing of a fairy riding a swallow, its gauze cape swirling with the bird's wings. Bob made a child-sized table and two little ladder-backed chairs with rush seats. The chairs are pushed into the table, and on the top is a begonia plant with delicate pink blossoms. Peter carved a flaming sun on the shelves. Everything shines with new varnish, including the floorboards and the shelves, on which I've piled the blankets and jumpsuits and diapers and Sprout's Christmas presents: a *Pat the Bunny* book, the Snugli, a blue rattle hammer, a floppy dog. I open the toy-box, rearrange the shower gifts that I keep there. I run my hand over the piles of soft flannel blankets, patterned with stars and moons, as if I'm stroking a cat. I pick up an ivory teething ring with a dented silver bell, which was Peter's, and a soft-bristled brush, which was mine, and a purple velveteen horse, which is Sprout's.

We've finally decided that a girl baby will be Molly Taintor, a family name. Only last night did we find a boy's name: Tate, old Anglo-Saxon (the book said), meaning "the cheerful."

The phone rings almost continuously, and I lumber downstairs, holding the bannister. People are calling, "checking." I'm expecting to start labour at any minute. I can think of nothing else. I read and re-read my Lamaze book. I pack my suitcase.

I go past my due date. We ski, one Friday, and I fall at the bottom of the hill, on my face. The snow is so deep that I can't get up until Peter reaches me. I hold his ski pole, and he helps me flounder to a kneeling position, and then to my feet.

The baby doesn't kick all weekend. Friends are visiting, and they hold their hands on my belly, eagerly waiting to feel the baby, but never do. On Monday, the baby still hasn't kicked. Peter presses his ear to my belly and thinks he can hear the heartbeat. I call Dr. Kay, who says not to worry; babies are often very quiet just before they're born. Two days later, we go to his office and I know the baby is fine: I can hear its heartbeat through the stethoscope. I picture it as black notes of music, sporadically jumping up and down.

On February eleventh, I receive ten phone calls. Everyone has a myth, a remedy, a story to share with me. I imagine myself stepping through a door into a room filled with women who are strong and whole, who have completed the initiation that I have still to undergo. There are children in the room, faces dusky in candlelight; there are sleeping babies drifting in and out on the sea of becoming, coming closer, all the time, to shore.

That night, Peter and I work in the studio. He's trimming pots on the wheel, and I'm dipping pots in glaze. When I'm done, at nine-thirty, I bundle up in my old air-force parka and go out into the freezing air. I stop in the door of the house before going in and look back at the windows of the pottery. Their light makes the icicles glitter and throws warm squares across the snowdrifts, which are almost as high as the windows. I'm suddenly filled with wonder. I'm amazed to think that Peter and I built that pottery, that this beautiful northern farm is our home and that we're expecting a child.

Chapter Five

I t's *February thirteenth.* We drive to town for a doctor's appointment. On our road, the snowbanks are higher than the roof of
our car. I notice how wind has made an archipelago of snow
islands on the fields; how each one casts a curved blue shadow.

Peter and I sit together in the waiting room until the nurse
calls my name. I go into the examining room; a young nurse helps
me lumber onto the table. Dr. Kay comes in, and we smile at one
another like partners, discuss inducing labour if this baby doesn't
decide to come out soon. I stare at the sterile green walls as he
presses the cold circle of the stethoscope into my belly. I've been
missing the baby, who has become so quiet. I need to hear the
small, dark drum of its heart, impassive and steadying as the break
of waves. I'm waiting for the moment when Dr. Kay's face shifts
from concentration to attentiveness, the moment when I sense
him quicken as he finds the heartbeat and listens intently,
acquainting himself with his new patient.

He moves the stethoscope, with increasing pressure and

precision, from place to place. I glance at him. His eyes are wide, inwardly focused. He's staring at the wall as he listens. He suddenly tears the stethoscope from his ear and steps to his desk, returns with a small black funnel. He presses it into my belly, hard. His face is towards me as he holds his ear on the funnel, but he doesn't see me. He moves the funnel on my belly, pressing it so deeply into the flesh that I'm afraid for the baby. He mutters something, and leaves the room abruptly. I stare at the ceiling. My heart begins to pound heavily, as if it has grown huge inside my chest. Dr. Kay returns instantly with another doctor. They are both intent, silent. The second doctor presses the black tube into my belly. His face is masked with the same anxious, inward intensity; he moves the funnel over and over, as if unwilling to stop.

He straightens; the two doctors look at one another. Neither one looks at me. They leave the room.

I swing my legs sideways, push myself up so I am sitting. Everything in the room slides away and adheres to walls that seem to have curved up around me like a Christmas ornament. The only thing I see is a plastic cube with school photos of Dr. Kay's children. The studio backdrop is turquoise; the false colour, the bright clothing, the camera smiles, all are part of another world, outside this moment. Their faces augment the thick surge of my heart.

Dr. Kay returns; Peter follows him.

I notice Peter's Save the Whales pin. It is on the blue army-surplus parka that he carries folded over one arm. The sun slices the gleaming stainless-steel trays on the work station. I can see, in Peter's shocked face, that Dr. Kay has told him something. Dr. Kay comes to the examining table and puts one hand on either side of me. I can smell his tobacco and the starch of his lab coat. I feel him trembling. There's a split second before he can pull his eyes up and stare into mine. Still he can't find any words. He seems as shocked as Peter.

Shadow Child

I find myself speaking words that would be appropriate only if I knew everything was all right, as if they will make it so. "Is there a baby in there, or not?"

He says, simply and gently, "I can't hear a heartbeat."

Peter helps me into my coat. We are being sent to the regional hospital in Saint John, where there is monitoring equipment that may hear what the doctors cannot. Dr. Kay leaves, makes arrangements, returns. He holds the very edge of Peter's whale pin, looking at it dumbly. He seems reluctant to leave us. I see him going down the hall with one hand out to the side, as if he's pushing something away.

We go out into the skin-freezing air, onto the slabs of dirt-flecked ice on the sidewalk. Car roofs glitter in the sun. We put our arms around each other and weep.

It's an hour drive to Saint John. We say nothing. I cry all the way, without sound, my eyes staring. We have nothing to speak of save our hope, which is inexpressible.

When we arrive at the Saint John hospital, we are separated. I see Peter standing at the desk, both our coats draped over his arm. He's admitting me; he looks numb, as if he can't make any sense of the papers before him. I'm in a wheelchair; the nurse swings the chair in a smooth, relentless arc that has no relation to my desire or fear. I am cargo, being delivered.

I'm in a room on the seventh floor. I can see out over the harbour; can see the soundless and remote furling of flags and the reptilian pluming of steam; can see derricks, bridges, highways, their glass and steel honed by winter light. Colours in the cold air are harsh, like advertisements.

I lie on an examining table. I'm wearing a green hospital gown, soft from countless washings. A young British intern gently pushes it up over my belly. Two other young men make adjustments to a machine that they've rolled close to the bed. The intern bends over me, holding a metal disc as if it's alive, the way a diviner grasps his forked wand. I close my eyes. I feel the cold flat steel, heavy on my flesh. I feel a vital stillness come into the room, as all our minds, like migratory birds, wing swiftly towards the same place.

I hear a gurgling rush, a liquid churning. It continues, unchanged, the monotonous gargling drone of digestion.

The intern moves the disc, deliberately pressing, methodically, on every square of an imaginary grid. Each time he moves it, my heart quickens. I tense. I can't believe the dark drum will not suddenly come tapping through, urgent, independent, continuing unabated somewhere deep in the soft waters.

There is no sound save the wash of fluids.

"I'm sorry," he says, finally. "I don't hear anything."

There is nowhere to go inside my head, so my brain shuts down my imagination. The moment assaults me, too loud, too bright, too fast, as if to compensate for the evanescent, shrouded images of past and future, which I've lost. I feel the corduroy lines of the footplates under my paper booties as I'm wheeled down to X-ray. I notice how bobby pins make tiny dents in the fabric of the nurses' white winged caps. The technician's voice, as I'm helped to the X-ray table, is so hearty that I can't understand her words but hear only her separation from me, her inclusion in this ongoing present through which I'm being transferred.

Peter comes towards me down the hall. My mind opens to receive him, and includes memory and hope, as my emotion rises and our hands clasp. The nurse leaves us in an examining room, and soon a doctor comes tilting in from the hall, carrying a file folder that contains my records and the X-rays. He's an older man with thinning hair; he's hurried and harried. He tells us that even though they have not been able to locate a fetal heartbeat, the X-rays show that the skull is not collapsed, and so there is a slim chance the baby is alive. He says I am going up to the maternity ward, where I'll be prepped and then put on an intravenous drip to induce labour. Extra blood has been put aside in case there are complications, but he expects a normal delivery.

Peter goes to buy me a new toothbrush, toothpaste, comb, deodorant, all of which are sitting in my suitcase back home. When he returns, I'm in a private room. It's six o'clock, and the pulp mill, the dock cranes and the Martello tower have turned to black silhouettes against the fiery sky and then gradually been absorbed by winter dusk, like piers at high tide. The city lights, without context, float and shimmer on the darkness like a ship's running lights, scattered and stretched on a night sea.

I have a needle taped to my left hand, a bag of pitocin drip on a stand next to my bed. The nurse has checked it and left. Peter closes the door. We are entirely alone.

He holds a bunch of daffodils to my nose, and I smell their cool, earthy fragrance. He puts them in a vase at the foot of my bed. Then he unpacks yoghurt, fruit juice, oranges, toiletries. I feel as if he's building a raft, gathering scarce materials with the resourcefulness of survival. He arranges everything on the bedside table, refolds the thin hospital blanket and settles it around my shoulders, shifts a few daffodils, tidies my clothes.

The small room, high above the night city, is warm and quiet. It is like a sanctuary; the daffodils are our offering. They are translucent, pure as sunshine; they radiate light, as if lit from within. I look at the trumpet faces with their papery petals. They carry me to wind, rain, soil; to the fields of their birth, where yellow tapestries beneath grey clouds ripple in sea wind.

The nurses glance at us as they come in; they leave quietly, without comment.

I drift away, knowing Peter is steering the raft.

Labour begins. I feel the cramps, low and deep, the purple-veined fruit of pain that I first felt when I was fifteen. The cramps come and go, and come again. I recognize the wringing darkness, the dragging heaviness in bowel, thigh and womb that has informed me for ten years of my unneeded nest, of my body's rhythmic preparations, of the mysterious vessel I inhabit. I concentrate on the daffodils; Peter begins to time the contractions. The nurses come in, watch us, adjust the drip. Labour proceeds rapidly, driven by the relentless drug. After only three hours, my mind begins to realign itself. I lose the edges of vision. I see the sweet flower faces; I cling fiercely to my image of the silent fields on the Scilly Isles and the sound of seagulls, and then the room falls away. I hear Peter's voice speaking to the nurse, but I have lost the flowers, too; my eyes are closed and I travel farther inside myself as the ache explodes, like rage, into pain, and I feel sucked into the curl of a massive wave. I'm tossed, flung, aware only of the fight to stay conscious. Someone puts ice in my mouth. I shrug the blanket from my shoulders. Hands touch me, brush hair from my sweating forehead, roll the bed down, check the dilation of my cervix. My mind begins to detach. I am panting, blowing, listening to Peter counting. I know that there is the room, the flowers, Peter; there was our quiet place, our sanctuary, where we were still poised, only moments ago, on the cusp of our dream. There is Peter, lifting grapefruit juice to my mouth, my lips closing on the straw. There is the road we've been following, its familiar territory, the terrain I've grown to expect. There are the things we are doing that we've been practising for weeks: my fingers, effleuraging my belly, down, around, up; me, sitting cross-legged, breathing in through my nose, out through my mouth. But my mind is ripping like cloth, the threads separating into rags that whirl, untethered, into territory without paths, or directions, or language, or symbols. It's a place of confusion and terror, where I hear my voice; where my eyes see my belly standing out from my body like something separate, hard and quivering; where something crashes to the floor and many hands lift me

Shadow Child

to a gurney and hot lights make a flesh-red flood as I'm crying out to Peter to kiss me, to hold me; where I'm holding my ankles and pushing and a voice says that the head is out; where I feel the passage of a great weight from my body, an exit, a leaving, and hear myself calling, as if in a place where I'm alone, "Is it alive?" and no one answers.

I'm in a bed in the maternity ward. It is very late. There is a curtain between my bed and the one next to me, where a mother nurses her baby.

I have been given a shot to stop my violent shaking, and another one to dry up my milk. Peter and I eat bread and cheese. He goes to make phone calls. He washes my face with a warm cloth. The nurses bring extra blankets.

Now everyone has left, even Peter.

In the next bed, the baby cries and cries. Its tiny mewing spirals, coils tighter and tighter, and then breaks. It begins again, tightening towards an inconsolable point that always reaches an apex. The mother makes whispery shushings. After a while, I hear only tiny wet suckling sounds.

I feel as if all the mothers and babies who nest together in the intimate circle of night-lights, cheek on soft head, tiny hand on breast, are a community from which I've been expelled. No one here will speak my language. I can't speak theirs.

I feel detached, weightless, connected to nothing more than my visceral reaction to exhaustion and freedom from pain. I am empty. Nothing weights my belly as I lie on my back. I feel the pillows coming up around my face and the blankets warming my body. My hand, with the needle still piercing it, lies on my chest.

I did not see my baby. I am told it was a perfect baby boy. The words mean nothing to me. The nurses are talking about someone else's baby.

I feel dry and empty, like a husk. I am myself again. I am only myself.

The sedative is like oil, smothering my mind, disconnecting my thoughts and making my feelings dissipate. I lie sleepless. I am always awake when the nurses come to take my temperature, check my blood pressure, change my bloody pads.

I can see pale smoke drifting across the black sky in one window-pane. I watch it, formless, randomly shifting, evolving, dispersing, like something alive that never begins or ends.

I lie awake all night, watching the drifting smoke, waiting for light.

Chapter Six

The next day is Valentine's Day, and my meal trays arrive decorated with red cardboard hearts. There are hearts on the paper napkins; hearts suspended from a string, looped over the nursing station.

Young men walk past my door. They're carrying flowers, red carnations and shasta daisies, bound with ribbons. They are young fathers and they're going to visit their sweethearts, who have become young mothers. Their faces are eager; they leave behind their toughness as they walk nervously through the maternity ward, restraining their excitement; they're on their way to see their new babies, with whom they'll be tender, silly, wondering.

Peter comes in at ten o'clock. He's carrying a backpack filled with everything he could think of that might make me more comfortable. He brings me a valentine that he drew himself that morning. It's a picture of him and me. We're a couple, in a place where everyone else has become a family.

He sits by my bed and we hold hands. He looks at me searchingly and seems relieved, as if he expected me to be in far worse shape. I'm still disconnected. I have no feelings except the strong sense of unreality. I drift in and out of consciousness, find myself waking from a sleep I didn't realize I'd fallen into. I'm vaguely aware of Peter's intensity. He is like a child who runs when hurt, as if to escape the pain. He is used to always being in charge, to being able to fix whatever is wrong. He goes out during the day and returns with the smell of winter on his coat. I stare at him as if he's been in another world while he shows me brochures he got from a travel agency and suggests we take a trip; then he tells me that he called social services about adoption. He's as far to one side of grief as I am on the other. He's running; I'm sleeping. He's had to make arrangements with the funeral parlour for the cremation; he's had to call our families and tell them the news; he's had to talk to friends and sleep alone in our house; he's had to deal with the hospital about the autopsy.

I'm given another sleeping pill with lunch.

My parents arrive; they drove half the night, six hundred miles up the eastern seaboard. Their concern is for me. I feel a shell coming over me when they arrive. I struggle out of bed. My IV stand rolls next to me as we walk slowly to the visitors' lounge, passing young women in bathrobes holding tiny bundles wrapped in pink or blue. I notice my mother putting her hand to the side of her face and making a soft sound of anguish as we walk by the glass windows of the nursery. She glances in with a haunted expression. I feel like a character in my own dream; I have no substance, no feeling. I am empty. I am inside a calloused hide. I look in the nursery as if it has nothing to do with me. I'm not a mother. My heart is empty.

Dr. Kay arrives, bringing me a little gift from him and his wife. He sits close to the bed and holds my hand. He is on the edge of tears. I watch him, feeling nothing. I don't understand, yet, what has happened. I'm just myself again. I don't realize I've had a baby. I feel as I did when I was first pregnant and everyone else was more excited than I was. I can't connect with Dr. Kay's emotion; I know that he is surprised and perhaps disappointed not to find me in tears, not to be able to comfort me. But I haven't arrived where he is yet; I'm still numb.

The next morning, a nurse arrives early, takes my blood and tells me I'm free to leave. I get up slowly, get dressed. I am packed and ready to go when Peter arrives. Today he is white, haggard. He can barely speak.

We walk down the hall past the mothers, who glance up at us. I am carrying the daffodils. Peter is carrying books, bags, suitcase.

A nurse speaks to us at the desk as we're going out. She is cold, impatient. She tells us we have to fill out a stillbirth form before we can be discharged. We put down our things. She pushes a pen and paper across the desk, which is so high I have to stand on tip-toe to see it. I feel the nurse's hostility. We are like blemishes on perfect fruit, and might infect the others. Peter's eyes fill with tears; he tightens his lips to keep them from falling. The form asks for the baby's name.

We stare at the paper in bewilderment. Because I have nothing that makes me understand that he was a real baby—no footprint, no lock of hair—because I didn't hold him, or even see him, I feel that the child I carried inside me has simply been reabsorbed into the ether from which he came. I want to keep him not yet begun, and so not yet finished. Naming him makes me face the truth of his death. Naming him takes him out of the place where I want to keep him.

All this whirls through my head as the nurse stirs and indicates without a single word that we are obstructing her.

Peter writes down a name that we had rejected as too grand,

too mythic, then shows it to me. I'm not sure, but we are being rushed and there is no one to advise us. I nod, pressing my lips together to keep from weeping. The nurse pulls the paper away.

We ride down from the maternity ward in the elevator.

We get into the car. Only then do I feel, for the first time, the feeling that will haunt me for the rest of my life. My arms ache with emptiness.

There is only us, going home, crying all the way.

There is no one in the house when we arrive. The kitchen is the same as it was three days ago. I walk through the house slowly, disoriented.

Nothing has changed. The winter sun still slants across the varnished spruce floorboards and haloes each geranium plant. The tea kettle still reflects a distorted room on its gleaming side. The wooden spoons still lean against one another in the pottery jar.

There is nothing to do. There is nothing to move towards. I walk into all the rooms, weeping. I go through the kitchen into the dining-room, where music is open on the piano, into the sunny living-room, where my desk, in the corner, is as tidy as I left it. I go on, slowly, up the stairs.

The nursery door is closed and the hall is dark without the sun that streams from the south-facing room.

Inside the sun-filled room is hope and love: the little toy chest; the shelves with the rising sun; the bright yellow walls, the soft nightgowns with their suns and moons; the fairy, trailing its gauze over the swallow's back; the velveteen horse and the Snugli; and the *Pat the Bunny* book.

I stand in the dark hall and then grief begins. It bursts from its seed, begins to wind its tenacious roots into my soul. I can't go into the room. I can't open the door. I think that if I keep the door shut, the pain will subside and then the baby, still and always a

Shadow Child

dream, will sail loose like the fairy on the swallow and take my grief with him.

Later, my parents are here. We hug, but do not weep. We are all thinking that we should protect one another, and we talk about food and sunshine, wrapping words like gauze bandages around the unnameable wound.

Peter and I take a nap after lunch and cry in each other's arms. We talk about the birth, trying to remember every detail. I try to describe the contractions to Peter, how I felt like a tree in a windstorm, or a flower being battered and bent by rain, or surf itself; how I became mindless, part of a dark power that was black but made of many colours; something warm, blind, painful, emotionless; something direct and deep, without sympathy. As long as we talk about the birth, I am still close to the strange rapture of creation.

Then we fall silent and I feel Peter's hard chest under my cheek. I feel his breathing. I hear the beating of his heart.

Now I sense a new presence. It holds me, bends close to me. It breathes a bitter breath that cloaks me, weights me. It mocks, drains the substance from everything: from Peter's chest under my cheek, from the wool blanket over my shoulder, from the snow-bright light on the plaster wall. Nothing is safe, nothing is exempt. Its choices are without meaning, beyond reason. Death reaches with cruel fingers, rips away the face of life. It fills our silent bedroom, watches over us, broods, waits.

I am like a prisoner. My mind darts from side to side and meets only bars. I can't believe our baby is not here. I want to know where he is. I need to hold him. I need him. I want him. He is not here with us. He is not downstairs with my parents. I can't believe he is gone. I can't believe we can't find him, bring him back.

I turn my mind back endlessly. I want to be waiting. I want to be sitting in the rocking chair with my hands on my belly, pushing, feeling the baby push back. A boy. A boy. I want to be waiting for the miracle, feeling the light inside me, the silver and green of a summer's morning.

He has slipped away without a sound.

No one counsels us. Someone tells us, in the hospital, not to have a funeral. The funeral home in Saint John is taking care of all the arrangements, whatever they might be. I don't want to know the details. Suddenly we are isolated. The eager phone calls that came every day, before the birth, have stopped. No one knows what to say or how to react. We don't talk to our families. We see only my parents and our closest friends. My pregnancy has ended. A child was born, but we hold no celebration of his life, no mourning of his death. He goes away like mist, touching the landscape with beauty, vanishing before the light of day.

I awake, two mornings after returning from the hospital, with my breasts hard and lopsided, so filled with milk that it seems the skin will split. Milk drips steadily from the dark nipples. My body reacts with fever; I shake with chills, my face burns. I am turning back on myself, consumed with futility.

My hands shake. I'm weeping as I strap on the nursing bra that I bought months ago. I go downstairs and sit in the rocking chair. I am beside myself with anguish. There is nothing to do with this milk; there is no baby to feed it to. I am ready, I am completely prepared for this child who is not here. Every day his absence is more painful. Peter drives me to Dr. Kay's office.

I sit on the examining table. The photo cube with pictures of his smiling children is distorted by my tears; my cheeks feel chapped. Dr. Kay comes in, and then I begin to sob. I show him my dripping breasts and tell him that on the day the baby stopped kicking, Peter and I were skiing and I fell forward onto my belly. I put my hands over my face, choke on my tears. I awoke, today, obsessed with guilt. I shouldn't have skiied when I was pregnant. I should have been more careful. I should have come to see Dr. Kay as soon as it happened. I fumble in my purse, wiping my nose with the back of my hand. I'm wearing towels under my shirt to absorb the milk. I'm flushed with fever. I show Dr. Kay the vitamins I was taking, certain that they are somehow to blame.

But my deepest guilt is something I can't tell Dr. Kay, because I am so ashamed of it, and because I know it is the real reason the baby died. I know the baby thought I didn't want him. I know he felt my misgivings when I was first pregnant. I know my love was not strong enough or true enough. He left me; he didn't want to meet me. He didn't want me to be his mother. I have an obscure sense of this baby as someone very old and wise, who considered me and found me unworthy.

"You're not to feel guilt," Dr. Kay says to me, holding my shoulder tightly. "Look at me. You're not to feel guilt. If anyone is to feel guilt, it is me. Okay? You are to feel sorrow. Only sorrow."

He asks his nurse to bring me tea. He writes a prescription for medication to dry up my milk. He tells me over and over, in various ways, that it wasn't my fault, and that he will try to determine the cause of the baby's death.

Peter and I drive home without talking. I stare out the window. The only word inside me is why. I can't ask Peter this question; he is absorbed in his own unspoken guilt. He is a man who couldn't save his son. We are people who "lost" a baby. We are people untouched by the finger of divinity.

I want to turn back time so badly I feel my mind will break. No one can drive away the despair. There is nothing I can do to help myself. There is no cure for a broken heart.

Our farm is fifteen miles south of town; the road follows the swale of a wide valley. Beside us, glittering fields spread up the hillsides, untouched by hoofprints or toboggan runs; spruce trees carry loads of snow on their curved boughs. Smoke rises from the chimneys of small farmhouses that have been redefined by snow, their shape changing with the wind-shifted drifts, rectangles of north windows cut by a curved lip of snow, a back door carved from a blue snow wall, shed roofs slanting from unbroken waves of snowdrift.

It is the blue heart of winter; the landscape seems frozen and complete, as if suspended in an icicle. Every surface is a prism, makes cold fire with the elements of light. The air is so cold, and so clear, that far-away things come close, distances vanish; trees are distinct, isolated from one another, quiver like mirages.

I see people, town-bound, bundled in wool toques and scarves, passing in cars. I see farmers ploughing driveways on their tractors. I see smoke coming from chimneys like steady flags, indicators of comfort. Life is going on as if nothing has changed. I watch it without comprehension. I'm in a place where there's no past, no future. The present is fragmented; nothing makes sense. The string that threads one moment to the next has snapped. I see the beauty of the winter day and it dazzles me with cold dread, like the point of a knife held to my face.

When we get home, my mother is baking bread, and my father is fussing with the firebox, sliding dampers, poking at the coals. They are trying so hard to be cheerful. They are being very loving to one another; it's the only way they can safely express their love for us, the only way they can safely staunch their own grief. And they have been preparing for their first grandchild; my father's love gathered as he built the blue toy-box; my mother knit hers into a soft blanket. Now it has nowhere to go, like my milk.

Kathy has dropped Erin off while she takes Bronwen to a doctor's appointment. He's asleep in our bedroom. I go upstairs to use the bathroom. I look into our room. I see his blond hair on the pillow, the red batik bedspread mounded over him. He rolls over suddenly, completely, and gazes at me. He is looking directly at me, as no one else does. His eyes are placid, sleepy. He takes his thumb out of his mouth. He says, hopefully, "Baby? Baby?"

We've lost our only chance to have our own child. Now I think about what this means, as I never did when it was still a possibility. Peter and I will never have a child who has my high forehead and Peter's generous mouth, my blonde hair and his long legs. We won't glimpse a grandfather's sense of humour in our son, or see how a daughter resembles her cousin. We'll never have a child who has germinated in the warm soil of our love for one another.

This anguish tangles with my grief and augments the endless ache of loss. I can't separate all the strands that are snarled within me: sorrow, rage, shock, longing, guilt, bewilderment, loneliness, rejection. I begin not to be able to look into Peter's eyes. One of my feelings meets one of his and is repelled; they clash, like dissonant phrases of music; they don't resolve, they don't blend and wreath around one another. Grief is lonely. We are two people sharing the same grief, and yet as the days pass, we spend less time crying in each other's arms. We hide our grief from our family and friends; and then, gradually, from one another.

Peter is obsessed with beginning adoption proceedings. It's his way of healing a wound; the future will absolve the past. He wants to set the framework for this in place. He wants to replace our baby with another one, like building a new barn. I know that he's making these phone calls. It's a pattern of our marriage; I'm not sure whether I agree with his plans, but I don't tell him not to make them. The idea of adoption, for me, is as abstract as the idea of pregnancy was before it began. And now I have a new set of fears: I want a baby in my arms, but I want a baby who is ours. I wonder if I can love an infant who arrives without nine months of living heart to heart, sharing blood, sharing breath.

My ears ring and make roaring sounds. I wonder when deafness will come down around me like a shroud.

My heart is so heavy I am weighted down by it; I can hardly walk. I feel like doubling over and holding my chest with my hands. Aside from my heart, my body feels so empty that it aches. I was a nest. I myself have been a nest, soft and warm, protecting a tiny life. My nest has been ripped open, the life wrenched away. I am torn, lacerated.

A week after the birth, or the death, I push open the door of the nursery.

The shelves are empty. All the baby clothes are gone, as are the little book, the horse, the folded corduroy backpack. I open the toy chest. It is empty. The plant has disappeared. Only the picture on the wall is still in place.

I look at the empty shelves. Someone is trying to protect me, but I want the baby clothes. I want to hold them in my arms. I want to bury my face in the soft diapers and let my tears soak into the sweet-smelling cotton.

I stand in the empty room. I want to hold my baby. It is all I want. I want to hold him.

I sit on the bottom step of the cellar stairs. I have shoved a log onto the pulsing embers and shut the furnace door. The flames begin to tick, to crackle. Light flickers through the grate. It is dark down here, far from the glittering snow-light. This is the only place that feels like my soul. Cobwebs make soft tents from beam to beam; there's frost on the stone walls, and water drips, sporadically, from a copper pipe. The dirt floor smells like potatoes and old bark.

I bury my face in my hands, drag my fingertips through my hair. I can't face another unstrung moment. I want to stop living.

Shadow Child

My head is filled with black rage and my thoughts pour like pebbles, sliding, striking one another.

I am afraid of my love for Peter. I am afraid of any attachment. I rage at death. I see him with his scythe and his faceless cloak. I feel his implacable mockery. I claw at his face, tell him I will never love again.

Rocking with my face in my hands, I say, in my mind, "Please, God, please, God, please, God." I want someone to help me. I have no faith, and yet I am broken. I am crying out, calling, by whatever name, to the green-and-silver light that has left me.

One night, when my parents are still with us, I look across the supper table at Peter. I watch his mannerisms; they could belong to no one else. His hands, which are so deft and strong when he's centring wet clay on his wheel, are clumsy handling fork and spoon, fishing coins from a wallet, shuffling cards. I watch him chasing a piece of cauliflower around his plate. I can see the boy he was and the man he's becoming. He's still somewhere in between, in his mid-twenties. He's beginning to lose his defensive edge; to lean back as if within the chair of his own authority; to listen, as he's doing now, to my father, who delights him.

Peter and I begin to make a shape together. It's the shape of the life that we're building, each taking the wet sand of experience and patting it against the shape the other is in the process of making. Sometimes my pile knocks down his; sometimes his undermines mine. But more often, we bolster one another, and so enable each tower, each buttress, each wall of our sand castle to grow.

I watch as his fork finally spears the cauliflower. I think, "We had a son." I feel a sudden, searing wonder. For a moment, and for the first time, I allow a radiant feeling to fill me. We are parents. Peter and I truly are parents. I feel light piercing my inner darkness, slanting towards a place I've never seen. The light comes unbidden, without warning, like the moment when I felt the baby's first kick. I'm suspended within it. I glimpse the truth: when a child is born, parents are born. I am a mother. Peter is a father.

I stare at Peter across the candle flame that burns between us, and I want to tell him this, but then the light inside me goes dark; another thought comes like a cold draught and snuffs it out. This thought warns me that I'm having a fantasy, and that I'll only hurt myself with it; it tells me to face the fact that we don't have a baby, we don't have a son, we don't have a child, we are not parents. It advises me to shield myself from the solid fact of our baby's death so I won't be haunted by it. It tells me that if I never think of myself as a mother, then I don't have to carry such a terrible burden. It tells me that our baby was only a dream; he never lived. His life never began, and so he never came to be.

I extinguish the light that tries to illuminate our baby, that would have let him come alive in my heart.

On the morning that my parents leave, Peter and I talk with them about adoption. They are encouraging, positive; we all try to fool each other into believing that we are going to look forward and not back, that we are going to be positive. We fold the death of our baby into a handkerchief that we stuff to the very bottom of our pockets.

I feel a thin snake of fear coiling in my bowel when I sense the distinctive silence that means it is time for us to say goodbye. Every goodbye makes me acknowledge the choice I made to leave the soil of my childhood. With each goodbye, the journey of separation begins anew.

My mother's softness envelops me as we put our arms around one another. It's as if her softness absorbs me, as if there are no boundaries between us. It is a feeling that comes from no one else; a strange absorption, so that my love has no definition, it is for us both, as if for one entity. Our eyes gaze nervously; I see in her eyes a courageous love that accepts and forgives all that I don't yet understand. Then I feel the steel arms of my father, restraining the full power of their strength. He holds me for a long time and makes little comforting sounds in his throat that say everything words cannot.

Car doors slam. Peter and I stand on the driveway, between the snowbanks, and wave as the car passes beneath the maple trees, turns left at the end of the long lane. We watch its roof pass between the high snowbanks of the fields, and then we see it, once more, as it passes the church and disappears, heading south.

It is three weeks since our baby's birth.

We go into the house. I feel the absence of their suitcases; of my father's tenor recorder on the piano, and his book of Telemann quartets; of my mother's blue nylon parka and grey wool gloves; of her glass jars of brewer's yeast and mint tea, labelled with masking tape. They have taken all these things away, left nothing behind.

There is an echo in the house, a reverberation. It is like the last rays of sunlight stretching across a field, shining in the awns of grasses, flashing on the wings of birds, sliding down window glass. It is the dance we made as we stepped through meals and dishwashing, as we made music and read out loud, as we heard the tap of toothbrush on sink and the murmur of voice from behind closed door, as we fed animals and watered plants and wove words over silence.

We stand in the kitchen and hold each other as the echo fades, as the house empties.

Then we go upstairs and sit on the floor in the baby's room. Sunshine slants up the yellow plaster walls. Varnish glistens on the pine shelves, on the spruce floorboards. The room is warm, peaceful. A fly buzzes.

I feel a sense of finality, an incremental shifting of events, so that some of them belong to the past. An entire life has passed, from conception to birth to death. Our baby has gone ahead of all of us, has skipped the long years that stretch before us, has returned to the dark sea without experiencing the joy and pain of passage.

I don't understand, but I think about this, without tears, my head buried in my arms, in the drowsy sunshine of the room that would have been his.

I shut myself away for most of March. I don't want to see anyone. Once, I go to town with Kathy. She is holding Bronwen in her arms. We stand together in the drugstore, waiting to pay, and the woman behind the counter says to me, "And where is *your* baby?"

It's what I dread the most. I dread her horror, when I feel my mouth saying, "My baby died." I dread the feeling of shame that follows. I have not fulfilled the promise of my blossoming body. I have no new life to kindle the glow of love in people's faces. I have only death to share. No one wants to see it.

One day I push open the hall door and find Peter going into the back shed. He is holding something. I follow him into the dark room where we keep our trash cans, our rakes, our snow shovels; where skis lean against the molasses-coloured walls in summer, and lawn chairs in winter. I sense instantly that he is protecting me, and I demand to know what he has in his hand. It is a small metal container. It came in the mail. It is from the funeral home.

I take it from his hands, pry it open. Inside is a wad of pink packing material, like insulation. I pull it out. Underneath, there is a handful of mica-like bits; not bone, not ashes, but grains like crushed rock, like sand glittering with broken shells.

We are both stunned. Peter tries to take the can from me. He wants to bear this particular horror for us both. I am fierce, sensing a need that is both irresistible and unseemly. I reach into the can and touch the ashes with the tips of my fingers.

We are so shocked that we can't untangle the knot of our impulses. We both want to hide the can. It is like the stillbirth form. It comes from unloving hands. It denies the baby. It seems a reduction that makes no sense. My mind and my heart refuse it, and I feel the sick, violated feeling that possesses me at funerals. There is nothing here of life, of random wild growth, of beginnings and endings, of transformation. This anonymity is obscene. In my hands, I'm holding a fear of death so deep that no one even wants to see me receive our child's ashes; an unknown person mails them in a plain brown carton, with a label typed by a secretary and tape secured by a packing clerk.

Spring is coming. The rooms of the house are changed by the sun's angle. Shadows are shorter, the light is less ponderous and arrives without effort. In the hall, rubber boots shed mud. Two of the goats are pregnant. Every morning, the robin-song is as complex as running water; I can hear it, faintly, coming from beyond the storm windows, which still seal us into the dusty house.

I go out into the windy morning to tap the sugar maples. I put my fingertip into the hole I've made in the bark with a hand drill; the tree's inner flesh is bright yellow. The flakes of sawdust are moist, come off in my mouth as I suck my finger, tasting the faint earthy sweetness. I hear red-winged blackbirds. I hear the freshets in the pastures and smell mud. Under the soles of my rubber boots, ice crumples like shell.

I am sealed inside myself. I can smell, taste, hear, but I feel as if I'm encased in clear jelly. Nothing reaches the part of me that might react. My eyes are not connected to my soul. My heart is wrung, exhausted. I seem to brood more and more, and the ache grows greater as time moves on.

The report comes from the pathology lab. They have found nothing wrong. Both the baby and the placenta were perfectly normal. I undergo many tests, but when the results are analyzed, no problem is revealed. Dr. Kay tells us that we will probably never know why the baby died.

I carry hopelessness. It is the heaviest burden I have ever borne, and it makes me far more tired than I ever was when I carried a full-term baby. It weights my arms, making them hard to lift; the effort of carrying it displaces resolution. It settles like sand in my shoes as I move slowly across the kitchen, going to stir the sap that boils in the black-speckled lobster steamer. It makes me sit in the rocking chair, gathering my will, which is scattered like spilled rice. I wait until I have scraped enough bits together to rise, walk down the hall and split wood.

I stand in the back door, holding the axe. I listen to the incessant ringing in my ears. I wonder what I'm not hearing. I long to be pregnant again.

Last fall, we met another couple who bought land at the end of three miles of uninhabited dirt road. He is a potter, she is a poet. They live in an old barn that overlooks a deep, wooded valley. They've partitioned off the south end of the barn; a step goes from the dry, crumbling dustiness of abandoned cow stanchions into two high-ceilinged rooms piled tower-like, one above the other, the upper room accessible by a ladder that goes through a trapdoor. The floors and walls and ceilings are made of raw lumber, and the place smells fresh, sappy, like a saw mill. They cook on a woodstove, draw their water from an old well. Out back, in the wild raspberries, they've built a wood-fired salt kiln.

We begin to visit them frequently the spring after the baby dies. We drink mint tea by the light of kerosene lamps, while the cold April night rises around us—woodcocks dive in the darkness, their wings whistling over the tangled brown grasses of the meadow. Lee and Mary wear overalls and work boots; their faces

Shadow Child

are tanned from days spent outdoors. She and I talk about Seamus Heaney and Sylvia Plath; he and Peter discuss downdraughts. We decide to open a pottery shop on Broad Street, across from the train station, in an old barber shop.

Life seizes me, impassively. I have only one choice: to continue or not. I begin to separate myself into parts that are not connected. One part of me goes to town, driving the Jeep over deep ruts on the dirt road; one part of me kneels and vigorously strips paint, hammers plinths, laughs with our friends, drinks tea in the sun, sits on the sidewalk with my back against the building's warm brick, watches porters suspending themselves on one foot from slowing trains, speaks to the old people who stop to watch us work and tell us of their lives. Another part begins to shut itself away, like a recluse who can't bear the light, who can't bear to see or be seen.

Then it is May, full-fledged spring, and there are five baby goats in the barn. Maisie, the white duck, misguidedly sits on twenty eggs. Warm rains come that turn the fields green, even as I watch.

It is a warm foggy morning, and I step outside to smell the day. Spruce trees spike the mists that wreathe the hillsides. I can feel the sun behind the fog; I can smell river mud and balsam, the wild scents that sharpen the farm morning of manure and tractor drone, of ploughed earth and worms.

I walk around the corner of the house and find a raccoon on the front lawn. He lies on his side. His front paws are folded, one over the other. He is strangely rich, opulent, lying so still on the grass.

I start, recoil. Then I approach quietly, and stand looking down at the little dead animal with his dark face, his bandit's mask. His loose-jointed intelligent paws are as limp as wilted flowers. I kneel and lift the thick tail, run it through my hand. I stroke the round ears. I pass my hand across the tips of the whiskers.

The mists are lifting from the hills and the sky lightens over the greening fields. The sound of the brooks comes louder on the quickening air. The birds are singing in the branches of the maples, as if nothing ever changes from year to year.

I sit back on one heel and rest my arms on my knee. I gaze at the raccoon for a long time, trying to understand his emptiness.

Chapter Seven

In early June, we find someone to take care of our place and we travel to New England so I can see an ear specialist who we've heard of recently. He is renowned for a micro-surgical technique that he's invented to implant a stainless-steel stapes in the middle ear.

At his office, I'm taken to a soundproof cubicle. A young woman puts earphones on my head and goes out, pulling the heavy door shut so I'm sealed inside. I see her in an adjoining cubicle, through a window; she's adjusting knobs and suddenly her voice is in my headset. "Click the button when you hear the sounds." I close my eyes, concentrate. The sounds are unmusical yet resonant, like the songs of humpback whales. They become fainter and fainter, and then vanish, although I can see the woman continuing to turn knobs for a long time.

When I've finished, I go into another office. Peter's already there. We're waiting for the surgeon to evaluate the tests. I stare at the pink folds of the inner ear on a glossy poster. Peter pats my hand, but I don't want to be reminded of my anxiety. I stare at a rack of long-handled, stainless-steel probes. The contrast between the efficiency of the office—its veneer of normalcy; its secretaries and nurses, who are not deaf, who are busy organizing the facts of my disease—and my own sweating palms and hammering heart, my own feeling that within this cold and impersonal place my fate hangs in the balance, this contrast makes everything seem prison-like.

The doctor strides through the door carrying a folder. He's short, vital with authority, his face tanned, monkey-like lips curved in a smile. He's warm and reassuring. He tells us he's done more than five thousand stapedectomies and has a 98 percent success rate. He says there's nothing wrong with me that he can't fix. According to him, pregnancy has no effect on the disease, and he dismisses what we were told with a grimace of contempt. I tell him we have applied for adoption. He shakes his head, wonderingly, amazed at the extent of our unnecessary pain. He gestures towards pictures of children on his desk. "Have your own!" he says. He looks at both of us. "Have your own," he repeats gently, and pats me on the shoulder.

I feel my mind stumbling, spinning. I feel a door opening onto a new future. I feel the light of its space pouring into the dark place where I've been trapped.

When we get home, summer, as it does in the north, seems to have come overnight. The poplar trees shimmer, their coin-shaped leaves light-filled; they dance like flames against the dark spruces.

I call social services and tell them that we won't be adopting, that we've been told I can get pregnant.

I have a second chance. I will not fail this time. I'll tell our friends the instant I know I'm pregnant. I'll have a party to celebrate the new life inside me. I won't be afraid. I won't resist. I'll embrace whatever happens with humility; I'll be sick without complaint, I'll sit quietly, I'll listen.

I think I'm looking forward eagerly, but really I'm looking back. Really I'm saying, *I'm sorry, I'm sorry, forgive me. I'll redeem myself.*

Peter and I never speak of our lost baby, and so neither does anyone else. No one knows the baby's name; we never even speak his name to each other, since we're not sure what it really is. If he'd lived, he would have been Tate. This is the name we chose for the little boy who would have ridden a tricycle; the young man who would have borrowed Peter's jeans, asked for the car, loaded clay and drunk beer. But we put another name on the stillbirth form, and obscurely we know that it represents only our own confusion.

I begin a deliberate process of forgetting. I want to deny what I know is true: that it is my fault the baby died. I put the baby who died far away inside me. He's not part of my life, he's not part of the days that rise and fall and expire as Peter and I and the rest of the world roll ahead through time.

One summer night, I dream that our baby mysteriously divides himself into twin boys. We name them Garth and Morgan. Peter and I are watching them, longing for them to wake up so we can play with them. Then they do wake up, and I am kissing and hugging them, as though I am in love for the first time. I breastfeed them and am filled with joy.

I awake, feel my conscious mind displacing the dream. I send tendrils of sleep after the dream and carefully transform it into memory. I lie with my eyes closed. Cool summer air comes through the open window, smelling of cut grass. I hear the persistent clarity of dawn birdsong. I stay as long as I can in that place where I am a mother nurturing my children.

One evening in June, we babysit Erin and Bronwen. The field grasses are long enough to carry the breeze; they surge, endlessly, like water. The weathered boards of the grey barns are steeped in the last rays of the setting sun; every nailhead glints, every rain-eroded ridge casts a shadow. The barns become as portentous as standing stones, light-held and significant in the expanse of grass. The spruce trees on the eastern hills hold the last ruddy light, but behind them shoals of pink clouds expire on the dusky blue sky; I can smell the summer night in cold pockets, the sharp scent of mud, ferns, moss, spruce needles. We walk out to the barn to show Erin a dead chicken. I'm carrying Bronwen, whose eyes glaze and widen with resisted sleep. Peter bends to hear Erin, who is wearing nothing but a T-shirt and red rubber boots. The eerie wing-fluting of the snipes begins; the frogs start their sweet, unsynchronized chime.

Erin squats by the dead chicken, fascinated. He lifts her head, pokes his finger in her beak. He spreads her claws, feels the leathery scales of her legs. He strokes the flat place between her wings. The swallows fly in and out over our heads, carrying insects to their babies.

Dusk has softened the house when we go in. Peter sits in the rocking chair with the poetry book his brother sent to our baby last Christmas. Erin puts his thumb in his mouth and his eyes lose focus. His legs dangle and one of the boots falls off.

I carry Bronwen upstairs to our bedroom, where I make a nest with the pillows. I sit on the bed cross-legged, rocking her and humming until she falls asleep. I see my tanned leg, her small brown hands on my arm. In the darkening room of the old farmhouse, beneath the sloped plaster ceiling, our bodies make soft curves in the shadows.

I feel peace come down around me like a soft comforter. I remember how I was afraid of my love for Peter last winter. How death mocked me. How I raged at death and told it I would never

Shadow Child

let it have another chance to take someone away from me. I look at the sleeping little girl in my arms and think that I'm holding both life and death in my embrace. I think of Dylan Thomas's poem "And Death Shall Have No Dominion." A tear runs down my cheek. I sit holding her for a long time after she has fallen asleep. I know the price of love.

I am astounded by beauty. Summer opens, blossoms, is as exuberant as naked children running in rain. Because I have been close to the dark side of nature, I appreciate the fierce power of its opposite. I'm filled with elation. Life strikes me like a salt wave in the face.

I rise early, put on overalls and sneakers. I write every morning. I say to myself, in my journal, that I'm writing a story about "the terrible beauty of age." I think about old people, about lives lived at the brink of death. I imagine the stubborn courage of loneliness, and the exacting perception of diminishing time. The story rises in me, vigorous and elastic as bread dough. I carry it inside me all day long. It is my response to death, a clarification of my rage.

Late one afternoon, we meet our friends Mark and Claude and their two little girls on the banks of the Kennebecasis River, behind the lumber mill. The river is still high; Peter and I load our lake kayaks with food, tent, sleeping bags. When we're ready, we swing out into the current. The family goes first, in their canoe; the girls are like tropical birds, their black hair glossy over their orange life jackets. Their canoe rides low; it seems delicate, like any leaf or pod carried by the black waters, but the family is snug, contained. In the stern, Mark sends them forward with a strong stroke, while Claude dips her paddle more delicately, watching for submerged logs.

I head into the river, and realize instantly that my kayak is overloaded. At the first bend in the river, I can't make the bow turn. I glimpse the bright colours of the family in their canoe as they easily vanish around the bend, but the current is carrying me straight towards alders that grow out from the shore and make a dense stand in the deep water. I lean far forward to pull hard, with my paddle. The kayak flips.

I'm underwater. I kick to the surface and encounter the kayak. The weight of the river is holding it against the alders. I kick and try again to swim to the surface, but still bump up against the bottom of the kayak. It traps me, keeps me underwater. I push upwards and feel the bottom of the boat with my hands. I'm forced back down. My mind begins to split. I'm becoming part of the black water, but I see a world of green light. It's the essence of life beyond this world, spinning, bubble-light, but I will not accept it; rage like murder or blood-lust rips me past the boat and my head emerges. I am pinned between the alders and the kayak with the river pounding me. Peter has plunged into the river from his kayak and swum to me. He's shouting, pulling at the boat, making inches of space for me to pull myself out. Then I'm acting without awareness; I scramble to the bank and stand with my face like a death mask, spitting at the kayak, screaming at it. I come back to myself lying in the grass with tears streaming down my face. I have no thoughts. I am conscious only of being alive, conscious only of the sky over me and the earth under my body.

The family comes back. We go to their house and Claude runs a hot tub and makes me get in it. She brings me a glass of red wine. She and the two little girls bring flowers from their garden; they pull the heads off and drop them in the water, so I'm surrounded with pink peony petals, roses, pansies.

But the horror remains inside me. Black water, alders, and the spinning green light of death. I can't listen to music. I am close to tears for days. I leave my diary page empty. Death seems to be stalking me.

The summer is increasingly busy. Company comes: Mère, who is eighty-four and gamely flies up to visit, forgetting her ailments for a week; Peter's sister and brother; my cousin; friends of friends. Maisie hatches three baby ducks from her twenty eggs; I make cream with a separator; the vet comes and removes our billy goat's horns; we hike to the coast with friends, sit on bone-dry driftwood watching the white spume of waves; the toads at the pond begin to quack like ducks. I work at our store two days a week. I read funny papers with a young boy who comes to visit me on his homemade bicycle; I try to decipher the hand-waving stories of a man with a cleft palate; I sit behind our counter of tea crates covered with burlap and elicit stories from ladies who make mittens, from the wives of doctors, from the old men who room at the hotel down the street. I garden, cook, glaze pots, stack kilns and write.

I begin to notice how, as the summer progresses, I cease to live in the moment. I don't see what is in front of my eyes since I'm always visualizing, anxiously, what I have to do next. I'm terrified of failure, and yet I'm obsessed with creation; all summer, I try to write. I want to make something that succeeds, that will endure. Peter, too, works with manic intensity, as if he is obsessed with creating things that he can control. He tears down both our kitchen and our living-room chimneys; our house is filled with old bricks, and we set our guests the task of chipping off the mortar so we can reuse them. He hires a mason and works with him, building two new fireplaces and a new flue. He plans a pond in the east pasture; backhoes, bulldozers and gravel trucks arrive. We go to craft fairs; Peter produces enormous quantities of pots for our shop, for fairs, for wholesale. We work all day, then work every night after supper, pressured by everything we've set in motion.

But none of my stories, after the first one, is any good; and I don't get pregnant.

One afternoon, I'm on my knees in the squash patch. I'm working fast, grubbing up weeds with my fingers and dropping them into a bushel basket. The warm wind smells of wildflowers. Suddenly, I find myself examining my purposes. If I left all my tasks unfinished, no one would care. No one would chastise me. I have time to breathe, and stop.

I make myself sit back on my heels. I clear the day's list from my mind like wiping a window clear of condensation. I look out over the pasture. I see my pony grazing in the lush grass down by the brook; the black-and-white goats bound away, but always come back to him, as if for safety. Daisies, buttercups and redtop grass all bounce in the same direction when the wind stirs. I hear the trickle of the brook and the sweet searing cry of birds. I look at the squash leaves, see the crepey orange trumpets of their flowers. I imagine the baskets of hard-skinned buttercup squash I will carry into the house in September. I imagine the onions I will braid and hang behind the stove.

I am making food to sustain my life. What I do with that life is another matter. I feel the spiky hairs on the squash leaves. I make myself look at the weeds my hands have been scrabbling; I take them out of the basket and sniff them. They hang over my hand like limp rabbits. I come back to the moment and then I see myself as part of the picture, kneeling in the squash patch. I am as mutable, as fleeting, as everything else, but the life force beats in me as steadily as it does in the swallows, in the worms.

Everything is in movement: leaves, flowers, the animals, the warm wind, the serene clouds, me, my busy mind. But if I sit back on my heels and look out across the rippling grasses, I sense that

Shadow Child

beneath the illusion of movement, of change, is the imperturbable rhythm of the life force, a heartbeat that does not stop.

I begin to understand that it is life I want, more than anything else. I want to be gathered by that mysterious force; I want to be transformed, embraced and cherished by it. I want to be part of it, included like the swallows, easy in the sky.

Three times, my period is so late that I'm sure I'm pregnant. Each time, I feel a profound and secret joy, lovely and lush as the armfuls of lilacs I pick at the old cellar hole by the side of the dirt road. Once, Peter brings me a rose and a card; and on a morning of warm summer mist, thinking I'm pregnant, I go into the baby's room. I feel it is a place of hope again, of possibility, no longer a cold shrine. I ache to unpack the clothes, but I resist, wanting to be sure.

Then my period begins, and is so heavy that I suspect I have miscarried.

I spend the summer like a sunflower, lifting hopefully towards the light, and then drooping. Lifting again.

We come to the days of late August, when clouds pile and make the sky seem vast, a realm of its own dominating the landscape. In the rich light, colours are of consummation, rather than inception: pink fireweed, furze-yellow goldenrod, white aster.

We are on the coast with friends. There are nine adults, four children, a dog, and we are all naked, our clothes in piles around picnic hampers and coolers. We scatter, browsing the rocky beach beneath the red sandstone cliffs, calling to one another to report on found treasures. Rocks rattle and slide beneath our feet. Seagulls mew, hover over us and slide away; the waves curl, crest, glitter with sunlight and then break.

Icy water numbs the sides of my feet as I stand in the surf-rattled pebbles. I watch the waves emerge from undifferentiated water, each one as distinct as the face of a pansy, each one gathered back by the ocean. I'm mesmerized by the disintegration of form.

I feel the clean space between me and my friends. I feel how we all become small and separate, and how the wind blows between us and snatches away the words we call to one another. Time, too, is absorbed by space and wind. I feel as clean as scoured driftwood; the day has no imposed pattern, no exigencies save those made by heat and cold, light and shadow, hunger and thirst; I'm calmed and steadied by the endless boom and hiss of surf, as a baby must be by its mother's heartbeat.

I'm relieved to be fifty miles away from our farm. Everything about it seems small and unimportant from this windy perspective on the edge of the sea: its garden ready to harvest; the pots that are cooling and will need to be priced and packed; my unfinished story, which is tormenting me. My life seems tiny, small as a beach pebble, and as insignificant. I'm feeling tired, defeated; my period has come again. I carry hope like a precious egg and am exhausted by the effort of keeping it safe, unbroken, warm, alive. My memory of grief threatens to destroy its fragile shell. I can't help looking at our friends' babies and calculating how old our baby would be. I think, "My baby," and then say to myself, "No, no," and I put the feeling away. I keep telling myself that I need to forget. The longer I go without speaking of my lost baby, the further away the event seems, and so I think I'm healing. I remember birth without fear; I remember pregnancy. But there is an emptiness at the end, like a book whose pages have been ripped away.

A seagull dips, tips his head sideways to examine me with one eye. The wind whips my hair, and I notice that Claude and the girls are opening the picnic basket. I feel, suddenly, a profound sense of passivity. I want to let myself be shaped, as the waves are shaped. I am exhausted with effort. I want to stop trying so hard. I feel how mystery is at work within my own body, and I want to release my will, cut it loose and let it sail away, out of my sight. I want to let the mysteries happen, if they will, as they will. I turn to look out to sea, far out over the dancing waters. I'm clutching a smooth white pebble. My hands relax and I hear the small plop of the stone falling. I imagine that to let it go is like being a woman, like embracing life, like learning wisdom.

On October twenty-fourth, when I call the hospital about a urine sample I took in the week before, the nurse says, "Congratulations!" Her voice is charged with warmth and excitement.

I am pregnant. The baby was conceived in late August. It will be born next May. This child will have its birthday when the daffodils are blooming, when the swallows have returned, when the wild cherries dance in the hedgerows.

My belly begins to swell. My pants become tight, my breasts grow. I am so ready for a baby that I hardly dare hope too much, for fear of being shattered again. But we have entered that sweet, exalted place. At a party where children swarm around heedless parents, Peter and I look at each other and see the shared excitement of our secret. I imagine the cell burrowed deep in its nest in the lining of the uterus, its villi roots attached; I picture its fins and eyes and little tail. This baby is real, and I am not afraid; and I will not send any messages to it that might make it go away. I think, "This baby *will* be born."

On October thirty-first, we wake to find the fields covered with a thin layer of snow. The sky is dark grey, but the clouds thin and the sun slices through; for an instant, the ice-encased branches of the maples glitter. I've put aside my writing for the day. I feel Christmassy; I light a fire in the woodstove. I want to make the kitchen cozy and warm; I am going to bake, fill the house with the smells of cinnamon and nutmeg. Before he goes out to the studio, Peter brings down the box of baby clothes from the attic. I am going to sit by the stove and embroider green vines and red roses on tiny baby T-shirts.

I'm alone in the kitchen. I hear the snap of the fire and notice that the air outside is filled with snowflakes. I unfold the flaps of the cardboard box. I see a soft blue baby sweater. The smell of lavender rises, as evocative as the scent of roses in a walled garden. Nothing has been disturbed or dispersed. The essence of another time lingers.

I don't allow myself to feel, to cry, to mourn. I allow only the memory of the ponderous matronliness of pregnancy, the slow competence that is coming back to my fingertips as they tiptoe through the box and pull out only the little shirts I am going to embroider. Next summer, I imagine, the baby will wear mostly diapers and T-shirts. I close the box and sit in the rocking chair, pawing through my skeins of embroidery thread. I called Mère last night; I told her Molly and Tristan were the names we'd chosen for the baby. I called Kathy. She said she will get pregnant again soon so we can raise children who will be playmates. I called my parents, Peter's parents, my brother. They were all thrilled; I could feel their efforts to hide their anxiety.

As my needle pokes in and pulls through, making the stitches that Mère told me the nuns in Quebec taught her, I sense that my life is on track again. My story about the old people was accepted by *Fiddlehead* magazine. Another was accepted by *Tamarack Review*. I count the stories that have succeeded; not very many, but I feel a small core of belief in myself. I imagine the future. I remember how last winter I could not imagine even the next minute. My wrist bends and my fingers hold the needle tenderly.

I remember Granny, and wish she could see my baby.

Shadow Child

The land folds in upon itself like a bear settling for winter—turning, shuffling, finding its place of repose—then, day by day, retreating deeper and deeper into stillness and silence.

The fields are white, the farmhouse is white, the skies are grey. It's November; the tamaracks have lost their yellow needles, the birch trees are like wishbones on the hills. I walk across the frozen earth, going to the barn to feed the animals, and know that the air is going to begin its spinning soon. The snow will come one night, like a blind woman who dances in a place set aside just for her; who makes her own beauty, in solitude and ecstasy.

I feel the familiar early-winter sense of containment; still a pleasure, not yet a prison. I return to the house and hold my hands over the stove. I'm glad to come inside, where the windows let me see the place I don't want to be; where I can watch the trees whipping in the wind, and be surrounded by warmth, music, the smell of black-bean soup and cornbread.

I have a sense of resumption, a sense that I am back in the place where I belong. I browse through knitting books; I am going to make matching sweaters for Peter and the baby. I feel released, no longer separate, no longer unattached, no longer excluded. On the table are the eggs I've just washed: brown hen eggs, white duck eggs. Beads of water dry on their satiny shells. The phone rings and I talk to a customer, laugh, chat about the weather, write down an order for a stoneware casserole. I shove the tea kettle to the back of the stove. I notice that a few flakes of snow are passing through the air like messengers.

I am contained in life, and life is contained in me. Once again, I am graced, and this time I am hungry for the gift.

On Tuesday, I am exhausted. I go to the bathroom and find tiny spots of blood. Terrified, I call the hospital. The nurse is calm, reassuring. She tells me to go to bed and stay there.

I dream all night that I am passing gouts of blood, but when I get up and stumble to the bathroom, nothing has happened. My heart is racing so violently that when I stand up, I feel myself blacking out; I fall, calling Peter, who finds me curled on the floor, crying.

I spend the next day on the couch. I feel kneading fingers of pain in my womb, like menstrual cramps. My mind touches on them and is repelled, shies and skips like water drops on a griddle. I write in my journal. There's a barrier separating every moment from the next. I read P.G. Wodehouse. Peter is in some similar place; he suggests I take a walk. I stare at him in amazement. He paces out to the studio, comes back in, sits next to me and runs his fingers through my hair until I make him go away. I need to stay behind my walls.

At four, the cramps intensify. I crab my way upstairs, sit on the toilet. I pass something large, rubbery. I brace myself to look, but see only four large black blood clots. I call Dr. Kay and he says that I must come instantly to the hospital.

We drive to town. It's a twenty-five minute drive and I lie on the back seat with my feet raised against the window. It is pitch dark, pouring rain.

They are waiting for me with a wheelchair. Everything seems askew, tipped sideways. A nurse takes my blood pressure; I hear the sharp rip of the sphygmomanometer as she removes it, raising her eyebrows at Dr. Kay. My heart is beating so fast I can barely breathe. My mouth tastes of blood.

Dr. Kay examines me. He tells me that I am threatening to abort, and that I may lose the baby. I'm given a sedative, wheeled to a private bedroom. I feel the cold support of a bedpan; I feel more blood come out. I close my eyes, grit my teeth; I can't stop it, am as helpless as the waves. I feel something leave my body that is slippery and juddering. I put my hands over my face. Then I look at the nurse; she's a small, older woman. She doesn't want

Shadow Child

to look but she does. Her practiced face tells me nothing. She says it's tissue. She covers the pan and takes it away.

All night, I can hear the rain.

Nurses take my pulse and temperature every hour. I have no more cramps, no more bleeding.

I awake to a dark day. Rain lashes the hospital, the former army barracks, whose low, connected buildings ramble along an exposed hill. Lights are on; I hear the clatter of food trolleys, smell toast, hear the soft squeak of rubber-soled shoes.

I'm not allowed to move. I have to lie passively, doing nothing. I can't think about myself, because I don't know who I am at this moment. I follow the threads of the pink blanket. I remember the metal pot-holder frame I had as a child, and how I'd loop the warp and then carry the stretchy fabric loops over, under, over, under. I read the label on the tampon box. I count the letters on a wall calendar, trying to make them come out evenly, in groups of two and then three.

Dr. Kay comes in. He tells me that they are going to send the material I passed to Saint John for analysis. He says he can't say whether I have miscarried, but holds out hope that I haven't; if I had, he thinks there would have been more blood. He tells me that they will take a pregnancy test on Friday.

He leaves for the OR. I eat breakfast, feeling calmer, and then lie back against the pillows. My bed is cranked to an upright position. The nurse takes away my tray, smoothes my blankets, shows me the buzzer safety-pinned to my pillow. I watch the rain coursing down the window. The runnels slide like oil and then change direction inexplicably.

I can't read. There is only one place I want to be, and I don't know if I'm there or not.

Dr. Kay returns after his first operation. He pulls a chair close

125

to my bed. I notice how tired he is; how his eyes open wide when he talks, so I can look nowhere but into them. He takes my hand. I can't imagine the rest of his life; even though I can see his green suit and the mask hanging around his neck, I feel as if I'm his only patient.

"I've been looking at the tissue," he says. "I want you to be braced for disappointment. I couldn't see a foetus, but there is so much of it that I don't know what else it could be."

He continues to talk to me for a long time in his understated English accent. He tries to be calm, to make me understand that this is a small event in the scheme of human tragedy. He tells me about last week's car accident and the child who died on the operating table. He tells me to think of women who lose babies at six or seven months, and then he stops suddenly, appalled.

I understand his intent. I want to say that no sorrow is relative to any other, but I don't, because I know he's using words to fill a space that neither one of us knows how to acknowledge.

How can you brace for disappointment? It means expecting the worst while hoping to be proven wrong. I can't do either of these things.

All afternoon, my friends come, so I am never alone. They bring books, fruit, flowers, magazines. They give me themselves, talk to me about their marriages, their fears. I'm accessible to them as I haven't ever been before. There is no way I can hide my helplessness.

That night, I begin to cry. I cry for a long time. Finally, I press my buzzer. A young nurse comes and stands by the bed, anxiously asking me how she can help. I don't know what to ask for; I can't stop crying. I say through my hands, "I can't sleep. I'm so tired and I can't sleep." She brings me cocoa. I take it from her. My cheeks are swollen and hot with tears. I lean forward to sip and she gently puts her hand behind my back. I have no mask. I weep before her as I could not weep before my friends. I accept her help as I could not accept, or ask for, theirs.

She assures me that she will come back whenever I need her, and then she leaves the room quietly, as if I'm already asleep. I drink my cocoa slowly. I put the empty mug on the bedside table and roll on my side. It is not the cocoa that makes me sleep, but the buzzer on my pillow that I have finally had the courage to use.

Nothing happens the next morning. A different nurse comes and takes my vital signs, tells me I still have to stay in bed. I stare at the ceiling. I don't want to eat. My heart begins to accelerate, to skitter and pound. I open a *Chatelaine* magazine to a picture of a child's room, bright toys on red shelves, a toddler sitting with legs splayed like a fat cat. I hurl the magazine across the room. Its slick pages fan as it flies; it hits the wall. I hurl another one, as hard as I can. I rip a page from my notebook and grind the paper into a ball, viciously. I sit with my head in my hands.

I am cracking. I can't hope, I can't grieve. I feel only rage.

Peter comes later that morning. We are expecting the results of the pregnancy test.

A few days ago, Peter and I were talking about how we would teach this child to read; I was embroidering its little shirts; we knew when its birthday would be. We had chosen names. We were imagining next summer. Our edges were softening, our separate sharp selves were unfolding like flowers to the sun.

Now I hunch in the hospital bed with my knees up, and Peter is again sitting at my side, without daffodils. My heart is pounding. Sweat rolls down my sides, chilling me. I don't know where to put my mind. The future is like a picture whose glass has been smashed by a rock, whose frame is twisted. We are waiting to see whether failure, loss and shame will replace the spindrift of dream.

Dr. Kay comes into the room wearing his green operating suit, a stethoscope around his neck. "Hello, Peter," he says kindly, and then comes up to the bed and puts his hand around my wrist, gently. He looks into my eyes. He pauses. He says evenly, "The test is negative." His grip on my wrist tightens.

Our relationship shifts. He has exhausted his store of possibilities. He knows nothing, now, that I do not know as well. I see his eyes betraying him, unable to suppress the fear of his own helplessness. Before he speaks, I sense him pleading for my forgiveness. He, too, feels that he has failed.

We are no longer doctor and patient, but have become fellow voyagers on this rudderless ship whose destination is unknown, whose wandering path makes no sense, and upon whose decks random storms break without mercy or justice.

Love bears its price of pain, and has no power against the implacable force that empties my womb.

The land is hard and grey. Nothing moves. There is a snow sky brooding over the frozen brooks, the brittle brown stems of wildflowers, the rotten cabbage leaves in the garden.

I clean the house. I feel empty, exhausted. I stand at the edge of futility; it's like a deep pit with a crumbling rim.

Peter goes to a meeting to organize opposition to a nuclear power plant. I stay home. I don't want to see anyone; I don't want to eat; I can't see any point in doing anything. I sit at the kitchen table with my head in my hands, staring at the scarred maple. I fear that I will never have children. I fear that if I ever get pregnant again, I will die in childbirth.

I have a sense of having passed into a new stage of life; all my bright, innocent illusions are gone, and life simply progresses from day to day. No wonderful surprise waits for me. I feel the burden of having to fill my own life with event, ritual, creativity.

Shadow Child

Nothing will happen unbidden. I realize now, why children enter a life at this point and make a blossom of hope and growth, why human beings need the long years of watching the lovely, shining maya of childhood.

The snow comes and it is December. A new feeling crystallizes within me, like the icicles that hang from the eaves and grow thicker and longer imperceptibly.

Fate, like an actual adversary, is testing me, toying with me, and I will deny it any further opportunities. I refuse to be vulnerable, to cast myself into the blood darkness. I take all my feelings—grief, despair, longing, shame, guilt—and package them like the tiny clothes into a box whose lid I seal shut. I shove them deep inside myself. I feel bitter and hard. My life is like a horse whose neck I will keep bent as I ride it; I will keep my seat balanced, my legs close against its sides. It will not break loose again.

I have no children but suddenly, strangely, I feel with this denial that I have become a woman.

III
1976–1977

Chapter Eight

After Christmas, Peter begins to awake in the night with his heart hammering. He sits up abruptly, flings back the covers and leaps violently out of bed; sometimes he doesn't fully wake up until he's already halfway down the stairs. He's dreaming of flames, crumbling walls, red light pulsing behind the studio's windows.

He's obsessed with the sense that he can't control his life. He hardly dares sleep for fear fate will come stealthily, in the night, when he's unaware. I am less afraid of disaster than exhausted by the effort of gathering the scattered shreds of my hope. We've lost our vision; we can't see the life that we imagined, and so we have no sense of the future. We work without joy or energy, like people who walk without a destination, eyes downcast, unaware of wind-blown wildflowers or the sun's shadow dance.

In February, a year after our baby's death, we realize that we need to disconnect ourselves from our own past. We need to put enough distance between us and our farm so that all the memories we've been so careful to cherish and gather, both good and bad, become as small and precious as a picture in a locket worn close to the heart. We decide to spend a year in Europe. Suddenly, there's a subtle shift in the alignment of events. It's as if we've thrust a stick into piled ice, and the pieces begin slowly, majestically, to swing into the river's current. Lee and Mary have bought a piece of land on our road; they want to live closer to town and be our neighbours as well as our business partners. They need a place to live while they're building a house, so they will live in ours and look after our animals. One piece follows another. My brother and his wife are making plans to hike in Switzerland, so we'll join them. Someone else wants to take over our share in the pottery shop for the time that we're away. Our resolve to make a life on the farm in New Brunswick is like a strong, long-held dam; once broken, it widens rapidly, its edges crumbling under the weight of freed water. I'm startled by the ease with which we become one of the pieces of ice, or sticks, that are carried by the leaping waters.

What we do is refocused; Peter makes a winter's worth of pots in a few months so their sale will support us while we're away. I drive to town nights and unpack box after box of stoneware goblets, mugs, bowls, vases, setting them on shelves in the dirt-floored basement of the shop. They're no longer beautiful things that I love for themselves; they lose distinction, individuality. There are so many of them, and they've been produced under such pressure, that they're like offerings, payments. What were once embodiments of our dream, each mug or vase made special by virtue of its place in our vision, have now become soulless: tickets to escape.

By April, there's nothing left to do but leave. Our plans are in place; we've found a Soviet ocean liner that sails from New York to London and have purchased round-trip tickets. We've determined that we'll spend the summer wandering in Europe, and then will settle down for the winter in London to study. One after-noon, our friends gather in our kitchen to say goodbye. I realize that we've already left our little community; as soon as our minds began to shape a new dream, the threads of the life we'd woven here began to fray. We're like a spiderweb shredded by wind. We're only a sketch of what we once were, only a vague shape of an intention. As we drive away, and our waving friends become smaller and smaller, shifting into the faceless figures of memory, I feel relief rather than regret. I have a strong feeling that I need to let myself be carried for a while; to cease struggling, resisting, wrestling, determining. I want to take the risk of giving up.

I stand at the railing of the *Mikhail Lermontov* as we swing away from the New York pier. I feel like a seagull, blown by winds so strong that I can't quite control my direction. But it doesn't mat-ter; I spread my wings and hold steady in the fresh, clean, salt-spray air. The deck vibrates under my feet, the yellow taxis on Forty-second Street suddenly become irrelevant, part of another world; we're no longer on the continent, we're heading for the open ocean. The past separates, slides away rapidly. The Statue of Liberty looms, seagull splattered; the World Trade Center be-comes two tiny, glittering towers that dwindle until they're absorbed by the white sea-light, replaced by the mewing purls of gulls and the chopping of spume-tipped green waves. I've chosen to be carried away. I don't want to be able to return. I want our farmhouse, surrounded by wind-tossed grasses, to assume a new size in my mind, to reduce and become insignificant, the way Manhattan has been absorbed by the sea. I want to be in a new place every day; to make no attachments; to put down no roots.

For the next four months, I make nothing. I don't plant seeds or make bread. I don't hoe my garden or braid onions. I don't give dinner parties, I nurture no friendships, tend no animals, clean no stall or bedroom. We stop planning, and we drift. We have noth-ing but our hiking clothes, our backpacks, one day's food and a little car, a wood-sided Morris Minor. We drive down through France, where it's so hot that we stop in a cool wood and pitch our tent by a gate made of woven sticks; we watch cows drifting in hazy light as we tear chunks from fresh baguettes. We hike through the Alps, sleeping in cow barns—we rinse our sweat-soaked socks in mountain streams, hang them in glassless windows that frame green meadows and snow-capped mountain peaks, and they reek the next morning of fresh cow manure. We climb high into the mountains. At eleven thousand feet, my heart pounds so violently that I have to stop after every twenty steps; I stand, panting, forearm braced on bent knee. As far as I can see, there is nothing but the inhospitable mass of rock, broken by scree, the knife-edge lips of cornices, snowfields, green icefalls. In the earth's thinnest air, I feel the darkness inside me being displaced by another feeling, which is new and bears no relationship to any emotion I can name. It's neither hope nor love, neither passion nor pain. It's clear as light, and carries me beyond my human smallness into the exalted silence of infinity. I feel it here, in the summer snows, in the trickling of pebbles over cliffs; but I soon realize that it's everywhere, not only in the mountains but also down in the lush valleys, in the smell of roasting coffee, in the sound of church bells, in the window-boxes of petunias and geraniums, in the faces of children.

After our Swiss trek, we ramble north, always seeking wild places. On the Outer Hebrides, off the west coast of Scotland, we pitch our tent on a rocky hillside overlooking treeless islands with white sand coves; cows wade belly-deep in the cold surf, smoke rises from stone crofts and seals bark, heads glistening as they bob up to watch us, like friendly dogs. I watch tide pools, mesmerized by the stately grasp of barnacle antennae, the curling arms of red starfish, the waving fronds of seaweed; and the feeling grips me again as I lie on wet rock with my chin cupped in my hands, gazing at the microcosm, and carries me into the vast silence of the universe. My eyes begin to see clearly; my soul begins to listen. Peter and I lie side by side on a beach where no other human being is in sight, only the surf-wading cows, and we hear the wild dissonant drone of bagpipes carried by the wind. Sometimes we hear it, and then the wind veers and we can hear only the boom and hiss of surf. And I learn to trust again in the possibility of the unexpected, of the wondrous.

In September, we find a ground-floor flat in Croydon, South London. French doors open onto a back garden whose earth is fine-grained, like river soil, dense and moist; its sparse grass is intensely green. The sun is shining, and I stand in the open doors and look out on the garden. All around the small patch of grass are brick walls; I see a cloth cap and an arm rising and falling as a hammer bangs nails. I see chimney-pots and hear the never-ending, wide-throated thrumming of London, spiked with horns, metallic clangings, canine barks, human shouts. I've hung our two blue towels on the clothesline. I lean against the door-frame, tanned, relaxed, smiling, thinking that the towels are like me and Peter; they have nothing to do with this place, any more than they had with the bushes I draped them on in the Hebrides, or the stone walls in Yorkshire, or a hotel window in Innsbruck. We've been wheeling through our days, carried by the winds of whim and chance. I'm still connected to this feeling of freedom, of unattached drifting; I go back into the flat and set out our few possessions, with pleasure, like a child playing house. I put our white-spackled blue-tin plates and mugs on a shelf in the dark kitchen, whose window overlooks a concrete yard filled with rubbish bins. I pull our sleeping bags out of their stuff sacks; they smell of damp soil, of ferns and bracken. I spread them on the double bed in the bedroom, and tack maps of Switzerland to the walls of the living-room. I set out my journal on a table next to the coal stove.

Peter is away, registering for classes at his art college. We have been each other's family and friends for months, bearing the entire weight of each other's love and concern. We've never been without one another. But I'm ready to have days alone now. I'm ready to stop wandering.

I sit at my new desk, feeling content. Sun spills across the floor; in the living-room, the roar of London becomes as remote as distant surf, and yet the birds seem part of the flat, their insistent chirping as intimate as the drip of water in the sink. I want the summer's freedom to grace me. I want to touch my pen to paper and find it moving as effortlessly as sea-grasses in wind. Mountains, Iron Age forts, window-boxes, wet cobblestones, cowbells, the smell of rain-wet streets and coal smoke, the taste of oat cakes, black tea and digestive biscuits; I feel these things in my heart. I make a shape with my hands, as if I'm holding a bowl. I close my eyes, hoping that I'll be able to weave these things into a narrative that conveys the essence of this time.

This morning milk arrived on our doorstep, three small glass bottles with foil caps. Letters slide through the door-slot twice daily, before breakfast and after lunch. The coal truck came yesterday and poured coal into our bin through a chute. I've bought plastic carry-bags to take with me when I go to the open-air market three blocks away. There's a park just around the corner. Tonight I'm going to enroll in adult-education classes: Writing, 19th-Century Poetry, the Modern British Novel.

In the hazy, late-summer sunshine, before the rains of winter, the space of the open road is close behind me. I still feel the exoneration of travel, the freedom of being committed only to contemplation of the moment. I've been on the perimeter of life, and thus, oddly, I've begun to find myself coming closer to its vital mystery. I sit at my desk with my eyes closed, imagining the taut line beneath my feet as I take my first step on the tightrope that stretches between past and future. I don't want to be absorbed by this temporary home, yet I need to make a balance between wandering and settling. I'm trying to retain freedom as I slowly reattach.

At first, we feel like tourists, though with the luxury of having our own place rather than a hotel room. I am engaged in my writing; I enjoy my courses, am inspired by my teachers; I'm reading poetry, myth, novels, literary criticism; I'm taking notes, following tangents, my mind alert and freed from obsession. Peter comes home at dusk, talking about the visiting artists who have come to the college; his love of experimentation returns once he's freed from production, and he learns how to make plaster moulds, photo silk-screen on clay, slip cast. We spend weekends visiting art galleries, seeing French films, attending concerts; we eat profiteroles and drink red wine at an Italian restaurant on Goodge Street; we ride double-decker buses, always on top. Once, we see the queen riding side-saddle on a white horse; we watch families in parks where chrysanthemums bloom late into the fall. I write letters home, describing the way the fog diffuses the lights out-side of Buckingham Palace at night, and how I feel that I've come home, that it's the place of my native tongue, of the language that shaped my imagination.

Then it begins to rain. It rains and rains. There are slugs on the walls of our bathroom. I sit so close to the coal fire, trying to get warm, that I make a scorch mark on my padded jacket. When I close my eyes at night, the first sight that rises in my mind is the blue and pink lights of neon signs, blurred by runnels of rain, their colours twisting in puddles or glistening on black umbrellas.

One day, after we've lived in London for several months, I'm standing before a glass case in the Museum of Mankind. Inside is a carved stick. A placard explains its vital role in the ceremonies of Australian aboriginals. I stand in the sound-deadened room while a guard by the door stares straight ahead, gloved hands behind his back. I try to imagine the hand that took the stick from the earth, that brushed soil from it; I try to imagine the huts where it has leaned, the firelight that cast shadow-feathers on its carved surface. I try to imagine the passion within the hearts of those who loved it, who feared it, who trusted its power.

I glimpse my own separation from earth and sky. I'm becoming a watcher, a listener, a reader. I sense that I'm being leached of life. I stand, staring at the magic stick made soulless by its removal from the possibility of ever being broken, or lost, or washed away in a flood, or burned. I try to imagine the empty beaches of Barra, the stone crofts of Yorkshire; I try to imagine the sound of the wind in New Brunswick, and the mad swirling of snow dervishes. All I can see in my mind's eye are chimney-pots and tile roofs extending to the horizon. I feel the enormous weight of London. It seems like a dominant personality that will keep us here forever, passively riding trains, discussing the lives of characters in books or the dilemmas of people in movies, visiting museums that celebrate culture as if it were something rare or exotic, and so is kept enshrined behind glass.

When I return home, nothing has moved in the flat. Its air is still; not even a cat's paw has shifted the papers on my desk. I stand, listening. It is what I wanted: a place where I could be entirely alone, and undisturbed; a place to work, to grow, to develop my craft. But it feels like the glass case in the museum.

Suddenly, the summer is part of another era, no longer connected to this one, and I begin to realize that I am being absorbed as I fall into an undeviating pattern. Week after week, I take a train to my classes in Drury Lane, my train crossing the surging brown waters of the Thames; and when I come home after dark has fallen in mid-afternoon, I stare out the rain-streaked window and see my own reflection. I've become part of a picture. I'm one of the commuters; and when I step off the train in Croydon, and lift my umbrella, and feel the key in my pocket, I'm in step with everyone else, head down, going home.

By November, I am beginning to long for the unexpected. Every day is exactly like the one before; the sky is dense with cloud. There's no violence, no mornings of swirling snow, no howling winds, no clean, ice-glittering light. I tell Peter that I'm enraged with the trees, which retain their limp leaves long after they're brown and rustling, like someone determined not to vomit. Peter is gone all day, and sometimes I walk in the suburbs of Croydon, wishing I knew someone. I look over brick retaining walls and see gardens where next spring's green shoots have already broken the soil and now are stalled. Frost shards on the walls are as large as moth's wings and more fragile. I come home to the empty flat and make myself a cup of tea. I pore over the day's letters. I try to figure out what it is I really want to write about.

Early one morning, I dream that I'm wandering in a warehouse. Dark rooms are filled with chaotic jumbles of furniture, crates, mirrors. I push into a room with a sense of guilt, as if I know that I shouldn't go there but am overcome by the desire to do so. A man is standing on a chair. He is one of our close friends. He is wearing brilliant clothing, like a parrot in a dark forest; he's stringing a noosed rope to the ceiling. He is furiously angry, shouts, "Go away! Go away!" His force and power strike me as strange; such life, such energy, at the moment before death. I leave instantly, feeling rejected and hideously sickened by the intimacy of his choice, and by the way this death is totally private and excludes me.

I awake from sleep and lie in our lumpy bed, hearing the drone of traffic, the dripping faucet. The dream is like a stone in my belly. I curve around it, trying to smother the pain. I'm beginning to remember futility and entrapment. Now that we've ceased drifting and have come to a dead stop, I sense that I haven't really changed; that somewhere inside myself, I feel profoundly unworthy; and that my desire to create, to give shape to experience, to make something that will outlast my life, is like a rat that gnaws me, rather than a song that I hear and want to sing.

Later that morning, I look up from my desk and see a white cat in the garden. He is paused in a cat's complete suspension of movement, one paw raised; he is staring at me with passionless green eyes. I freeze as well, afraid to frighten him away. The garden changes to incorporate his soft, white wildness. It becomes a jungle where anything is possible. When the cat turns, suddenly, and leaps onto the wall, I go to the doors and open them. I feel the damp air on my face, smell petrol, toast, coal smoke. I glimpse my yearning, soft-pawed and elusive.

I want to take care of the cat, to feed him, to hold him in my lap. I want his supple body to flow like water over the static furniture of my life. I long to look up from my reading and see him curled in his own chair, possessing his space with an absent-minded flex of his padded paws.

Peter and I have learned that the purest form of freedom is being unattached: no one to love; no animal, child, parent or friend who needs our care. We've also learned that the price of freedom is loneliness.

The child comes like the cat in the garden. We don't expect its appearance; we aren't waiting for it. We can't say, or remember, the exact moment it begins. We find ourselves held by a gaze as steady as the unblinking green eyes of the cat; one day a child enters our minds and never leaves.

I look up from my reading. Peter is sitting by the coal fire, one leg tucked beneath him, the other bouncing slightly, channelling his restlessness; he is absorbed in a book, one finger on the page.

Shadow Child

I watch him, thinking that he reads like a child, swept up by the words, entirely unaware of what surrounds him, although I know his finger will stop on the word and he will come to attention the instant I speak. I hear the soft hiss of flame, see the red throb on the mica window of the stove door.

I imagine a child trotting from me to Peter with its arms out for balance.

The care we would like to expend on parents, friends, animals, gardens, business, place takes shape between us in the silent flat. Our energies slide like berries on a board, tumbling towards the same place.

I don't think about being pregnant. I feel the inception of this child in my heart, not my womb.

It is as if there are already three of us. As if we are a family: me, Peter and our love for one another, which, like a idea, seeks form. As if over the summer, we both followed the same inner pathway, took the same turns without discussion, arrived at the same place, at the same time. There is no need to retrace the route.

I remember my rage last year at this time. I remember my bitter resolution, and the power I felt as I turned my anger into reins, as I compressed my feelings like hands packing snow. Over the summer, my fingers have fallen open, my rage has been shouldered aside by the world's wild places. Life unfolds before me, even when I do nothing. I have recovered trust by following paths that seem to lead nowhere.

The days are closing in, and we realize how much farther north we are, in spite of the rain and fog. I sit in my class in the Adult Education Centre listening to my teacher, a thin, grey-haired, unmarried woman whose passion settles unhealthily into the Edwin Muir poem she reads aloud; the lights in the classroom are on at three-thirty in the afternoon. I step out, afterwards, into wet

London dusk. I meet Peter, and we take the bus to Victoria Station, looking down onto the turtling wet umbrellas, the end-of-day jostling, people so numerous that I'm no longer intrigued by their faces.

As we travel back to the flat together, on bus and train, we remind each other of the places we've hiked in the British Isles: Grassington, Appletreewick, Arncliffe, Malham Tarn. The names, like music, quicken memory. They evoke the smell of peaty earth, of sun-soft foxgloves growing from fissures in stone walls; the piercing cries of curlews, the dart of swallow over clear stream; the dispassionate bleating of sheep, and a herd of wild rabbits grazing in the filtered light of oaks; slate roofs, rubber-booted farmers, manure-caked Land Rovers; sheep dogs, sharp-eyed, black-and-white, grinning over panting tongues.

I make blinkers with my hands on the train window so I can see the Thames rather than my own reflection. Long fluting twists of colour stretch across the water, city lights abstracted and rippling like lures endlessly tugged by the current.

We decide to make our baby in Yorkshire.

Chapter Nine

P eter and I are sitting on sheep-cropped grass, leaning against
  a stone wall. Below us, the afternoon sun glints on the slate
roof of our bed and breakfast, one of a cluster of houses tucked in
a fold of the moors. A road and a river unfurl down the valley, coiling between green fields whose stone walls make a complex grid,
like the remains of Roman forts. A stone bridge spans the river;
from our vantage point high up on the windy moor, a red phone
booth by the bridge is the size of a matchbox. Blue-grey coal
smoke rises from chimney-pots, seeps into the air and tinges it
with its acrid bite, a smell that will forever after make me think of
tufts of wool caught on gate hinges, of back gardens where only
submissive brassicas remain, limp-leaved. Other than the smoke,
nothing moves; no cars crawl down the road, no Land Rovers or
tractors traverse the fields. There are no flowers in the village gardens; no yellow pansies or pink roses, no purple clematis cloaking
shed walls. This is a place of greens, blacks, greys, scoured and
still, like a gull's skeleton in sand, brushed by beach grass.

After three months in the city, I realize for the first time what it's like to be a visitor to the country, where it's silence, rather than the roar of traffic, that assaults you. I wonder how long it will take for the wind to blow the sound of London out of my head.

I lean forward with my arms around my knees. I feel like myself here, the way I felt as a child when I curled on my rock or sat cross-legged beneath sun-filled ferns. Last winter, in the dead-frozen month of January, I studied guidebooks and read Virginia Woolf's diaries until I was convinced that some dormant part of myself would be quickened and brought alive in London. But I see clearly, on this November afternoon in Yorkshire, that the cry of a crow, striking like flint on the silence of the countryside, is more fraught, complex and moving to me than any of the symphonies I've heard in the Albert Hall. This is the life I want our child to know.

We've been walking all day. We parked our car in a lay-by early this morning, climbed over a stile and followed a valley that gradually narrowed into a rock-strewn path overhung by cliffs. We scrambled over rocks, called clinks and grikes, that were deeply fissured, close-set as cobblestones, then came to a high moor where we could see the lands of Britain laid out below us, just as the Romans would have seen them. I imagined centurions striding along the same walled track that we followed as we sought the stone circle where we would conceive our child.

I close my eyes and feel the wan sun on my face. Peter touches the skin at the corners of my eyes. "You've got thirties lines," he says. "They look good." I glance at him. I'm happy that he likes the signs of age on my body. I see his broad face, his blue eyes, the character lines that are developing in his cheeks, creases that deepen as his face becomes thinner. He is vivid, here, where behind him the land falls away and his wind-stirred hair is the only thing moving. I take his hand and burrow my head against his chest. He's so much bigger than I am; he wraps his arms

Shadow Child

around me and we look out, together, across the moors. We're not going to say to one another how we hope that they contain some ancient magic that will bless our child. We won't touch, stir, or mention this; it's like seeded soil that must remain unturned.

After a while, we go down the hill, stepping over sheep droppings, following narrow tracks in the sod cut by mussel-shaped hoofs. We go down to the tea that our hostess said she would have for us in the front parlour, behind drawn red curtains, by a fire.

Three weeks later I'm sitting in a dark theatre. A naked young man leaps around the stage, thrusting an imaginary knife deep into the eye sockets of horses. Actors wear wire hoofs and massive papier-mâché horse heads. As the great masked horses rear back in agony, I feel black lines fissuring my womb. They zigzag, link, multiply, spear me with tiny pains, swift as thought.

I put my hands on my stomach, amazed. I wonder if I am pregnant so quickly. I wonder if this is the child of the Yorkshire moors, present within me.

In the dark theatre, held within the intimacy of shared concentration, absorbing the smells of perfume and clean clothing, someone's shoulder brushing mine, I continue to stare at the young actor whose character is bent on destroying the unbridled forces of nature, but my mind has sheered sideways like a bird caught by wind.

I'm alert, feeling the tiny dark lines. They are deep, deep as the fissures of the clinks and grikes. I close my eyes, picturing a wondrously complex web being spun at inconceivable speed. I feel myself becoming still, the way I suspended myself, hardly breathing, when the white cat appeared in the garden.

My heart quickens with fear, but another feeling comes like a flood of sunlight into a cold room. I close my eyes, assuaged by its calm. I won't be a victim. I'll go steadily, holding this child's soul like an egg in the palm of my hand.

My period does not come and I feel the flickering black lines in my womb. I try to continue as if nothing has changed, but my attention is diverted. I've come to a sudden stop inside, like a snake on a garden path; my energy has not ceased but has been concentrated. I fear the consequences of any motion.

There's no single moment when I realize that I'm pregnant. The strange ache in my uterus comes and goes every day, from the moment I first notice it. I tell Peter about every twinge, every flicker, of both my body and my emotions. After I've missed my first period, in early December, I go to a pregnancy clinic. We sit in a waiting room where many of the women wear saris and speak softly in languages other than English. A doctor gives me an internal exam and tells me she's fairly certain that I'm pregnant.

By the time my parents send us airline tickets so we can spend Christmas with them in Connecticut, I am sure that I'm carrying a baby. But I don't return to the clinic. I don't want to see a doctor; I want no concern, no advice, no one else's fear or protection. Something else will guard and nurture this child; some wordless spell woven by Yorkshire wind, hoof-cloven soil, fern spine, bone shard, river song.

I write one last story. It is called "Aliens." I write it in four days, and it comes from the current I've been seeking all fall; I'm graced, like sea-grasses, by one long sweet breath. Then I close my notebooks, tidy my desk, pack a suitcase, and we go home for Christmas.

It's a strange visit because I tell no one the news. Peter smuggles crackers to me, in the mornings, before I can get out of bed. I don't want to be pitied, or pampered, or worried about; I don't want the anxious looks of those who wonder if this time I will bear a living child. I don't want assurances that I know bear no certainties. I don't want to be reminded of the memories I try to keep locked in my internal closet.

I have some idea that I will have the baby in England, before we come home; that no one will ever know I'm pregnant until I call to tell them we have a son or a daughter. That way, if I fail again, no one will know that I tried. Most of all, I feel a precious link between me and Peter and our baby. We're a family, and I don't want anyone else's apprehension to shatter this dream.

It snows, thick, wet New England flakes. Peter and I roll a snowball so huge that we leave erratic bare patches on the lawn, like mole-runs. We make a fertility goddess, with huge breasts and fat snow-fingers on the ends of her stumpy arms. Her arms are outstretched in an embracing gesture of acceptance and blessing. When she's done, we call her the Venus of Willendorf.

I stand looking at her, this creature risen from the snowy field. The bare branches of the pear tree behind her rake the scudding white clouds. I put my arms around her and lay my cheek on the icy snow of her face. My belly is pressed against hers.

I try to shift my vision, like twisting the end of a kaleidoscope, so all the pieces of perception are realigned and make an entirely new configuration. I want neither to expect, nor *not* to expect. I want to be, like the snow goddess, a creature of the moment, subject to shaping elements, neither becoming nor dissolving, but bearing both forces in every cell and fearing neither.

She is my carved stick; I take my memory of her glittering power back to the cold flat when we return, in early January, to finish our term.

Our intention was to remain away for a full year, to return in June on the *Mikhail Lermontov;* to complete a cycle of seasons. I remember the words we spoke to describe our fantasy; they seem, in retrospect, as one-dimensional as the Golden Books of my childhood: *sailing to Europe, hiking in the Swiss Alps, living in London for a winter.*

The flat, when we return, feels strangely like home. I push aside the dark blue drapes, look into the garden. The young daffodils are still spearing the black soil, thick green nubs that postpone their eruption, unrushed by this winter that is more a queasiness than a season. On the bulletin board in the kitchen are black-and-white photographs of me and Peter in knickers and hiking boots on the Blümlisalp, standing before an expanse of snowfields. On the wall behind the steamer trunk is a survey map of the Outer Hebrides. On my desk, a pile of orange-spined Penguin paperbacks.

We're like the daffodils, suspended in a strange place where one epoch is ending and another is beginning and we're not sure which one we're in.

Nothing germinates in my mind. I sit over my desk with increasing desperation until I give up and close my journal. I'm sick, with both pregnancy and flu, which makes me cough until I crack a rib. I increasingly isolate myself from the outside world. I give up my classes and spend hours lying in the damp bed; branches stir vaguely over the brick walls, against clouds that hang over the southern coast like an incurable disease.

I've crossed what I thought would be the hardest barrier: the decision to try, once more, to have a child. But no one has prepared me for the mental anguish of balancing hope and desire against a fear that is deeply grounded in memory, and that never ceases to grow and gain strength. Fear is the dark counterpart of hope. I have no tools, no support except Peter; and he, too, is anxious.

I go to see a doctor whose office is just around the corner. He

Shadow Child

is as grizzled as a terrier. He eyes me speculatively over his glasses, grey moustache accentuating the slant of his upper lip as he warms his hands over his electric fire. I lie on a tartan blanket. There's no nurse in attendance, and a teacup the size of a soup bowl is on his cluttered desk. He croons as he passes his hands over my belly, "It's a little baby. It's a little baby." His face reddens, and he's excited. I feel violated. I miss Dr. Kay. I walk home, jostled by crowds of people. I wonder if the baby can hear the roar of buses shifting gears at the traffic light. I look at the slice of sky between buildings. I smell diesel fumes; cars careen by, their drivers looking straight ahead. I still have to make myself think which way to look when I step onto the zebra-striped crosswalk. I turn onto the relative quiet of Chatsworth Road, walking past identical windows where an occasional cat sits wide-eyed between glass and net curtain, motionless as a caged tiger.

Right now, at home in New Brunswick, the air smells of spruce trees, even when blizzards have bent their boughs with loads of sparkling snow. I try to recall the silence, so profound that I can hear the shirring of snow on snow, spindrifts ghosting over the snowy fields, random as tumbling dandelion seeds in summer.

The city has taught me my needs, helped me understand my desires. No road leads nowhere. At the heart of this city, I have discovered why I want to go home.

The baby claims me from the instant of conception. I am never in a hinterland where I separate my needs from its. We are one. The baby takes me on its voyage; its feet lead the way through darkness. It is I who follow.

Near the end of the first trimester, I make myself shake open my umbrella and go out into the rain-runneled afternoon. I walk past the meat store where brown rabbits hang suspended by their back paws, eyes crusted with clots of black blood. I stop to look.

Rain taps the drumskin of my black umbrella. I feel as if my own eyes are filled with darkness, clotted with anxiety. I tell no one of my pregnancy, and yet it is all I can think about. I imagine the huddled rabbits, minds slanted on the frozen moment, thinking themselves safely hidden, safely secret. I had thought that this place would be my burrow; that I would hole up, hide, peacefully nurture my baby. But I feel like a hunted creature. Eventually, those rabbits couldn't bear their own fear and broke cover.

I go into a bookstore and find the medical section. I am hungry to know what is happening. I need the measured cadences of facts. I'm unprepared for the dimensions of my fear, for the mind-tearing work of carrying this baby, who is spinning towards life and does not know its danger. I have underestimated the strain of never thinking *when*; always, instead, thinking *if*.

I dream I'm on an island. It's a remote place, and I know how difficult it is to get here. I'm surrounded by unfriendly strangers. I'm having a miscarriage. I stretch out my hands. The people look at me with disinterested eyes. I feel their contempt.

During the day, I fight panic. I keep the coal fire going. I wear a baggy blue sweater and curl up in a chair, drinking tea and reading books about mountain-climbing expeditions so I can imagine, and remember, the silence of the Alps, where the hollow rattle of pebble-fall cracks the thin air like an event of extreme significance; so I can relive the splendid sight of the Jungfrau, Monch and Eiger as we reach the top of a pass; so I can imagine the clanging cowbells, fields of daisies and clover, hand-cradled bowls of coffee, hot round loaves of white bread wrapped in paper, and eaten with chocolate as we sit in the sunshine at the side of our path; so I can return to all those places where my heart found light and spirit, and so sought this child.

I spend a week in bed during the end of the third month,

terrified of miscarrying. I cry every day. I'm still sick, coughing, sneezing. Peter tries to reassure me, brings me books, does the shopping. He goes to the art college with increasing reluctance.

One morning, the doorbell rings. I open our flat door, go into the vestibule. I see a shadow on the pebbled glass of the apartment-house door. I fumble with the locks, open the door. A small gypsy woman is standing on the wet doorstep. She is my height, thin, plumaged in a vivid silk head scarf the colour of butterflies, lemons, mangoes; a flowered shawl flows over the shoulders of her grey wool coat, is loosely knotted over its buttons. Gold bracelets rest on the bones of her brown hand. Ornate silver loops weight her ears. She seems remote and yet keenly present, like a bird captured in one's hands. She is pulling a child's red wagon; it is heaped with bunches of pussywillows. My eyes leap to the grey buds, soft as kitten paws. They cluster together, a grey cloud latticed with spring-tender wands.

"Would you like to buy a bunch?" she says, and tells me the price.

I go back into the flat for money, and when I return, she hands me a bunch of pussywillows so large, so long-stemmed, that I have to cradle them in my arms sideways.

She leans forward. She reaches out with her bangled hand and brushes the back of mine with one finger. "Good luck," she says, her eyes grazing mine and jagging away. Then she leans to the handle of her little wagon and goes away down the pavement.

I close the door, go back into the flat and stand in the room where the drapes are closed to conserve heat. The coal fire makes tiny tickings, flickers feebly. The room is changed by the presence of these pussywillows on their graceful stems; by the appearance of the unexpected. I hold the pussywillows against my belly. I close my eyes. I'm collecting omens, and this one tells me that it's time to go home.

Chapter Ten

We arrive home one afternoon in March. Everything continues peacefully, as if we'd never left: the English ivy on the wood cookstove; pottery bowls, mugs, pitchers; drowsy cats nested in rocking chairs; plants on windowsills.

I stand in the south living-room. Sun slants across the varnished spruce floorboards; the red geranium petals are edged with a wing-blur of light. I realize that this house is patient; it endures and grows, gaining character. After the worst storm of the decade, on Groundhog Day, its sinews were loosened; it groans now in certain winds. It has loomed like an iceberg through winter storms, been veiled and slashed by icy dervishes. Its stone-and-mortar foundation has been heaved by frozen soil; the plaster walls either bulge outward or crack apart in lightning forks that expose dusty lathes. The walls have folded around successions of lives and are mute, although as I stand in the high-ceilinged room, smelling the singular odour of mice and old wood smoke, I can feel the ripeness of the room's silence, its fertility.

Shadow Child

As I go slowly up the stairs, I glimpse the yellow plaster walls of the nursery. I stand still for a minute. Memories come like a shower of spears; then, like the moment when I felt the first flickerings in my womb, an answering feeling wraps around me. These walls are innocent. Sunlight washes them like hands scrubbing linen. I won't poison the present with pain that doesn't belong to it.

I walk steadily up the stairs, feeling our baby stirring inside my womb.

The nursery is empty, as we left it. I stand leaning against the door-frame, gazing into the room. Suddenly I realize that I have not moved for ten minutes; I've been imagining myself kneeling beside a narrow grey cradle with a baby lying in it; I'm gazing at the baby, humming a sleeping song, rocking the cradle and both of us are balanced on the edge of dream. I've brought back a child to its home. I see the house through this thought, and listen to the peaceful quiet. Then the baby becomes still, as if it, too, is listening to the sound of its new home. Instantly, my mind is shocked from its calm and sheers to the motionless baby, like a mother knocking anxiously at a locked door. I stand, my eyes unseeing, fingers exploring my belly, suspended in uneasy hiatus until I feel a little nudge from the baby, and then I relax. What I know, I can't allow myself to think; this baby will be born, but it will be either alive or dead. This is the knife-point against which my heart presses.

I sense a new presence within myself, a luminous stillness. It is something deeper than hope; it is stronger and darker. I feel myself folding endurance, like a blanket, around love.

It continues to snow through the end of March and the beginning of April, but the snow spins down through a warmer light, and the flakes are like flower petals, soft, melting even as they fall. At dusk, I come from the barn, a bucket of warm milk swinging from the metal bail in my hand; I can hear the waters of the brook chuckling, garbling, as it runs like a warm-blooded animal, black and alive between the wind-hardened folds of snow.

I feel the baby swimming and surging. It is growing like the northern spring, which comes unseen, hidden by sudden blizzards and wind-sculpted snow, unchecked in spite of our discouragement. Orion steps over the northwest hill. I watch him striding farther into the tree-tops, night by night, until only one shoulder star is left. Snow fleas teem like black pepper. The snow separates, in the fields, into bone-shaped islands. Red-tipped grasses needle the puddles in the roadside ditch; snow slants on a moist wind, and pussywillows paw the air with their grey buds.

Now that I've experienced life in a London flat, I can hardly believe that this place once felt like an alley without exit, or that I could have been wearied by things that now seem like treasures: the seeds I'm planting in flats, the bread dough I press with the heels of my hand on the knife-scarred wooden table, the friends who call on the phone or stop by to visit, the manure that steams in the morning light as I clean the barn, the pots coated in chalky glaze that Peter and I load in the kiln, the sticks of wood that I work into the firebox while embers tumble through the grate.

I'm no longer alone with this pregnancy. I stepped off the airplane in Boston proud of my belly, which swelled beneath my jacket. I'm delighted with the amazement and dawning wonder I see in the faces of my parents, my brother, my friends. I know now that privacy is not what I need. I slot back into my life and feel the warm, blind, instinctive safety that I felt as a child, with my cousins, in the warren-like halls, attics, barns and gardens of the family homestead. Peter and I, and our baby, need to feel our place within our families, within the landscape we've grown to love, within the continuity of our own dream, which blossoms again like a long-dormant seed.

My mood swings between two poles. In one, I curl comfortably

Shadow Child

on my side in our four-poster bed. I pull a red batik feather quilt over my shoulders. Through the door, I see the peaceful angles of floor, bannister, plaster walls, shadows. My cat, Sam, has made a nest at my feet; I feel his heat and heaviness. I know the baby is here with me and Sam. I let myself imagine the determined little creature who is swimming its way towards the light. I dare to relax my vigilance. I feel a warmth steal over me, like sun on my shoulders. I close my eyes and drift in the secret place. I feel the baby's determination, its boundless energy. I think of wool sweaters and snowsuits. I think of tiny moccasins, child-sized cross-country skis. I think of Beatrix Potter, of Paddington Bear.

At the other pole, I'm seeking the baby, constantly, standing with my hands on my belly and my eyes closed, waiting to feel a kick, a stirring, the uncontrollable surge that is as thrilling as the sight of a heron rising from mists or a fox steady-eyed in bracken. When I feel the baby, I go on for awhile, reassured; but then I'm afraid again, and stop: listening, waiting, praying. I glimpse the shape of my fear. I feel it rushing towards my love, like wind guttering a nascent flame. I will not name the fear. I will not allow it to take shape. I weep, instead, and call it exhaustion. I don't want to see the knife-point that still presses against my heart, pinching, making me breathless; the knife is wielded by a foe I have met.

Thursdays, I run the store. People talk to me about my pregnancy with veiled compassion; they ask me easy questions whose answers they already know. They really want to know if I'm frightened, if there's any way I can be sure this baby will be born safely, if it was hard to decide to get pregnant again, how I'm dealing with my anxiety. But they don't know how to ask these things, and I give them no openings. Their excitement for me is stretched, like a tent, over a framework of sympathy. I drive home at the end of the day, wrung by all the answers I did not give.

It's a cruel time of year in the north, when spring tries to come and is endlessly frustrated by the thwarting breath of winter. *"April is the cruellest month,"* I chant to Peter, like a bitter litany, *"breeding / Lilacs out of the dead land, mixing / Memory and desire . . . ."* The season mirrors my emotions.

It's May eighth. Peter is tossing a salad; steam swirls from the pasta kettle; there's a soft slapping of tomato sauce, and the smell of garlic and oregano. I put my head back against the wicker rocking chair, my hands hanging from its armrests like empty gloves, and I'm wrenched with sudden misgiving. I feel the grieving truth of time, can hear the silence of all the moments that have ended. I can't bear the weight and texture of this moment as it slides, like all the others, into memory. I long for my parents and my brother, for my grandparents, for the sultry trees of a gentler climate, for the past life that pushes against the walls of my heart. I fight, with tears, with closed eyes, the idea of endings. It's like my fear; I don't want to face its implications.

Life, in the wet early spring evening, in the quiet water-bubbling kitchen, seems to me a pointless passage; spring releases the soil, stretches the spiralling buds, sharpens the raven's eye—but then another summer breaks, like a wave, towards another winter.

Tears salt my food and Peter is powerless to help me. I can't articulate how anxiety tips my inner scales, sends me plummeting towards despair.

After supper, we make a fire in the fireplace we built the summer after our first baby was born; it was the summer that Peter made a pond, and a dock, and a new chimney; the summer we worked so frenziedly, like spiders repairing a torn web with new threads. Now we hang, again, in the delicate geometry. I sit cross-legged in the corner of the couch, and my finger loops grey wool around my knitting needle. I'm knitting a sweater, one row knit, one row purl, grey with red stripes. I spread the square of furled wool over my knee to see what is growing from my small stitches.

Shadow Child

The baby is taking its post-supper exercise. I put both hands on my belly, and Peter looks up from his reading. "He's really busy," I say, trying to smile. My voice is husky, trailing its sorrow like an old sweater dragged by one sleeve. I watch the fire licking round the maple logs; the flames are leaf-shaped, and I can never see one distinctly. They meld and separate, leap and quail. Shadows lap the walls, and the room rocks around the steady centre of us in our chairs; the fire parches my face and I travel to the baby's place, where nothing is remembered and everything begins. I sit with my hands on my belly, feeling the baby stretching, battering the walls of its home with its soft feet, its tender elbows. Its urgency pummels me to its present, where there is neither light nor dark, neither time nor space, neither endings nor beginnings.

I wonder if I will miss my own past less when I become a mother. I wonder if a child will lighten me, make me less prone to feelings of pointlessness and futility. I wonder what it will be like to show the world to this baby, if it will reawaken my own sense of its mystery and strangeness. I wonder if this baby will come as inevitably, and seemingly against all odds, as seasons do.

My own sense of the passing of all things leaps up, like a dancing shadow, and vanishes. I wait for the next kick, the next nudge, the next querulous shift of this child who wants me to carry him safely, who surely wants to be born.

Summer erupts, miraculously, from the thighs of winter. Peter and I mark the transition by moving into our summer bedroom, a big room over the kitchen that we keep shut up and unheated over the winter; two narrow windows overlook the east pasture, the pond and the hardwood ridge whose trees are friezed by both the rising sun and the rising moon. We wake with the sun dazzling in our eyelashes, the chatter of swallows so close under the eaves that they seem to be in the bedroom with us.

I spend most mornings writing in the front parlour, with the windows wide open to breezes carrying the smells of cows and wildflowers; every afternoon I put my blonde hair in a pony-tail, pin it to my head, go to the garden carrying a bushel basket of tools. I hoe between the rows of green beans. I've put yellow saw-dust around their stalks for mulch. I move on to the broccoli patch, where I've set the plants in a latticed pattern. I squat, my belly between my knees; I pull a blue-green leaf gently through my fingers. Each plant wears a tar-paper collar. I started these plants as soon as we got home from London; I've been amazed by their steady progression from purply-brown round seeds to sprouts that push up the Saran Wrap tent I tuck over their flats, to gangly plants whose roots are so intertwined that I wince as I tear them apart, separating them, resettling them in peat pots; and now they soar, in the garden, like cage-bound birds set free.

There's not a weed in the garden. The rhubarb leaves are the size of elephant ears. Scarlet runner beans have sent their first ten-drils round the wires of my bean teepee. Beyond a bed of tubular onions, there's dark brown earth, then chicken-wire stretched be-tween posts where peas are beginning to snake their wiry tendrils between the octagons; at the end is the squash patch, where silver-haired stalks thrust from the centres of the little hills I've hoed and hold their wide leaves over the straw I've gathered round them like blankets.

I've set all this in motion, dreamed it, planned it, seeded it. Now I hoe and water and mulch so the plants can grow in eccen-tric directions and become a tangle of overlapping impulses. The squash vines will roam over the manure pile and grasp, like boa constrictors, the Russian sunflower stalks. The nasturtiums will fill the spaces between the red cabbages, and bachelor's buttons will shoot up beneath the dill. By fall, I'll have to push my way through stems and vines, carrying my basket, gathering my fruits.

I've loved gardens ever since my mother gave me my own little

plot of Johnny-jump-ups. I loved the flowers for themselves—
each purple-and-yellow face was like a tiny lion—and I would
touch them gently with my finger and explain, when I picked four
or five, why they were specially privileged, by way of apology. I
feel the same way about this garden. I love it for itself, not
because I might show it to someone, or even because of the food
that it will give us. I simply love to watch it grow. And I am
amazed by its evolution; by its nascent peas, floating like embryos
within the veined shells of their pods; by the dewdrop that rolls
into the centre of a nasturtium leaf and trembles there, stretching
the reflection of golden flowers on its convex globe. I wander
down the centre aisle, looking right and left. I learn faith from my
garden, as I wait for basil seedlings to sprout; they'll come, but
only after the soil has been as warm as an incubator for days. I
learn patience and acceptance; frost settles on baby beans, their
translucent green leaves turn black as the sun rises, and I plant
them again. I understand my own tenderness, my own need to
participate in the miracle of creation, to push a seed into soil, to
feel astonishment when its shoot comes winging through.

My garden is my sanctuary, a place where I feel freed from
ambition, striving, self-expression, personal evolution. And yet,
when I walk peacefully between its rambling flowers and shiny-
skinned vegetables, the garden fulfils all of these needs; it gives
me myself.

I am the mother of this garden.

The rain comes in fat drops that trickle through my scalp and
twist like screws as they hit the dirt. I kick off my sandals. There's
a soft roar on the metal roof of the barn, and a clap of thunder.
My muslin blouse clings to my body and I can see the shape of
my belly, with its navel nubbin. The broccoli leaves bounce and
rebound, funnel the rain to their centres. Peter comes to the door
of the studio with his hands covered in clay. We yell to each other
over the drumming, tapping, splashing, trickling. I hear the goats

baaing. I feel like the earth itself, my toes spread, my baby safely carried in its watery sac, my plants submitting and gathering.

It rains, unprecedentedly, for nineteen days. The salt seeps; I can't sprinkle it on my egg. I see Erin and Bronwen splashing sturdily down the driveway between the lush rain-jewelled timothy grasses, wearing rubber boots, their T-shirts soaked.

Then, in late June, sun reveals the opulent splendour that the rain has wrought. Wind chases shadows through the hayfields. Leaves flutter, spill light from their sap-tight skins. Here and there, a single grasshopper sings searingly, forecasting heat. Mid-summer arrives, full-blown, like a ship rounding a headland with sails bellied.

We build a shelter for the goats and the pony. It's like a kid's treehouse, made from scrap lumber. When it's done, I sit beneath it in the slatted shade and the animals cluster around me. We look out at the shining grasses, the blue-flag iris by the brook, the diving birds. This morning, in bed, Peter and I decided on a boy's name: Jacob. I hug my knees and think, "Jacob. Molly." The goats nuzzle the back of my neck with their neat mouths. Clara is pregnant. I can feel her kid kicking. Her belly is taut; her neck seems as frail as a flower stalk as she waddles patiently, her udder swollen.

When we bought the farm, we found a pile of narrow screens in the attic; they slide sideways, fit any width sill. I set them in all the windows. The daisy-scented wind whishes through the stiff mesh; I can poke my finger through holes where the screen has rusted, leaving barbed ends as sharp as fish hooks. Successions of visitors, like wildflowers, replace one another in the big house. I work in the studio unstacking the kilns, pricing pots, writing orders and invoices; I cook, milk the goats, weed, run the store, listen to life stories, put laundry through my wringer washer, make bread in the woodstove, read, try to write. Mornings, the sun is pale, lemony, hangs dimly in a white sky; heat hovers over the land like a dragonfly. The garden path burns my bare feet.

I feel enormous. My breasts rest on my belly; I wipe sweat from beneath them with toilet paper. I sit with my legs spread, my belly ballooning between them. Peter's youngest brother laughs when he sees me for the first time in my overalls. Bronwen loves my stomach; she rubs it, fascinated, while she and Erin talk about the baby, oblivious to my presence. I'm increasingly exhausted, because it becomes harder and harder to sleep. It's too hot for even a sheet. We keep a fan by the bed; it reminds me of the comforting throb of the engine on the *Mikhail Lermontov*. Dr. Kay is monitoring the health of my baby by urine analysis; I have to collect every drop of urine in a peanut butter jar; we take turns delivering it to the hospital, daily. Several times a night, I lumber downstairs through the silent house, pour the hot liquid into a plastic jug that was given to us by the hospital lab and is inexplicably labelled "This Is Your Usual Product." The jug is in the refrigerator, next to the orange juice. My legs are seized with cramps so severe I wake Peter to knead them. My stomach is so compressed that I have continuous heartburn. There is no comfortable position in which to sleep.

I put a rocking chair by the bedroom window. I sit there, watching the moon, while Peter sleeps. I'm deep inside the vessel of myself. My body is the ship coming round the headland. My belly is her sails. The baby and I ride in her hold. I can't control the passage, I'm not at the helm, I can't see the captain or crew. Our keel may be rent, at any moment, by icebergs. I know this; I feel the insubstantiality of the shell that leans to these waters, that leaps to this wind.

The moon, however, sails the night sky with impunity.

Night after night, I watch it rising. I see it draw steadily past the spruce trees, which etch the silver light like black frost ferns. I see it cut loose from the earth's rim and soar, deflecting the sun's light without heat, without violence, without imperative. Fields, rose petals, cows, my sleeping husband—everything is touched by the unearthly light of the vanished sun. I feel as if I'm seeing life's reverse; not death, but a hint, a feather-brush, a dream-glimpse, of the place in which we all drifted once and will drift again.

My hands lie on my belly, over the thin nightgown, and I push the hard place I can feel by my belly button. A heel? After a moment it pushes back. I can't shelter myself from my love for this child. I'm like a pianist executing an increasingly difficult piece: if I allow my concentration to break, I will be lost; if I become aware of my concentration, it will vanish. My mind narrows, pinpoints; I think of Jacob, of Molly, of hands and feet, of soft hair. I hum songs of life. My inner eye refuses its peripheral vision. I will not allow myself to remember what I have already experienced, and cannot help expecting.

Every day, as my skin expands beyond belief—as I walk more slowly, sit more often, try to gather enough breath from my beleaguered lungs—it is not my body's job that is most difficult, and most exhausting, but my mind's.

I close my eyes, rocking, learning patience in the only way possible. The baby, like the moon, swims in its dark sea, progressing steadily towards fullness.

On a clear, fall-like day in late July, I go to see an obstetrician in Saint John. If the baby hasn't been born by August eleventh, I'll go to the regional hospital; labour will be induced and equipment will monitor the baby as it is being born. I like this idea. I want to be supported by nurses, specialists, machines; I think of this as a team that will surround me, making a wall so death can't get past. Dr. Hill tells me that the baby is fine, and has strong reactions to external pressure, a good sign. Peter's in the waiting room; as we walk out into the bracing air, which smells of the sea, our long-suppressed emotion breaks through. We allow ourselves to feel excited.

I stand with both hands on my belly, wind whipping my hair. "The baby will be here in *two weeks!*"

"I wish there was a window in your belly," says Peter.

I have a sense of having walked for so long that I'm almost unable to continue, and yet I know that I'm nearing the end of the journey. I have been struggling for so long to get to this place, and yet I don't really know anything about it, except that I sense its deep familiarity. I've experienced my own birth, so it's a place I've been but can't remember, like a dream whose story vanishes, leaving, like lingering perfume, only its essence.

I get Peter to bring the box of baby clothes down from the attic once again, and I take out all the summer clothes: white cotton undershirts, nightgowns with smocked yokes, receiving blankets. I stand in our cool north bedroom. I unfold and refold each thing, and all the while the baby is elbowing, stretching, kicking. For a lovely, loose, untethered time, we're in the dream-place together, me and the baby. It's like being in a walled garden where rose petals steep, infused by the sun; where no one can find us, and yet we're not hiding.

The clothes seem different. They seem ordinary, sturdy. They belong to this day, to the smell of goldenrod on the cool breeze, to the jars of urine in the refrigerator. They belong to the baby in my belly.

Still, I will not dangle any lures before the mouth of fate, and I leave the piles of clothes and diapers on our bed in the shady room. We leave the cradle in the attic. In the little yellow baby room, flies bumble against the windowpanes and their droning buzz echoes in the hollow, unfilled space.

There's a day of wild west winds. Leaves cling to their stems upside down. The lush grass by the manure pile tosses silver blades of light. Sheets on the clothesline billow and crack; I hear them spelling the shape of the air all afternoon.

The wind dies with the coming of dusk. There are no more peepers or snipes as I walk out to the barn, only the thin trickling of brook-water fingering steadily between the stems of forget-me-nots. I hear the crunch of my sneakers on the driveway. The barn looms before me, its roof black under the Big Dipper. I smell the dried-clover, tangled-vetch, crushed-daisy sweetness of new-mown hay.

Late this afternoon, I noticed how the nanny-goat Clara lay under the shelter without moving, how she nosed her belly and chewed her cud rapidly, her square-pupilled eyes staring straight ahead. I put her in a box-stall filled with fresh hay, and I have trundled out to the barn six times since; she's always lying in the hay, chewing, waiting.

I walk through the barn door, and a swallow flits in over my head at the same time; I hear the sudden chittering of bird babies, high in the rafters over the hay mow. I open the Dutch door into the low-ceilinged section of the barn, where I can see the dim shapes of stalls, mangers and stanchions. I hear the small sounds of sleepy animals: rustle of hay, hen's throat-croon, crunching of cuds.

In the moonlit stall, Clara is standing with her back legs spread and her sides shrunken. She is no longer alone. She is licking and licking the tiny doe kid that tries to stand, falls and struggles back onto its soft white hoofs. The glistening amniotic sac hangs between Clara's legs. There's a pool of blood on the hay. I go into the stall, manoeuvring my belly through the narrow gate. I've brought clean tea towels. I drop heavily to my knees by the kid and help Clara fluff its wet fur.

I scratch her bony head. Her eyes are anxious. She seems entirely unaware of the swinging amniotic sac, of her own long

Shadow Child

day of waiting. Her eyes are dark, and she tries to lick the baby everywhere at once. The kid staggers and lifts her blind face, eyes closed; she is searching and lost, and her cry breaks on the night, quivering and trailing loneliness.

When I leave the barn, the moon is veiled by a shoal of dappled, smoke-blue clouds.

I watch it, my night's companion. *Will I be a graceful mother?* I ask it, silently. *Will I gather my child back to me after it is born and heal its anguish? How deep is my well of love?*

August. It's grey, much cooler. The summer wildflowers are gone. I get a slight headache when I drive to town on the dusty dirt roads. Sturdy, stick-stemmed flowers thrive in hedgerows at the edges of mown fields: goldenrod, blue aster, fireweed, meadowsweet, turtlehead, Joe-Pye-weed. Grasshoppers click and snap; crickets pulse rhythmically, the hidden heartbeat of the dry grasses.

My belly is seized with cramps so strong that I have to stop and lean forward, breathing deeply, until they are over. Then I check my child. My hands know the flat sides of my belly, the shelf under my breasts; I can find arms and legs, and I push one of them, wait anxiously for a reaction.

I can think of nothing else but the baby and the birth to come. I dream I am being tossed in huge waves that fling me against a shore and then suck me back again; I am reaching for purchase, and my hands grasp helplessly at slippery rock. I awake to a red sunrise. I'm attacked by diarrhea so painful that I lie in bed afterwards, exhausted, curled on my side, rocking, longing to be through, to be past, to know the result, to unclench my teeth which bite back fear. The baby is kicking so vigorously that I can't believe he doesn't somehow know that it is time, now, for him to be born. I feel sorry for the baby in a way. He's so free and spontaneous, so perfectly adapted to his environment—and so secret, such a mystery to us all. This is how I have grown to know him; us, together, safe in our walled garden. But now he is going to leave me. The most perilous part of the voyage is still ahead of us. We're going to tear apart. I know why my arms ached last time. Already, I am preparing myself for our reunion.

I cry that morning, August eighth, until my heart's storm loses its force, and leaves me shaken, calm.

The next day is cool and breezy. The swallows fly high in the sky, beyond the insect zone; they seem restless, agitated. They are withdrawing, leaving doorway and eave, pond and brook; their job is done. I can't tell babies from adults.

I sit on the doorstep of the pottery studio. I'm in the shade, looking out at the raspberry patch, whose red berries shine in the August light. I can see my belly shifting under the blue flowers of my maternity dress.

There's a bowl of peas in my lap, but my hands are idle. I can't think ahead any more. I can't live as I have learned to live, doing something now while my mind works on the next step of the process. I can no longer shell peas that must then be blanched, bagged, carried to the freezer. I can't bear looking at the raspberries and thinking that I should pick them because they'll be over-ripe by tomorrow. I have been *expecting* for too long. My stomach twists, my heart begins to race.

I take the peas to the kitchen and leave them on the table. I get the old battered bucket that was my granny's and a straw sun hat. I walk away—past the pottery, past the barns, up through the cricketing fields, over the rock pile in the hedgerow, under the mountain-ash tree, through the waist-high hay-scented ferns in the birch grove—until the valley lies far below me, its houses and barns the size of toys, its quilt of fields and copses spread over the

Shadow Child

tilted hills, its farthest hills blue as whales. I'm in the highest meadow, where all I can hear is the swishing sigh of wind in the spruce trees and the far-off fluting of a thrush; where sleek light is tossed from green spruce needles, slides from the bent necks of feathery grasses, makes tiny oblongs on the juniper berries.

I sit in the prickly grass, belly between my legs, picking wild blueberries. They are low-bush blueberries, four inches high. The berries are fat, dusty. I hold my hand under a clump and roll the berries forward with my thumb. They fall from their stems into my palm. At first, they plink when they drop into the bucket, but soon the bottom is covered and they settle, berry on berry, without sound. I trickle some into my mouth, taste a few leathery leaves. The wind lifts my hair, cools my scalp. A clump of reindeer moss scratches my thigh; it's tinder dry, crunchy.

The wind douses the flame of my fear, keeps blowing until it has put it out. I feel my heart lighten when it is finally gone. Then there is nothing inside me but this moment; me, and the baby, and the wild blueberries, and the August wind, and the glossy wings of a raven who dips low, curious, and the goldenrod sweeping in the breeze, and the pink seas of fireweed down in the hollow by the green fern beds.

I pick methodically, as if I'm a gatherer and this is my only crop. When a bush is clean, I let my hands fall into my lap and lift my face to the sun. I wonder if the baby can feel my peace. My fingers relax. Like the blueberries dropping silently onto a bed of other berries, my fears, desires, grievances and worries are absorbed by their larger context, blown away by the wind, gathered by the clouds. I sit in the high meadow and know my baby is alive. His inevitable and eventual death becomes an event as remote as my own; it's nothing more than a fact, as clear as the light on the grasses, and something that I must learn to love for the shining edge it gives to this moment.

Chapter Eleven

The next day, Peter and I are in the pottery shop. We came to town to do errands, but I can't maintain any more the effort of containing my fear. I can't stand at a counter and count my change; I can't walk down the street and greet people with a smile and discuss my due date as if I were not at the end of my mental strength, about to break under the unrelenting responsibility of believing, of trusting, of loving when my mind cautions otherwise.

I call Dr. Hill from the store phone, speaking quietly so no one will hear. I can perceive the strain in my voice as I try to sound matter-of-fact; I tell him that I can still feel the baby kicking, but that I'm getting nervous. He understands everything I'm not saying. He's a tall, laconic man; he says, in his dry, kindly voice and as if it's the simplest thing, "Come down this afternoon. We'll keep you here overnight, and start labour tomorrow morning."

One of our partners is running the shop. It's busy, filled with friends and customers. Peter and I say nothing to anyone, but make a quiet exit. We go home and pack suitcases. I take a shower. We go out to the garden and prop the camera on a chair; Peter sets the timer, runs to put his arm around me. I stand with my hands on my great belly. We're in a bower of sunflowers and scarlet runner beans. I wonder if this is our first family portrait.

The sky has clouded over, and I have the strange feeling, as I get in the car, that I am leaving for a long absence, or perhaps forever, without having made any preparations for departure.

In Saint John we go out to supper, but I am too nervous to eat. We go to an early movie; my heart begins to race, my eyes are darkening at the edges. I'm suffocating; anxiety shortens my breath, hammers in my pulse, beads my scalp with sweat. We get up to leave, stumble down the dark aisle.

As soon as I am settled in my private room on the sixth floor of the Saint John General Hospital, I feel this is where I'm supposed to be, and I begin to relax. Nurses listen to the baby's heartbeat and smile. "Your baby's fine," they tell us. I wonder what the baby is thinking, or sensing. I wonder if it knows that its warm, dark peace is about to end. I feel its dignity, its mystery, as it lives its last hours of unknowing absorption, carried in my womb as effortlessly as a hawk on wind.

My window is open to the city night. I can hear police sirens, trucks changing gears, a foghorn in the harbour. The distant threaded sounds make my room seem bright, quiet, safe. There is nowhere else I want to be. I have brought my baby, safely, this far, and we are in other hands now.

Peter has to leave me at eleven, when visiting hours are over. He's reserved a hotel room. He sits on the side of the bed and carefully puts his arms around me and my huge belly. He hates having to leave; he goes over everything I might need: juice, extra pillows and blankets, book, magazines. He adjusts the lamp and the bed's angle. He checks the window, twitches the curtains.

Finally, at the door, he smiles at me lovingly one last time, letting me see that he's convinced himself that I'll be fine.

I feel the peculiar strength of aloneness once he's gone. I have no choice but to hold myself together. I anchor myself in the moment, hook myself on everything that surrounds me: the nurses who pass my half-open door, walking rapidly on their squeaky soft-soled shoes; the pool of light from my bedside lamp, which lights a plastic cup of grapefruit juice with its jointed straw; the pale blue walls. A young male intern comes to examine me, takes my vital signs, listens for a long time to the baby. It's one o'clock and he's tired, so he sits on the foot of my bed with his stethoscope hanging from his neck and tells me about his problematic marriage. I'm glad of his company; he's like a fire at which I warm myself. I sense the dark strength that exists within me like the eggs I was born with. It infuses me, slowly, as I absorb this young man's distress; it makes my heart feel stronger and larger; it makes me feel resilient, as if nothing can make me break, as if I have no brittle edges, as if I'm as deep as goose down. When he leaves, I swallow the sleeping pill he insisted I take. In the next room, I hear the low fluid moans of a woman in labour. I listen, detached, unafraid. It seems to have nothing to do with me and Molly/Jacob. We are waiting for our journey, but it will be ours, and so unlike anyone else's. The moans break into a bellow that is without emotion, that is the sound of human life, neither joy nor anguish, but deeper than either. I hear this sound at the edge of consciousness, just as I'm plunging into darkness.

When a brisk older woman with a Scottish accent wakes me at six, I feel refreshed, ready to take each step as it comes. I'm still cushioned by the feathers of my resilient darkness and I submit to each procedure with detached calm. My concentration has reknit; it has given up the task of balancing hope and fear: now I dare to believe. There is no more shred of *if*. Every sting, every discomfort, every intrusion into my body of hand or instrument is part of this fierce conversion, an inward effort so consuming that I feel as if I'm in deep meditation. I feel myself responding to questions as if I've split in two. One part of my mind takes care of what is happening in the room, makes me speak briefly to the nurse as she inserts the intravenous needle into the back of my hand, makes me glance up at the bag of pitocin drip; another part of my mind travels deep into the darkness, where a new soul is poised on life's threshold. In this warm, dark, light-flecked place, I'm waiting, gathering my strength. I'm as stern, wise, keen and blind as the child who waits with me.

At seven o'clock, Peter arrives. He pulls a chair close to the bed and kisses my forehead. I reach for his hand. My other hand lies next to one of two small black boxes that are strapped across my belly. The upper one, the tocotransducer, registers my contractions, which come sporadically and are not yet strong; the lower one, a smaller transducer, records the fetal heartbeat. Peter and I watch, fascinated, as two lines of black ink scrawl steadily across graph paper. Two nurses stay with us. They never leave, but adjust the pitocin drip, increasing its strength; they take my blood pressure, make minute adjustments to the monitor, write notes on the paper as it scrolls from the machine and watch me critically. I never let go of Peter's hand. It's the only way I can connect him to the place I'm in with our child. We're like parents in an audience, mesmerized by the sight of our own child. We murmur to each other when the heartbeat augments. These are the days before ultrasound, so this is the first time we've seen proof of our baby's existence. We watch the pen jag and dip as contractions begin. The baby kicks so strongly that the tocotransducer is dislodged and has to be readjusted, and the nurses laugh and talk about the baby as if it is not a mysterious creature, as if they have already made the transition between unseen and seen, as if this is a baby and not the possibility of one. Later, the nurse watches the monitor intently, and then listens to my belly with a stethoscope. My cheeks numb with terror, but she smiles and shakes her head. "Don't worry." She jiggles my belly with her hands and listens again. "Your baby's asleep," she says. "We have to wake him up." Even though everyone seems calm, there's a taut intensity in the room, as if we're all aware that we are second-guessing nature, trying to forestall any possibility of random disaster.

Dr. Hill arrives, speaks to me reassuringly and then breaks my waters. My uterus responds almost instantly, beginning its wringing pull, opening the place that has stayed shut for so long; it's as if massive muscled arms in my belly are wrenching at something that resists, resting between each pull and then redoubling their violent effort. My focus shifts. I lose awareness of the baby, of the room, of the nurses, of the monitoring machine, of everything except Peter's voice, which is recounting, as we'd planned, every step of our most arduous hike up the Blümlisalp. He murmurs steadily of blue-green lakes, of narrow paths under overhangs, of sun glittering on glaciers. "Now we're passing the lake. The sun is shining. The water's green. We see Mark up ahead. He's waving at us. Relax," he whispers, wiping my face with a wet cloth. "Relax." I feel his body crouched tensely at my side, working with me. I say nothing because I am fighting the impulse to flee. One part of my mind tells me to scream, to run away from my body, to twist and thrash and resist. The trained part of me fights to accept the contractions, to let them work, to lie motionless and be passive. I'm fighting to stay in the place I went to two hours ago, when the baby and I were together, waiting, but my own body has become a boat flung by a violent storm and my mind slides and crashes like a loose crate sliding on the deck.

I'm almost fully dilated after three hours; a nurse's small hand enters my vagina to clip the monitor to the baby's soft scalp so we won't lose touch with the heartbeat when the baby is in the birth canal. The contractions are losing definition and I begin to feel confused; I don't know how to breathe. My distress signals a swift

Shadow Child

decision and hands help slide me onto a stretcher. Dr. Hill comes into the room and talks quietly to the nurses while Peter goes out; he returns almost immediately, dressed in a green robe, a surgical mask hastily adjusted over his face. Then we are rolling down the corridor, the nurses pushing the monitor next to me; Peter carries pillows under both arms. The delivery room is cool and very quiet. I'm shifted onto the high table. I ask breathlessly if the baby's heart is still beating and a nurse reassures me that it is. I'm aware of Dr. Hill, remote beneath his mask, pulling on rubber gloves, whistling "Greensleeves" softly. The nurses are silent; their eyes shift over their hidden mouths. I grip my knees with my hands while Peter puts his arms around me and lifts me to a sitting position, and I push, teeth gritted. I fall back into Peter's arms; then he helps me sit up again; I push, fall back; sit, push, fall back. I hear snatches of the doctor's calm whistling and Peter's voice in my ear, his controlled calm now charged with excitement, telling me I'm doing well, I'm doing really well, it won't be long now, the baby is okay. Suddenly everything changes, there is a sense of acceleration; I am loose and falling, lifted by a great wave and flung, lost and free within it, as we roll forward together, me, the wave, the baby, and I feel the head passing through and then the soft, minnow-quiver of the body. I hear the unbelievable sound of a mewing cry cracking the quiet, and I struggle to rise, totally oblivious of my own body. The nurses step round quickly and lay the baby on my breast and I see him, I see Jacob, my son, and I am astounded to feel my heart wring with compassion, with love, with pity, as I see his tiny mouth opening and shutting, as I see his trembling clenched fists, as I meet my child, no longer the emperor of his kingdom, but arrived, so precipitously, to start another life in a new element, without darkness, without walls.

Peter's arms are around me, and together we are watching the nurses taking care of our baby. My body is forgotten, like a caddis-fly's husk. An intern shows us the placenta and the stretchy pink bag that held Jacob; the doctor puts a few sutures in my vagina, but neither can I feel the prick of the needle, nor can Peter and I see anything but the child who has entered our lives. The nurse lays him on my breast again, and this time he takes the nipple in his mouth. His eyes are open. They are dark blue. They are calm, alert; he slides them around as though he's unsurprised by anything he sees, as if he's been here before and already knows everything of importance.

I'm put on a stretcher and wheeled into the hall, and then we're left alone for a while; someone brings Peter a chair and he sits holding Jacob in his arms. Summer sunlight slants from a window. It gleams on the waxed floor and is luminous in my husband's hair as I see, for the first time, someone else entering the secret garden with my child. Peter bends over his son and his face is open, almost shocked; wonder has no form but stillness, no expression but silence. I lie on the pillows that Peter propped beneath my head, and watch peacefully as my husband changes before my eyes into a father.

Then we're whisked apart. Nurses take Jacob to the neonatal unit, where he'll be kept during our hospital stay; there's no such thing, yet, as lying-in. We decide rapidly that Peter should go with the baby, and an orderly wheels me to a double room in the maternity wing.

I'm shaking, cold, hungry, and my needs are satisfied one by one. There's a young woman on the other side of the thin blue curtain. It's very quiet on her side of the room, and the nurse whispers to me, as she dips a washcloth into warm water and gently washes the dried sweat from my body, that my roommate has just had a stillborn baby. The nurse tells me this as if she'd rather not have to, as if it is a contaminating piece of information, but feels that she should so I won't "say" anything, so I can join everyone else's sympathetic silence.

There's a phone on my bedside table and I call my parents. I feel a shadow looming over me as I roll away from the other woman's side of the room and cup my hand over the mouthpiece of the phone, listening to it ring in my parents' house. The shadow is dark, and I resent its presence. It hovers over me as my mother and father answer the phone anxiously, and I am torn between the pure joy of my news and the need to mute it, for the sake of the childless mother who shares my room.

I have never heard my parents sound so happy, so excited. Their voices break open like Peter's face, have no ambivalence, hold nothing back. Peter returns, tells me that a specialist is examining Jacob, and that they will bring him to me soon. Then we call Peter's mother, Peg; she is with her own mother, and we can hear the phone hit the floor as she runs to call out the news. Then we hear them crying and laughing, and Peg returns breathlessly to the phone and tells us that they joined hands and danced around the room. I call Mère, hear her carefully modulated hello, as if I might be the queen calling; I tell her she's a great-grandmother. We tell brothers that they are uncles, Peter's sister that she is an aunt. Jacob is the first grandchild, the first nephew, the first great-grandchild. Everyone cries, and then laughs, and then wants to know every detail, with compulsive fascination, as if these facts are the first gatherings of a rich harvest, like berries whose round firmness confirm the rest to come.

The afternoon passes in a jumble of events. I am both tired and happy beyond anything I've ever experienced. I feel clear, euphoric. The oppressive weight of the last few years is lifting from my heart. I'm like a bird that has been beating against a closed window. A compassionate hand has opened it and I'm flying free, my wings stretching into light-filled air. Nothing holds me down except the silence of my roommate.

When we talk finally, I tell her that I, too, have lost a baby. She asks me if the baby felt stiff when it was born. I am amazed by my inability to recall, at this moment, anything about what I have come to think of as "the first birth." Her husband comes and sits on her bed, and I notice how they don't cry, how they talk quietly, how they are separated from me by the ending of anticipation. No visitors come to see them, they make no phone calls, the nurses are not occupied with them, no counsellor comes to their bedside.

I don't want them to be there. I don't want to remember. Yet I have no choice, and as I lie impatiently waiting for the nurses to bring me my baby, as the moment hangs taut and weightless as Christmas morning, I am listening to her sad, brave voice telling me of the only things she has left to expect: the funeral they are going to have in the hospital chapel, the name they gave their baby girl, the stone they are putting in the family plot. I want to turn away from her, but compassion keeps me listening. She stops speaking abruptly, and I see the nurses coming through the door, carrying a blue bundle. I feel, even as I gather my baby, bend my head over his, feel his solid, breathing body fill the boat-shape of my arms, that my attention is divided. I want to think of nothing in the world except this beautiful child, but I feel the despair of my roommate. I lower my voice as I speak to the nurses. My baby will never again have me as his entire world. As we begin our separate passages, he and I have no choice but to hear the anguish of our fellow voyagers.

A nurse wakes me at two a.m. The room is dark save for the bedside lamp. The hospital is quiet. She rolls up my bed, helps me arrange myself so I'm sitting cross-legged with the thin blanket over my lap, and then she lowers Jacob into my arms. He is jaundiced and they're keeping him under fluorescent lights. She helps me peel away the cotton balls that protect his eyes. I feel the sudden strong pull as his tiny mouth closes around my nipple and he begins to suck.

The nurse tiptoes away. It's the first time the baby and I have been truly alone. On the other side of the curtain, my roommate is asleep. No one passes our door.

I stroke the peach fuzz on his forehead. His body fits in the curve of my arm as if the two shapes had grown side by side, like feathers on a wing. His eyes open. They are the colour of blueberries. I stroke his forehead, over and over. I feel as if I know everything he needs, exactly how to hold him, just how softly to touch his skin. I lower my head so I am whispering into the snail-curves of his ear.

"Do you remember when we were picking blueberries? We were way up on the top of the hill and all we could hear was the wind in the trees and a beautiful thrush singing. And then I went to the pond and lay in the inner tube, and you could hear the water rushing past my belly. Do you remember?"

I watch him sucking, and feel anxious whenever he stops and calm when he begins again. Finally, he is finished and his eyes fold shut in his face. I lift him from my breast and lie down, cradling him at my side. I feel, for the first time, the mother's deep calm, terribly hinged to the fulfilment of a child's needs.

My love has no measure, and nothing within me can censor it any more. I lie looking at this tiny baby at my side, my son, and am amazed at how natural it seems to have him here, finally arrived. His face is both serene and strangely distressed, as though he is seeking, in sleep, his lost kingdom. He seems both wise and innocent. His beauty is as heartbreaking and majestic as the pure stillness that separates nightfall from sunrise, as the windless pink clouds of pre-dawn and the unbroken spiderwebs with their trembling, unfallen globes of dew.

I think of the beauty of the world, of all the things I am going to show this child. I think of books, dandelions, baby goats, rasp-berries, sun on frost ferns, snowsuits. I feel my face softening as it has never softened before; I know it is the wonder, the boundless awe that I saw in Peter's face, heard in my parents' voices. I know this baby has brought it here for us, from somewhere.

IV

1977–1993

Chapter Twelve

My *parents drive, as they* did the last time I was in this hospital, straight up the seaboard without stopping. Jacob is in the nursery when they arrive, and I watch them as they stand at the glass window. Their faces seem clear, like furniture stripped of layers of cloudy varnish. They look like children. They exclaim to one another without taking their eyes off the tiny baby who lies stark naked in his bassinet, bathed in light, cotton balls taped to his eyes. They are speaking to everyone and to no one. My father wants anyone listening to notice the astonishing length of his little red feet. My mother describes him from head down, skipping from one feature to the next with the amazement of fresh discovery, each wonder adding to the next until she is overwhelmed and stands speechless. They can't take their eyes from him. They have forgotten everything: their rumpled clothing, their tiredness, their illegally parked car. I hear Poppy's voice, suddenly, in my father's. It's a slight crack, a fissure that opens onto the past. My mother's face is alight with love, as simple as Granny's.

When they turn to me finally, I feel a new distance between us, a good space, the breathing room that motherhood provides me. I'm no longer only their daughter. I'm Jacob's mother. I feel as if the dark strength that carried me through his birth still surrounds me, like a new skin. I feel older than they are, as if for the first time I have experienced something before they have. I know this child whom they are just meeting. I've carried his soul within mine. I feel the strangeness of their obligation, their dependency upon me for their own growth. I have slid us all forward into a new configuration. I've allowed them to take their place at the top of the family pyramid.

I have never seen them so purely happy.

We're at the mercy of the neo-natal specialist, a tense woman who won't let us go home until she's absolutely certain that this baby is completely healthy. She comes to my room on the day after Jacob's birth to give me a report on the state of his jaundice. I look anxiously at her face; I see only worry, the weight of her responsibilities. She gives me no reassurances, but says I must make him eat as much as possible.

When she leaves, my spirits plunge. I'm sure there's something wrong with my baby that she's not telling me; I'm swept with a feeling that's familiar and frightening. It's up to me to feed this baby with my mother's milk; only I have the ability to protect him, to save him from whatever danger is threatening. Dark clouds brew in my soul; they race over my heart, darken my vision. Like any storm, this one is composed of many elements that come together in the same place and collude. I can't name, or analyze, any of them; I know, though, that there's a remembered taste, texture and shape to the grief that constricts my throat, floods my eyes with tears, makes me curl sideways and clench my fists. *He's going to leave me.*

I begin to weep.

A passing nurse pauses at the door, glances, comes in and

stands by my bed. I am shaken with sobs, which I try to stifle. She stands stiffly; she doesn't sit on the bed, put her arm around me, pat my shoulder. She asks me what's wrong. Her voice is cold, remote. She makes me feel childish and inconsiderate. My voice breaks from me, and it's as if someone else is speaking.

"I lost a baby in this hospital. I had a . . . . stillborn . . . . baby." It's a word I will never be able to say for the rest of my life without a twist of pain. I am surprised to hear my choking voice saying these words. I thought I was crying about Jacob. And I am.

The nurse says nothing. She seems helpless, and irritated with me for making her feel this way. Her silence reprimands me, tells me no one wants to hear about this, it is a fact that has no place here and now. She stands waiting for me to get myself under control. I tell her I'm worried about my baby's jaundice; then she's able to tell me I'm being silly, it's not a life-threatening condition, I shouldn't be worrying.

After she leaves, I lie drained, with my head on the pillow and my arm over my face. I summon reason, the way I might sit up and stare at all the things in my room after a nightmare. I put the facts of my life in place. I have a baby boy. Peter is coming back in an hour. My parents are at the house, weeding my garden, mowing the lawn. I build a framework with these facts, something with form and outline to contain the dark chaos that has broken over me like a random storm. I don't want to examine the conditions that brewed this storm into being. I wait, staring at the wall, willing it to move on, to leave me in peace.

My mother prepares the house for my arrival. She has brought the white wool blankets that lived on the beds in the rose pink room at Aunt Bernice's, where my brother and I went to play after tea. She spreads them onto my bed, smoothes them until there is not one wrinkle, runs her hand over the satin edging before she folds the sheet down over it. She takes scissors and a basket and goes outside to gather flowers; she wanders down the nasturtium-trailed paths of my vegetable garden, pushes through the waist-high cricketing grasses around the house; she picks goldenrod, bachelor's buttons, blue aster, borage, and mixes them all, domestic and wild, in Peter's pottery vases. She sweeps under the beds, squeezes lemon oil onto a piece of torn sheet and rubs down the piano, the mantelpiece, the rocking chair that was her father's. She washes all the laundry she can find and pegs the wet clothes to the clothesline. She is small, like an insect absorbed in some repetitive wing-rubbing, dwarfed by the maple trees that pass their leaves over one another like meditative hands and by the late-summer clouds that pile over the sere fields. She's thinking all the time about me, her little girl whose heart has been stolen, as it should be, as hers was.

I have my birthday in the hospital, four days after Jacob's. I'm twenty-eight. It seems quite an age, nearing thirty. My father and Peter swoop through the door of my room like two hawks descending from the freedom of the skies and bring me a cupcake with one candle in it. They tell me I have to wait for my party.

I see signs of strain on Peter's face. He feels like the useless father. He is between roles; one has ended and he wants the next one to start. We chafe at our enforced stay in hospital, but Jacob gradually loses his extreme golden-brown skin tones, and the day after my birthday, when Jacob is five days old, I call Peter, my voice trembling with excitement, and tell him to come get us, we're free.

It is the strangest feeling to drive away from the Saint John General Hospital. I can hardly believe that they're letting us take this fragile baby away from their charts, needles, IV stands, bandages, thermometers, tubes, lights, cotton balls. I can't believe that they are letting us have this baby for our own, to take home, for good.

Shadow Child

I hold him in my arms and he sleeps all the way. I make a hood with the blanket to keep the sun from his face, but I repeatedly lift it and gaze at him. His little face is as amazing to me as are the deep colours of the world, which I'm seeing like a blind person whose sight has been miraculously restored. The hospital, like a ship, drifted in white sea fog for all the days of my stay there. Today, the blue sky is as strident as the grasshoppers that I can hear threading the rush of sweet-smelling wind that comes through the car window. I see the shadows of hawks flick over the yellow stubble of cut oat fields, while wildflowers in swales toss and bend in a long, continuous passage like the clouds.

We come down our valley and our house looks as it did the first time I ever saw it: improbable, surprising, crouched in its fields beneath the forested hills. It seems both humble and stubborn, existing side by side with the wild, its white clapboards enduring the same storms as the rocks but with less resilience. We turn down the long driveway, rumble over the planks of the bridge. The place lies in the sun like a cat, tidily curled round its recent cleaning; the lawn is freshly mowed, the grass is clipped under the picket fence around the kitchen garden. I step out of the car and my delighted parents draw back at the door, ushering me so that I go through first, carrying Jacob. I feel as if I am seeing our home for the first time. There is a bassinet against the wall behind the woodstove. It's from my childhood, resurrected from my parents' attic; there are pouches to hold diaper pins and cotton balls. The dining-room table is covered with presents; my heart leaps with the never-lost childhood excitement sparked by bows, ribbons and shiny paper. There are new blue candles in the pottery holders; flowers, in vases, on every table.

After being closed away from the world in my hospital room, I'm surprised to realize that time has been lilting forward, that the summer is five days older. I walk from room to room carrying Jacob, showing him the house even though he's asleep. Every door and window is open to the dry, grass-roots chitter of insects, the whish of wind in the late-summer leaves. Sun slants across the hall floor. The house feels bigger; the walls seem to lean back, allowing more light. The curtains furl and relax, lazily gathering the sweet air into their folds. Nothing is finished; one thing leads to another. There's a stack of diapers on the chest upstairs, a book face down on my father's pillow in the guest room, and Sam, sleeping on the quilt at the foot of their bed, yawns so I can see the corrugated pink cave of his mouth, and sniffs disinterestedly at the baby. The yellow baby room is as we left it, empty but filled with light.

I go into our summer bedroom and sit in the rocking chair by the east window, where I spent so many sleepless nights, waiting for time to pass, watching the moon. My arms are sweating slightly under the blue blanket, and I lean back, knowing that downstairs they're waiting for me to conclude some ritual they must be assuming I'm performing, since they've left me alone. I let my head fall back against the brocade and I rock, and the baby rocks, too, clasped solid and soft to my heart. I feel as if I could sleep for days, sleep like the baby in my arms, travel with him to some place that drifts and spins like the Milky Way, a dream world without limits or dimension.

Nothing seems to have changed; it's the same rocking chair whose upright padded back held my head when I didn't know yet whether Jacob would be safely born; I'm seeing the same line of spruce trees, their tips sharp in the afternoon light; and I'm just me again, unswollen, comfortable. But now, since I'm holding my precious son, I sense that the world is different. It's a subtle change, like the smell of new snow. I look at the child-sized door to the attic, the mirror that reflects the bedposts in its tarnished glass, the stovepipe hole and the sloping plaster ceilings. I wonder what this room will look like to our child. I can't imagine the texture of his childhood, or the transfiguration he will make of this mosaic. Even as Jacob sleeps, the house is changed by his presence in it.

I feel a passion of tenderness, then I hear my dad lift the stove lid with a clatter and I smile, standing, and see the new blankets on our bed.

For the first time, I understand what it means to be someone's child.

The baby progresses day by day, like the beans that mature on the vines, the goldenrod that goes to seed, the cold mornings that presage frost, and our days are built around his rhythms. Peter and I find slices of time in which to do the things we did before Jacob was born: he runs out to the pottery to trim bowls, fire a bisque; I get my dad to help me squat in the unruly bush beans and strip green beans from their woody stems. There's suddenly so much more to do—everything there was before, plus a baby's needs. And yet when Peter and I wake up, in the night, hearing the cry of a baby in our bedroom, and I prop my pillows against the headboard and Peter puts Jacob in my arms, when we watch him nursing in the circle of light thrown by the bedside lamp, we are living in the heart of life, around whose centre everything else is peripheral.

The house, like our lives, is in a continual state of chaos; nothing is ever finished, as I observed about the homes of our friends some years ago, when Peter and I were wondering if we would have children; and yet I forget how I thought, then, that these parents seemed harassed, uncentred, without peace or serenity. The messiness of our house is like the turmoil of first love; its source is divine, and so gathers us into its blessedness. Peter and I sit on the living-room floor, surrounded by piles of sweet-smelling diapers that Jacob's grandparents are industriously folding; our hands are lifting and folding as well, but haphazardly, because we're watching our sleeping child, fascinated by every shadow of expression that plays across his smooth-skinned face, and we are lost to everything around us.

I feel released. My body is light, strong; I can bend, twist, run; my breasts are lovely, filled with abundance, and I can press beneath one nipple and spray Peter in the face. My mind is moving easily, too. It feels agile, as if it had been bound like a fly in a web, wrapped round with threads of anxiety, and now flies free; darts, hovers, lights on new ideas. Our house is filled with friends who come to visit Jacob, who are attracted to our happiness in equal measure to the way in which our darkness, two years ago, shrouded us and kept us alone.

One day, my dad and I carry bushel baskets of snap beans into the kitchen, where my mother is keeping an eye on the boiling kettles and the baby. Jacob is lying in a cradle that has been passed down through our family for six generations. It's high-sided, painted grey, extremely narrow; in the 1700s, people believed in easing the baby's transition from womb to boundless space, and kept their babies in secure, confined places. Jacob wears diapers and one of the undershirts that I embroidered with pink and green flowers. His mottled legs are bathed in sunlight. Already his face is expanding; he's losing his compressed, old-man look. He's asleep, and I squat by the cradle, watching him, wishing he would wake up and look at me.

Peter is working overtime getting pots ready for the annual fall craft fair. My dad splits wood, keeps the woodstove stoked. He clomps in and out of the kitchen in his leather boots, dropping armloads of wood into the scarred red box behind the stove. He sings in a tuneless voice; we hear the axe falling through logs out in the back shed, the thunking clatter as the severed pieces tumble to the floor. My mother and I sit across from one another at the kitchen table that Peter made from a maple tree we cut on the northeast hill. Our fingers move like running cats' legs: fluidly, softly. She snaps the stem ends from the beans, I slice them and we talk quietly, enjoying the calm efficiency that comes from some ancient womanly impulse to gather, organize and store.

The water boils. Logs in the firebox shift, there's a dry crunch and the rustle of embers falling into the ash pan. Through the screen door, we can hear the desultory snap of diapers on the clothesline; they're pegged, one to the next, like shining shingles, almost all the way to the maple trees.

Jacob cries out suddenly, his face crumpled with distress. The volume and intensity of his trembling, hiccuping cries increase as I squat by the cradle, calling him nonsense names, scooping him like a pea from its pod, sitting in the rocking chair next to the kettle whose lid rattles over the puffing steam, watching the baby's blind frantic nuzzle until his lips find the nipple and then hearing the instant, profound quiet of gratification.

I stroke the soft spot on his head. His dark blue eyes open, slide slyly from side to side and then close, as if in concentration. His lips tighten and relax, tighten and relax. My body, I think, was this baby's first home. I feel I am his shelter, imagine that there is nothing I can't protect him from. I'm looking down at him, feeling the curve of his body, how it fits there so perfectly. He is my home, too, my shelter; I've been wandering in the dark, seeking my way, searching for something. He's healed me. I feel my throat ache suddenly. I remember our special closeness when I rocked in the moonlit bedroom, pregnant, knowing he was alive, hoping he would survive his passage. I think of the infinite preciousness of this perfect child, of how vulnerable he is and of how my job is to send him away.

Then I think, with sudden wonder, that I will be as special to him as he is to me. That no matter where he goes, how far he roams, how many years he lives, I will always be his only mother.

Someday his love for me will make him feel as strong and tender as I feel now.

In September, after my parents have gone, we put Jacob in a blue corduroy baby-carrier that straps onto Peter's chest. I carefully fish his little legs though the holes. He's sprawled heart to heart against his father. Peter strokes his son's head, putting his own head to one side and tucking in his chin so he can see the little face pressed against his chest. We have no idea what anyone else is doing at this moment, friends, family or neighbours. We are totally absorbed in whether to put a cotton cap on the baby's head, whether to protect his bare feet from insects or let the wind cool them, whether I should take a little wool sweater in my day-pack.

Finally we set forth. We stride up the hill through the dry grass, seed pods rattling against our boots. The blueberries are shrivelled amid their brilliant red leaves. In the hedgerows, the ferns no longer wave, but trail over rock cairns that are veined with sprawling blackberry vines. When we reach the top of the hill, we stop to look back down the valley. The fields are the colour of fresh-baked bread and seem to radiate light. The hardwood trees are either fire red, or the intense yellow of an ember's heart.

At the edge of the field, we brush past prickly spruce branches and follow a footpath that leads us into the cool, quiet woods. Our steps are silenced by layers of fallen needles. Mushrooms grow in the damp hollows between scaly roots. Tiny white ones spread over the moss like stars on a black night, their stems as delicate as threads. The sun shafts into clearings where yellow ferns make pockets of glowing light.

Beside our path, there's a clearing with no ferns, only green sphagnum moss so dense that I can sink my fingers into it and they don't reach the soil. I spread a cotton baby blanket on the moss; Peter lifts Jacob from the pack and gently settles him on the blanket.

Jacob's eyes are open. He's been blinking as we walked, watching the play of light. He lies now on his back, with his legs and arms turned out as if he's still pressed against another body. I watch shadows flick across him. I wonder if he's smelling ferns, mushrooms, moss roots, spruce gum. I wonder if his blue eyes are seeing the stirring branches, are glimpsing the sky far above. I wonder if he's hearing the thrush that's fluting, dropping its resonant notes into the wind-brushed quiet and then falling silent, as if waiting for an answer.

Then, without warning, I am seeing not Jacob but our first son. For the first time, I truly understand that he was a baby, not the dream of one. I realize that he was solid, that he must have looked very much like Jacob, that he was his brother. He is born, for me, at this instant. My heart pinches so that I lean forward and put my face in my hands.

"What's wrong?" says Peter.

"What did he look like?" I ask through my hands.

He knows what I mean. He doesn't answer for a long time. My eyes are closed, but I'm seeing the baby that someone must have held, that Peter saw emerging from my body.

When he speaks, his voice has to overcome an inertia of pain, and begs my forgiveness for what he has seen and I have not. "He looked more like me."

"More than Jacob does?"

"Yes."

My grief, which I thought had been healed, doused and put to rest, seizes me. Tears come from a source that I thought had been exhausted.

We say no more. I uncover my face and look at Jacob, but I'm remembering the night I lay in the hospital, after I'd borne my first child and was alone. For the first time, I can imagine his tiny body, I know what it must have looked like. I wonder where he was taken that night. I think of his hair and his feet, of the seed-sized teeth waiting to come through his gums. I realize I have nothing of him, not even a memory of what he looked like.

At this moment, a shadow child begins to grow along with Jacob. Over the coming years, he will grow unseen, silently, whether I choose to acknowledge him or not.

I can't bear the implications of what I have just understood. It's so enormous a pain—the fact that I did not hold or see a baby who was whole, real, solid—that I can glimpse the truth for only an instant before I begin to shred it, like a dreadful letter that I daren't read, but whose words I can't help seeing even as as I destroy them.

Jacob is staring up, his eyes open. He is completely absorbed in this moment, cushioned by moss, surrounded by the forest trees that lift and fall on the wind like great breathing creatures. His eyes are losing their dreamy other-world obliviousness. I see wonder awakening in them already. He begins to look out, to enter our world.

I stroke the bottom of his foot. It's the very foot I used to trace under my blouse, the one that pressed against the wall of my uterus. It's as velvety as the mushroom caps.

The other baby, the one Jacob has awakened within me, vanishes like a wind whose passage I can see only by the branches that lift, stir restlessly and then settle back, rearranged.

The summer birds have gone, and frost has put an end to my garden. The ravens fly low and gather in flocks in the copse, quarrelling loudly, like victors apportioning spoils. They don't gather to leave, like the great flocks of blackbirds do, but seem to consolidate, considering the landscape that's theirs now. I can hear, it seems, the silence of my garden, as if its growing had sound.

Shadow Child

Jacob lies in a white plastic baby-carrier; it has handles on the sides and a mattress fit into its bottom, and I can carry him around in it to wherever I happen to be working: woodpile, garden, pottery. I lug him to the garden, where he sleeps, surrounded by lambs' quarter weeds, while I dig the last potatoes.

Jacob's babyhood fleets past so rapidly that just as I feel I've recognized a pattern, it changes. I am astounded by my love for him, and how it intensifies as his eyes open wider and become rounder; as he sees and then tracks with fascination the little clowns that revolve on a mobile over his crib; as his cheeks become red from the hours he spends with us outdoors; as his hands begin to close around things, a rattle, a plastic dog bone, measuring spoons; as he begins to make sounds, and they become joyful; as he gives me his first, great, gummy smile and I know he knows who I am.

My heart aches for him. I'm learning one of the many prices of love: now I want to stop time, to arrest change, not for me, but for my child. I know how his childhood will fly past, how his own heart will break as he mourns, so soon, its passing. I bear the parents' peculiar anguish of foresight; much that this child will suffer, I will have suffered, too, in my own way, and I have to watch as he tumbles innocently towards pain.

A month after Jacob's birth, my best friend leaves her husband. I say goodbye to her in the autumn sunshine and realize, when she's gone, why women need women. I fill my journal with all the things I would have told her, things that we would have shared, feelings that only she would understand: glancing, glimpsed evocations of joy and darkness. I miss her so much that I feel as if I, too, have been divorced. Other upheavals follow. Some mornings, when I first wake up, I lie in bed and try to remember who is in the guest-room: the mason who comes to fix our chimney and is in the midst of a marriage breakdown; Peter's brother, who has driven from Maine to ask our advice on whether he should marry his girlfriend; guests from Germany; Peter's cousin, en route to France, haunted by his past. People arrive, bearing their stories like knotted yarn that they spread on our kitchen table after supper, over wine, night after night. Within myself, I feel a strange ebb and flow of emotion; sometimes I'm sailing, weightless, carried by an inexplicable happiness like early morning sunlight, and then I'm weighted by the convoluted snarls of the lives around us, and wonder if adult life is nothing more than the keeping of desperation at bay.

My attention, as it was from the minute I met my roommate in the hospital, is divided. I wonder if all women feel this way, torn, called upon for their sympathy, for their attentive listening, lured from the one creature whom they know, without question, needs them the most. I hold Jacob, my cheek on his soft head, listening to stories of infidelity, of childhood cruelties, of mental illness and haunting tragedies. Part of me feels gratified by these confidences, not realizing the toll they are taking on me or how my compliant listening shields me from my need to tell my own story. But as I breastfeed Jacob, I can smell anxiety coming from my own body, from the smell of my sweat. I watch his peaceful face, the curve of his eyelids like the convolutions of shell, and wonder if he absorbs the emotions that fill the room: anger, fear, betrayal, mourning.

Yet we proceed, Peter and Jacob and I; we become a family. Our life together is like a rock in the sea; something anchors us, we're held steady by some great weight that I won't be able to see, or name, for many years.

I am not prepared for the terrible paradox of parenthood. Our job is to help Jacob grow up. We have to protect him at the same time as teaching him how to survive without us. Yet as my love increases, so does my mother-tiger desire to keep him from pain, to surround him with peace. However, Peter and I are delighted with each new accomplishment, each minute change. And he grows as swiftly as the passing of summer.

We take him to visit Harry and Inez. They are seventy-eight years old and were our first friends in the valley. Harry is totally bald and wears a fedora hat that he often removes so he can pass his hand, which is missing its index finger, over his brown head, as if smoothing his hair before resettling the cap. Inez unties her apron when we arrive, standing in the door of her kitchen on sturdy legs; she's taller than Harry, and strong-armed. She went with Harry to wherever his work took him: cooked in lumber camps, was caretaker for a fish-company lodge on an island in the Bay of Fundy while he tended weirs. They've retired here, to the valley of their births, where her mother was a midwife when more babies were born at home than in hospitals, especially in winter. Their grey-shingled house is on a hillside surrounded by elms that have not yet died, but will soon. Begonias grow in a tidy row along the east side of the house; round plots of bachelor's buttons and white phlox stud the lawn. Lush and weedless vegetable gardens run up the steep hill behind the house. Harry's pea vines are six feet tall; his potatoes are twice as big as mine, and he grins at my astonishment, telling me that he puts in seeds only so he can stand in his garden and watch it grow. In the kitchen, glass bottles line the shelves above Inez's green-and-cream-coloured wood-stove; a colour photograph of the covered bridge in St. Martin's hangs from a nail on the cellar door, and painted wooden chairs with turned rungs are pushed against a table that's covered with a yellow-and-white checked oil cloth. There are blueberry pies in the warming oven. The room smells of freshly steeped King Cole tea and hot berries. We can see our house, framed by their lilac-friezed window, and I feel as if our lives are somehow contained in this kitchen, along with theirs.

We come soon after Jacob is born, bearing him like a prince.

We lay him on the couch, and they bend over him, gazing with delight as if he is the first baby they have ever seen. Their malevolent tom cat stalks into the room, furry paws tapping the linoleum, loose slab of belly almost touching the rag rug. He glances at the baby with disinterested green eyes, jumps onto the plaid La-Z-Boy.

"Well, now," Inez says, firmly. "That's a fine boy." But Harry shakes his head as if he knows less, and is more amazed, the older he gets. His false teeth are white in his tanned face. I can see sharp whiskers in the folds of his cheeks. He looks at Jacob and grins. Then he shakes his head again and puts his hand over his mouth. The skin of his hand is shiny, like a leather glove that's been left outside all winter; his fingers are twisted.

"He's got a lot of hard old things to go through," he says musingly. His voice is softened by the wonder and strangeness of life. "A lot of hard old things."

Jacob's first two years of life pass, and I record everything he does in my diary because I know I will never remember it otherwise. He changes from a fragile wondrous creature who floats on my arms light as a leaf, still lost in the mystery of becoming, to a merry, apple-cheeked, blond baby boy who does push-ups with his arms, like a baby coming out of a manhole, and then begins to crawl, first backwards (vanishing, one day, out of the kitchen and under the piano) and then frontwards, spilling the cats' water dishes, pulling himself up on chairs, reaching for electric cords, bowls of steaming soup, long-stemmed glasses of wine. He enters eating trances when presented with yogurt and mashed bananas; slaps at his bath water; beams at me as though he's delighted by the sight of me; talks to his cloth elephants in a guttural monotone, pulls off their ears and chews them, chuckling to himself; gazes wonderingly at the black shadow of diapers on a patch of light on the living-room floor and laughs in a crowing cackle when I make the shadow twitch. I wonder how much of this time he will remember: the cardboard box he sits in, covered with a blanket, his eyes shining excitedly from its darkness; the wooden spoon he waves at me through its little window; how he bangs on the piano keys and discovers, with great seriousness, that he can make sounds; telling simulated stories in his own ba-ba language, and then, astonishingly, pronouncing words that we understand: duck, hot, book. I wonder if he will remember the time he industriously carries all his mittens from his bedroom into the bathroom and drops them in the bathwater; he is delighted with how they float about, red and blue, making beautiful patterns. Or if he will remember the day he learns to walk because he loves the softness of Bronwen's velour shirt; he stands with his hands on her, as if she's a chair, but she moves backwards and he goes with her until suddenly he is standing by himself, alone, springy and elastic, in the middle of the floor. He rushes five steps forward and falls face first on the couch. Bronwen and Erin lift him by his hands and walk him forward. He takes off, tilting like a baby bird on uncertain wings, his stumpy legs toddling down the long living-room, arms out, while the children squeal and giggle and Peter and I are beside ourselves with excitement. I wonder if he'll remember the cold winter nights coming home from Bob and Kathy's log house: walking over the frozen fields, I step around behind Peter to see Jacob's little face peering over the frame of the pack. Only his eyes show. He's muffled in wool scarf, toque and hood, his arms and legs stiff as a doll's in his snowsuit, but he doesn't seem to mind. His eyes are sleepy, wide, profound. He watches the moonlit fields tipping and flashing as his dad's snowshoes rhythmically rise and fall; he sees the icicles shimmering on the tips of spruce boughs, and then the nails on the unpainted boards of the back shed where we hang our snowshoes, and the cracked grey paint on the hall door that creaks on its hinges as we push into the kitchen. He feels the cloud-float of stairs. His eyes are closed as the crib comes up to take his warm body and the blanket tucks around his shoulders.

When he's two years old, I lie on the floor next to him and watch him sitting with his legs spread, gazing in amazement at the Christmas tree. His wide eyes study one thing and then another, resting on popcorn, cranberries, a straw doll, the tiny white lights, the shimmering tinsel. I'm quickened by him, stripped of habit. Seeing the world through his eyes imbues it with depth, dimension, quality. On Christmas morning, he carefully lifts the first present from the top of his stocking; it's a net bag filled with tiny farm animals. He takes each one from the bag with fingers that work as precisely as calipers. He is fascinated with each animal, spends a long time inspecting the ant-sized pig before we urge him to take out the brown horse, the black-and-white cow, the sheep. He becomes profoundly absorbed in walking each animal across the floor. He makes them tip-tap up chair legs, through Sam's fur, across my cheek. He expects nothing else.

His innocence fills my heart with anguish. He reaches for the world with such faith, such trust, such pure joy. I read children's books to him; there are guns, treacherous pigs, monsters, child-eating witches. My voice falters and I want to turn the page, but he doesn't want me to hide anything that he's already glimpsed. His little hands pat the pages; he exclaims with deep interest, traces the shape of evil with his tiny fingers.

The following spring, Peter makes a swing in the maple tree. We put Jacob on the wooden seat. He hooks his arms around the chains and hangs forward, mesmerized by the green grass, the yellow dandelions, coming up and past and falling away. He puts his head back, points up excitedly into the tree. He's becoming himself, a boy, a separate soul. I see his little teeth, his fine blond hair, his striped overalls and blue hooded sweatshirt as he flies into the sky, away from me, becoming smaller and more vulnerable; and then he comes back into my hands. I push him away, catch him when he returns, push him away again, back into the sky, over and over, listening to him laugh with delight as he flies free.

Chapter Thirteen

I feel a hand patting my face in the morning, and open my eyes to see a red-cheeked face smiling at me. Jacob is standing on tiptoe, puts an empty cup on my pillow. He pats my cheek again. "Who'sat?" "Mummy," I say sleepily. "Who's *that?*" I ask him. He clasps his arms around his stomach. "Jacob," he says. He points to Peter's back. "Daddy. Mummy. Jacob. BABY." He nods vigorously. I close my eyes and hear him trot out to the hall, where the bannisters and the newel post, like motionless marsh birds, are surfacing from darkness. The frost crystals on Jacob's south-facing window begin their slow molten sparkle in the rising winter sun. "Door," he says. He is speaking to his world. "Sun!"

He picks up words like shells on a beach. He listens the way he might scoop handfuls of sand; lets sound tumble back like pebbles flung from both hands. He holds books upside down and reads them out loud. When he realizes that a sound is a word, he hoards it, says it over and over again. "Bath!" he says excitedly, slapping at the shadow-mottled water that he sits in, neck-deep, his soapy hair ridged into a crest, making him look like a cockatoo. "Bath, bath, bath, bath!"

As the world spills its treasures, his reaction to them reveals his character. He turns rags into dolls, makes a family of snakes with clay, holds a knife and fork to his nose and tells us they're his whiskers. He listens to Holst's *The Planets* and runs around the house, shouting, waving his arms. He lies on the kitchen floor drawing, his pencil or crayon following his mind; his eyes see what he imagines, rather than what emerges on the paper. When Peter and I gather in his bedroom at bedtime, for our "family read," he watches the shifting shadows on the plaster wall, dusty grey, soft in candlelight, and he listens to words as if they are music, hearing their emotion, not questioning their meaning. I read to Jacob whatever I'm reading myself: Shakespeare, Yeats, Wordsworth, parts of *Great Expectations*. Peter and I read him all three volumes of *The Lord of the Rings*.

I love to name the world for him. I love Jacob's dawning fascination with the fact that each object has its own special sound that he can retrieve, that he can toss out like a spark into dry kindling. He can cause reactions, describe his power. "I walk on Mummy's shadow." Peter makes a huge planter and Jacob calls it "Big Lady." He hangs a dishcloth on her for a dress and squats in front of her. "Big Lady got breasts?" He sits in the rocking chair with his arm around Clancy, our tailless yellow cat. "Rock, rock," he sings abstractedly. I tell him to put his wooden rooster and chicken in their little box and his face lights with astonished pleasure when he understands—he trots off busily to do what I've asked.

He spends hours of his childhood on the periphery of our work. While Peter and I throw firewood from the woodpile into the cellar in thin November sunshine, he's bundled in sweater, toque and mittens, making Green Arrow and Superman save Paddington who hangs by one leg in the lilac bush; he comes to the shop with me and sprawls on the floor behind the sales desk, drawing while I set pottery on shelves; he talks to the chickens through the wire mesh of their stall as I shovel manure. And he plays alone for hours. These are the conditions of his life; often, I'm guilty, thinking I should be spending more time with him, should be working less hard, should be more in touch with what's happening inside his mind. But when I peek into his bedroom, where he's making something with string and scissors and a cast of characters—Batman or teddy bears or paper horses—he tells me to go away, please, he's busy. And he *is* busy. He takes one thing and turns it into something else. Everything is potent: pebbles, sticks, cardboard, string, hats, water, boxes. He turns dirt into mountains, bushes into caves, puddles into oceans; he makes cloth parachutes, wooden pistols, cardboard houses.

His creativity is spontaneous and fluid, inseparable from who he is. He doesn't make things for other people to see or admire or praise. He's not seeking judgement or approval. He wants to give form to feelings, and has no idea that this is a difficult thing to do; when I tell him one morning that I had a dream that Dad and I went to a convent, ate boiled lettuce and were accompanied by a ghost child, Jacob listens intently and then scrambles out of bed, gets paper, crayon and scissors, and makes a ghost family. He sets up the firescreen and makes shows with his ghosts; he takes them to bed with him. He invites us to watch his ghosts speaking to one another in strange, guttural voices. His life is dominated by ghosts for two days, until he abandons them, easily, in the growing pile of cast-off projects that litters the floor of his bedroom. Creativity is nothing more to him than the freedom to play with life, to see its strangeness and wonder, to take for granted his own power to turn one thing into another, just as he sees wind carving snow or frost ferns jungling his window. He's discovered that he is not wind, water or light, but a human boy, alone and separate; and yet he's free as these things. He lets music make him

shout; he sets his hand loose to trace the dreams he hardly realizes he's imagining.

After Jacob is born, a new tension comes into our lives; time
seems more precious, there's less of it. Peter and I have arguments
about the division of labour: who should do the breakfast dishes,
who should make the bed. What we're really arguing about is
whose time is more valuable, which job is more important. The
fact is that Peter's pots are what make us our money. My writing
does not.

I perceive that Peter is on a growth curve like Jacob's. He
spends all day in the studio, and his work becomes more accomplished; he uses different glazes, experiments with form and technique, takes weekend workshops, has colleagues with whom he
discusses slipcasting and marketing, is president of the provincial
craft council. He makes things that people, increasingly, want to
own. They want to buy more than just a stoneware bowl, however. When I sit behind the sales desk, I see customers turning
each vase or teapot upside down, making sure that his signature is
on the bottom.

Peter is juggling his own needs; he wants to prove himself both
as a provider and as an artist. He's a son still seeking approval.
He's a father trying to understand what his son needs from him.
He's a husband, bewildered and frustrated by my resentment of
his success.

I'm selling his pots, pots whose bottoms I have waxed and dry-
footed, pots that I've handed to Peter as he stacks the kiln and
taken from his hands as he unloads it again, that I've priced and
catalogued and wrapped and unwrapped and put on shelves and
wrapped again after a sale; and at that time, I smile and agree with
people as they tell me how talented and creative my husband is,
am enigmatic when they wonder how he can possibly produce so

much work. When they leave the shop, I feel as if I'm a towel saturated with falseness, and I want to wring myself out.

I do love the shop, with its plants and sunshine; I do love listening, smiling, chin on hand, to the people who stop by just to talk with me. I do love the pots themselves; I enjoy setting teapots on shelves, nesting mugs around them, adding a cream-and-sugar set to the group. I do love Peter.

But a slow anger simmers within me. I don't show it to anyone but Peter and Jacob, with whom it manifests itself as irritability, impatience, occasional rage. I feel the way I did when, as a child, I put on my best clothes and had to walk demurely in treacherous shoes that had no heels and no traction, were as smooth on the bottom as plastic. I had to spread my skirts to either side and sit on scratchy petticoats. The role I played, when I wore my Sunday clothes, was strangely safe; I knew the words to say, the face to make, the way to hold my fork. I'm doing it again at the age of thirty. At the hardware store, the bills are made out in my husband's name, never in mine. It's not my truck, but Peter's. It's Peter's pottery studio.

I wonder why no one ever asks me about myself. I don't realize that I never give them a chance.

My work is taken by an agent in New York. He shows my short-story collection to publishers; their reaction is positive, but they want to see a novel. I'm deeply excited. At five in the morning, when Peter and Jacob are still asleep, when the house is silent and moonlight falls on my desk, I crouch in the intimate pool of light thrown by my lamp and enter a world that's as magical to me as Jacob's imaginary worlds are to him; and I dream of the day when an editor will read what I've written and be as moved, as delighted, as filled with joy as I was when I pulled those words from the warm darkness behind my eyes.

I feel like two different people. The one who writes is trying to make something that will endure and remain constant, like music

Shadow Child

that evokes a particular epoch. The other person is like the swallows who return to our barn every year within three or four days of the date they returned the year before. Repetition makes the years fly by faster and faster. I think, Here I am, piling the winter squash in the wheelbarrow again. I'm squatting on the wood floor of the back barn, laying onions in rows to dry, while the smell of goldenrod comes again, on a wind just as apple-sweet and frost-sharp as it was last year at this time. I'm in the kitchen, and I'm watching my reflection in the window, red-and-black wool shirt, hair piled on head; I'm seeing my hands pulling dough, pushing it away, shaping loaves, dropping them in pans, lifting the lid of the firebox, ratcheting in another log. It's like a dance that I've performed for years on the same stage, the choreography so familiar that my mind is elsewhere. There's always more to do than can possibly be finished.

Yet I add more tasks, as if the life that everyone sees me living—mother, potter's assistant, shopkeeper, gardener, breadmaker, bookkeeper—might compensate, with its visible but repetitive accomplishments, for the silence of the other life that's trying to emerge.

In the country, cows mate in fields, kittens are born in hay mows, sows eat their piglets. We find stinking corpses; flies swarm on glazed birds' eyes; snakes are paper-thin, flattened by tractor tires. There are rabbit guts with iridescent livers on the back steps. Jacob sees his cat torturing a field mouse and he seizes a stick; incensed, he chases the cat, who races down the driveway with its tail in the air, the mouse flopping in its jaws. On our walks, we find raccoon skulls, mossy cow bones, raven feathers and deer jaws. Andy, our duck—who browsed grass on the lawn near me as I weeded my flower garden, watching me with his intelligent, old-man's eyes; who waddled down the driveway behind us, tugging at our pantlegs with his bill—is killed by a dog when he strays to our neighbour's farm, and Jacob asks us, several days later, if Russell has chopped that dog's head off yet. My youngest nanny-goat has her first kidding and one of the kids is born dead; we find it in the slimy hay at the back of the stall, flattened. When I pick it up, its legs and its head dangle, as loose as a marionette. Jacob sees it, but is soon absorbed in towelling down the other kid, who is staggering as her mother licks her, making tiny baaings that seem to come from somewhere else, like the sound of ice cracking.

When Jacob is three, he and I fly to Boston to be with my parents, as Mère is dying in a nursing home. I take Jacob to see his great-grandmother for the last time. She's lying on her back and I sit next to her with Jacob on my lap. "It's Jacob, Mère," I say. Jacob is interested in her, curious; he's not afraid. She's like anything else in his life. He sees her as she is now: teeth removed, white hairs on her chin, her mind snapped loose from its moorings and roaming in memory. She rolls her head over and looks into his clear blue child's eyes; at first her expression is confused, but then it clarifies and intensifies, like a starving person who sees food but can't reach it. She lifts her hands and puts them on either side of his face. She pulls his face close to hers. He watches her calmly; she stares deep into his eyes as if she is watching a tiny movie, seeing every person she loved, everything that breathed, sang, lifted on a wind, shone in the light. I watch this peculiar, vibrant exchange, astounded by Jacob's lack of fear. She takes something from him that lets her relax, gradually, and fall back on the pillow. She closes her eyes as if she's given away her soul and knows it will be cherished. She seems both released and exhausted; she sleeps, and never wakes up.

Jacob seems unaffected by this, but we take him, when he is four, to see a movie about the British poet Stevie, who lived with her mother and died young; he is silent until, as Peter is buckling the straps of his car seat, he bursts out angrily with "I hate the thing that makes old ladies die," and begins to cry. I wish we hadn't taken him to the movie. I try to comfort him; he puts his thumb in his mouth and stares out the window, mute and desolate, as we drive home.

We ride silently through the night, all of us aware of the current that flows so strongly, the thing that makes old ladies die. Mère was the last of my grandparents, and Jacob is the first of the grandchildren. I wonder if he's feeling, in his four-year-old soul, the beginning of the strange sensation that is both the curse and beauty of human consciousness: the knowledge that every instant dies at the moment of its birth. Time swallows itself. We're fireflies in an infinite night, succeeding one another, doing little more than keeping the darkness lit.

I decide to tell Jacob about his brother when he is small enough that he will never remember the time when it was something he did not know. It's after his bath, several weeks later, and I'm towelling him down. I take a breath and then tell him that we had another baby before we had him, but that it died. He watches me curiously. My eyes fill with tears and slide away from his. The longer this baby is unnamed, unacknowledged, the harder it is to speak of him. My mouth warps as I say, "It was a boy." I wipe the tears from my face with both hands and glance quickly at my little son. He's staring at me as if I've suddenly gone very far away, or become someone else. He seems cautious, stoutly alone. He's amazed by my sudden grief. I realize he feels no sadness yet for the brother he will never know. I wonder how what I've just told him will spread itself through his being, how it will change him, how it will accompany him through his life.

Our first child had no chance to know the exquisite beauty of being one of the fireflies. I don't know what to do with the knowledge that a child was born who might have lived in this house, who might have seen the moon silvering the hardwood forest or felt, with his little hands, the soft tiger fur of our cats. Every year, the child grows. When Jacob's four, he would have been six. This fall, he'd be starting school. He's always older than Jacob. He's his big brother whose spirit will not leave. He grows no matter how hard I try to keep him in the silent place where I think grief is meant to be contained.

I never tell new acquaintances that we had another baby before Jacob. Sometimes I'm confused when I blunder into a statement about being pregnant in winter and have to explain that I'm remembering my first pregnancy. I steer the topic when anyone asks me if we're going to have a second child. I don't want to explain why I feel that one child is miracle enough.

I have no idea how strong a spirit can be; especially one who never had a chance to shine.

There's nothing in the house to remind me of our lost baby: no pictures of me during my first pregnancy, no scrapbook of sympathy cards, no birth certificate or even death certificate. There's no gravestone in the cemetery. We have no ceremonies of remembrance. We never mention his name or talk about him with our families.

I want to treasure my growing child. As we read to Jacob at night, I gaze at him in bewilderment. It is another of life's surprises, the unearthly beauty and radiance of a child, and the pain, fear and power of my love. I wonder if my love for this child will be the most intense and heart-rending experience of my life.

We are still so close, mother and child. He registers, like a barometer, the slightest fluctuations of my moods. I find him sunk in dumb misery on the couch, sucking his thumb, when I have had another story rejected. I feel a quicksilver spear of anger towards him, and then I'm guilty. I realize that above all I want my child to be happy. I need him to be happy, just as he needs me to be happy. We are manoeuvring around one another, holding and pushing, needing and rejecting.

What surprises me is that we are both growing. When I was a child, I thought that my mother was fixed, complete; she was a "grown-up." She had finished the voyage, had arrived at the place I was heading towards. But I realize there's no such thing as a grown-up. No voyage ever ends; both Jacob and I are engaged in the same passage, the same strange quest, only we're at different stages of it.

We wonder about the same mysteries. He wants to know where the world came from, who made it. He wants to know where we go when we die. He asks us who moves the clouds. He tells me confidentially, "Cats and dogs have secret feelings." He wonders if sheep and ducks can understand each other's languages. He tells us he wants to be a large seabird when he dies. His wonder, and supposition, frees my mind, untethers it from the square facts that have anchored it. I float with him like a dandelion seed, glistening in the sun. His child speculations are wise, wild, delightful. He teaches me how to forget what I've learned and to begin, again, to see.

We are confused by the same contradictions. He tells me that he used to be God's child, that he lived in the sky with him, on sandy islands near the sun, and that God created this sky-island sunworld; only now, he said, he can't get back to God and God can't get here because they've lost their special whistle. He travels to special places at night, and tells me and Peter at breakfast where he went. I listen to his cheerful voice, prattling on as he waves his spoon in the winter sunlight. I wonder why even a small child seeks a place that is perfect; I'm amazed that he senses that even if he's able to get there, he can't stay. I wonder if the womb is the only perfect place, and remember the distress on Jacob's face hours after he had left his dark kingdom. I imagine his life, his search for the special whistle, his search for the sandy islands near the sun with his god.

I notice how he begins to deliberately gather comforts around him in bed, needing, just as Peter and I do, warmth and companionship. He lies, bathed, relaxed, his head cradled by a pillow, his stuffed animals, without whom he would be less himself, nested around him: a floppy grey donkey, Paddington Bear with his blue felt jacket, a yellow dog with a wind-up key in its back, a huge rabbit. After I've read him *Goodnight, Moon* and I think he's asleep, I pause at the top of the stairs, hearing his little voice. He's talking sleepily to a picture we drew during the day and pinned up over his bed. "Goodnight, cats! Goodnight, elephants! Goodnight, flowers!" And then: "Goodnight, Jacob!"

I want to tell him about everything in the great world that I find fascinating and strange. I want to tell him about deserts and cactus, Sherpas, lunar eclipses, Stonehenge and Druids, polar bears; I want to teach him to count and read. At the same time, I want to prolong his innocence, keep him tender. I watch his face light like sunrise on a wall when he sees something for the first time: a butterfly, a wasp's nest, the scales of a garter snake. I see his delight, his pure wonder; I can hardly bear the tenderness I feel as I watch his luminous astonishment at the world's mystery, as I watch him unfold, coaxed forward by time.

I finish writing a novel, then I write it again. I send it to my agent, who is still trying to place my short-story collection. For a while, I stop writing. I'm waiting, suspended, poised between hope and despair. It's the same feeling I carried through Jacob's pregnancy. It's a state of mind that grows increasingly familiar as I grow older. I take nothing for granted. I'm always hoping for the best and expecting the worst.

One day in March I get a large envelope in the mail. I carry it down the driveway. I don't open it until I'm sitting in the rocking chair, by the woodstove. Inside is a letter from my agent. He encloses six letters from editors of large New York publishing companies. I'll find them self-explanatory, he says. My heart is racing. I read the letters. All the editors praise my writing, but are bewildered by my novel, which they say is so dark that it won't sell. My heart twists the way it did when I was chastised as a child; I feel a peculiar stab of anguish. I've been wrong, bad, have failed, overstepped my bounds, tried to do something I should have known I couldn't. I drop the letters on the floor and lean forward with my face in my hands. I'm listening to the beating of my heart. I know I'm at one of life's crossroads.

Jacob comes running down the stairs, bursts into the kitchen, a model spaceship in his hands. I kick the papers aside, put my cheek on the top of his head as he stands by my knee, explaining. It's such a good feeling. I'm not listening to a thing he says, but he's like cool salve, taking away my pain.

Two months later, I stop at the mailbox as I'm driving to town. I slide out a box wrapped in brown paper. Inside is my short-story manuscript and a form letter. "Although we are happy to have had a chance to consider . . . ."

I stand on the dirt road staring at the letter. A warm breeze lifts my hair. It smells of spruce trees and freshly turned soil. My neighbour has turned his cows into our pasture, and before I opened the mailbox, I stood grinning, watching the calves prance stiff-legged over the dandelions, their tails held straight up.

I open the trunk of the car and hurl the manuscript in. Inside myself, I slam a door shut with such rage that the door splinters, its frame is destroyed. It's the end. It's the end, absolutely. I feel exactly the way I felt when I decided I would never allow myself to get pregnant again. I'm saying to some unknown person, "You will never hear from me again. I will never again let you have any power over my life." I leave the short-story manuscript in the trunk for the rest of the summer. I don't want to touch it. I'm glad when it's so thoroughly buried beneath bottles of windshield-washer fluid, empty pop cans and broken toys that I can't see it.

The next morning, I write to my agent and sever my connection with him. I take a black garbage bag to my desk and scoop everything into it except my journal: short stories, pen, rejection letters, notebooks. I take it to the attic. I shut the door of the living-room and for weeks I can't look into that room. The sight of my desk makes me feel sick to my stomach. My hidden writing life is like a room inside myself, the room whose door I smashed; everything that was inside it gradually vanishes: editors of literary magazines, agent, publishers, grants, competitions. No ongoing story makes me feel as if I'm riding a see-saw, one day rising high and weightless, the next landing on the unforgiving ground.

It takes months for the room to empty itself, years before its door will be reopened.

Summer comes sweeping over us, gathers us into its green curl. Mornings, I lie in bed listening to the swallows who perch on the phone line outside our window. They shrug their shoulders, peck their wing-pits, make chipping bursts that seem conversational and peaceful. I gaze at the ripple of sun on white plaster and think about how there seems to be a rhythm to my life. I wonder if I can glimpse a pattern emerging from the seemingly random chaos of days and months, of events and dreams. I've been filled with desire and determination, trying with passion to forge the raw materials of my life into the shape of my vision; and then there's a neap tide, and I'm cast far up on the shore. I'm shoaled. I feel as empty and shocked as the survivor of a shipwreck. I lie staring at the sky, and eventually I begin to feel the wind on my face, to realize that I'm alive and that the sea has no regard for me, that I'm as insignificant as pebble or feather; it continues to gather and break, to advance and retreat, without pause, without passion. My own passion seems surprising, unnecessary. Into my shocked stillness, the world comes foam-edged, shining, like the easy purl of expiring waves.

I swing my legs over the edge of the bed and see the green fields framed by the small-paned window, their grasses running like water in the morning light. Jacob is rummaging in his toybox in the next room. I hear the crack of sheets on the clothesline and my day begins to shape itself in my head, structured by the clear necessities of summer. Thin the carrots, weed the green beans, wash clothes while it's sunny.

After sunset, I see the evening star above the mist-filled valley. I hear the winnowing of snipes, the hooting of the great horned owl. Mists shift, eddy, creep over the corn patch. I smell wild roses and see my horse sniffing over the fence at Jacob's cat, who crouches white, gargoyle-like, on a pea stake. I realize that I see the world's beauty more clearly once I've relinquished my desire to capture it.

Jacob turns five this summer, and there is one year left before he starts school. All during his childhood, I have exhausted myself by what I never saw as the gruelling and necessary apprenticeship of a craft. Now my effort seems insane; I've wasted my time. I have so little to show for all my striving. I replace my writing with intense involvements, new projects. I learn to throw pots. I make a line of blue porcelain ware. I become involved in community projects, volunteer work, peace activism. And just as Jacob's time with us is running out, I finally relax into being a mother.

I drive Jacob to kindergarten in town, three mornings a week, during the autumn of his fifth year. After his morning spent with other children, we go to the library and then have lunch together at a tea room on Main Street, where the tables are built around fake trees and Jacob delights in pointing out the stuffed owls in their branches. He's a good companion. We talk to each other

215

about the things we'll continue to discuss for the rest of our lives: animals, history, books, dreams, his friends, ourselves. He makes me grapple with questions that extend me, make me examine my preconceptions, expand my boundaries. He is curious about other people. We sit in the window booth of the restaurant; he's eating a grilled cheese sandwich and chips and we're trying to think of reasons why a good friend of his might be unhappy, and why his unhappiness might make him angry and want to hit people. We drive home, and I turn off the car's engine and sit in the sudden quiet with my door open, gazing at the clouds, which are shining like a shoal of minnows; I tell him that the clouds make me happy. He runs into the house and says to Peter, confidentially, "Mummy's getting herself in order by sitting in the car and looking at the sky." He, too, is expanded by our friendship.

As the weather turns cold in October, I put a fire in the stove when we get home from kindergarten. I put music on the stereo; I bake bread and oatmeal cookies; I cook wrinkled apples for sauce, roll out pie dough on the scarred wooden table, flop it into Pyrex pans and flute the edges. I make a squirrel costume for Jacob, and he and Peter, one evening, spread newspapers on the floor and carve pumpkins. I watch them, father and son intensely curled over their pumpkins, and see how they are both artists; neither one has the slightest hesitation, they both plunge their knives into the juicy flesh and turn the bland orange globes into leering monsters, upside-down faces, one-toothed simpletons. We take long family walks, and I fall behind so I can watch Peter and Jacob engaging in the more spirited dialogue that differs from that of mother and son; already, Jacob disputes whatever Peter says, and Peter is anxious to prove his points. They aren't yet intense. Peter is still indulgent and Jacob isn't adamant. When it snows, we cross-country ski through the woods, over the fields. He skis ahead across the open fields, small and vividly coloured in the white world.

Shadow Child

Jacob is still completely comfortable with aloneness; I suspect it is not a concept he would yet understand, never having known its opposite. He makes private places and does not always invite me or Peter to visit. We might be in the same room, but still inhabit separate worlds; on a snowy winter day, he drags the wicker chair with its red corduroy cushions close to the glass door. Inches away, there's nothing but whirling whiteness, snow-flakes tracing wind currents as they will later reveal twigs. He makes a cave with an old green sleeping bag whose feathers prick out around a duct-tape repair; he puts on a pair of glacier goggles left over from our hike in Switzerland, and a Tibetan wool cap with earflaps. He's perusing *Tintin au Tibet*. I sit with my feet on the edge of the woodstove, whose heat begins to make my wool socks feel thin, and write a letter. The kettle wheezes. The house, our home, is like a warm nest, and I feel myself quieting inside it, like a bird accepting the brief time she must tend the smooth eggs beneath her body, patiently bending her neck to preen the only feathers she can reach.

Then it's the summer Jacob turns six. My brother's family comes; Jacob plays with his cousins. Under the high sky, the three chil-dren walk to the pond, pick raspberries, put peapods on their fingers for claws. They play in the treehouse. They take naps curled in the sunny, wood-smelling upstairs rooms, the breeze making the curtains tap. They don't need me, except when they want food, or have lost something, or want me to catch and bri-dle the pony. I see the children the same way I glimpse birds shearing across the sky; their voices edge the wind, their hair glints in the sun, they're part of wind and sky and wind-raked grasses as easily and mysteriously as the birds, and as contained in their own world.

Jacob's slipping ahead, riding on, outgrowing us. He lashes out at us at suppertime, and says he hates every bit of food on his plate. He is beside himself with rage if he finds me sorting through what I perceive as chaos in his room. He stubbornly refuses to do what he's told. One day, he decides to rearrange his room. I help him shove his bed against the north wall and his bookshelf against the east wall, and we take all the toys off the shelves and replace them with the clean, vertical spines of books. He seems serene and remote that night, tucked into bed, and has me shut the door so that his kitten, now a large cat, will stay there with him, in this place that he's reshaped. He wants to be in places that are his own. In June, Peter builds a treehouse in one of the maples at the edge of the lawn. Its boards are yellow, splintery, smell of sap; Peter hangs flags, makes a railing and a ladder, makes a pulley for a basket that Jacob lowers for an odd collection of gear he gathers on the moss at the base of the tree: French coins, dice, seashells, comic books, a knife sheath, a defunct pocket watch. Peter and I sit in canvas chairs on the concrete slab outside the back door, the white phlox head-high and alive with bees, lunch plates in our laps; and we call across the sea of lawn to our son, who seems as self-contained in his tree, as perfectly placed, as a captain, wide-legged, hands at nine and one on the great wheel of his ship.

He spends hours in his hidden places. When I'm working in the garden, I'm dimly aware of his activity at the corners of my concentration. I straighten from chopping the hoe into the soil, hear Jacob's voice calling from the corn patch. I can't see him. His voice comes sing-song from the dry stalks whose parchment leaves scratch against one another, making a dry rasping that accompanies the clicking and chirring of insects. I drop to my hands and knees and crawl into the secret place he's made with pillows and blankets, with crackers and Tintin books, walled by the swaying, bamboo-like stalks, his roof the blue sky glimpsed through pollen-dusty tassels. I lie next to him with my head on

Shadow Child

his pillow. The grey barn, slicing the sky, seems very far away, as does my hoe, lying between the chard and the cabbages, and the studio, where we can hear the hum of Peter's wheel. While Jacob chatters to me, I'm remembering my own childhood nests: a hay-bale fort where I left library books out in the rain; or the corner of the house, behind the lilac bush, where there were blunted shards of Willowware crockery; or my treehouse over the stone wall, where the sun-warmed boards dipped and rose when the wind blew. My fists uncurl. I close my eyes and see the shadows of cornstalks on the insides of my eyelids. I'm glad I came to visit, although I know I am not inside his world really. This is the place of his childhood, whose magic is singular, is something I can see and imagine, but can't experience.

At the end of the summer, I begin to feel like a pasture, a nesting ground, an island, a place that provides sustenance and nourishment. I realize that my child will take what he needs from me, and then roam away. He's like a young elk, drifting south for the winter, leaving his summer meadows. What I have yet to learn is that his needs will return over the years, and then so will he. They will be different, more complex, less easily satisfied. But then so will I have changed, grown, deepened; my soil fed with the decayed grasses of years, my rock honed and crevassed by storm and sun. When he is five years old, almost six, he's wandering at the edges of his feeding grounds; he's sniffing the wind. He's rested and restless, nourished and hungry. He doesn't think about what he's leaving behind. And all I can think of, as I'm gathering the materials for my son's next voyage—shopping for school clothes, consulting my list of supplies sent by the school board— is how I'll bake cookies in the afternoons, or put potatoes in the woodstove, or start a soup at noon so that when he kicks through the leaves and the low, hazy autumn light at the end of the day, he'll return to the place he started from and find that it remained in his absence. I don't know yet what I'm going to do on the day when I leave Jacob at the end of the driveway, waving as the schoolbus goes down the valley. I don't know what the house is going to feel like when I go back into it and he's not lying on his stomach on the kitchen floor, absorbed in the world that emerges from the soft lead of his pencil. I don't know yet if my own potential is harbouring any seeds in its dark loam.

But he's left something with me, for me. His child-spirit sways in the bathwater, rises on the smell of lilacs, lies across the floorboards in dusty sunlight. It lives in the strength of my hands, the complex gaze of my eyes, the lift of my smile. It's the shape I sought at my desk, in early mornings of my child's childhood, and could not find there.

Shadow Child

Chapter Fourteen

School comes slicing like a knife through our days. It cuts our lives into pieces, selecting segments that we're allowed to have or not to have, chooses their size and quality.

The elementary school is brand new; it's at the mouth of a valley, flanked by cornfields; every window frames a view of blue hills whose lower slopes are neatly skirted with fields. In fall, there are green pastures speckled with black-and-white cows and golden fields of ripe oats. I stand in the Grade One room on visitors' day, imagining my son's life here. The floor is carpeted, and there's a red geranium blooming on the bookcase. The teacher is young and smiley, and the walls are bordered with pieces of brightly coloured construction paper, hung high up near the ceiling, with a French phonic written on each one.

I watch as the teacher takes Jacob around the room. She's showing him coat hooks, the shelf where he'll keep his lunchbox, bookshelves, a bin of crayons and coloured pencils. He's entranced by everything new, as always. I watch him trotting eagerly behind his new teacher.

We're excited to see him becoming Canadian, learning to sing "O Canada" beneath a faded colour photograph of Queen Elizabeth. We want him to speak both official languages, French and English, and have enrolled him in a program where he'll be taught entirely in French. We want him to be a cub scout; to participate in Christmas pageants, Easter teas, book fairs; to know this world as we never will, no matter how long we live here. We want to be part of the history of our community, to discuss with neighbours our children's slice of the school's evolution: homework and teachers, proms, plays, fund-raisers, trips. We want to give our son a sense of belonging. We have no idea that we are using him to dispel our own feelings of estrangement, no idea that our hopes for his integration are entangled with our own needs.

Sometimes, once school has started, either Peter or I saunter down the driveway with Jacob to wait for the schoolbus. Usually, though, we're running late and there's an irritated scramble of unfinished cereal, lost mittens, schoolbooks left upstairs, snowsuit-zipping, backpack-finding. Once Jacob finally gets out the door, Peter and I make megaphones with our hands and encourage him to hurry; then I go to the west window to watch his progress down the long driveway. I see his black-and-yellow wool hat, his red backpack, his blond hair; he trots steadily, absorbed in his passage and unaware of my watching; he crosses the bridge and runs fast down the final stretch of the gravel lane as the bus waits for him, exhaust wisping from its tailpipe like white rags. I watch him lean sideways to take the big step, and I see the driver bend forward with his hand on the door lever, and then the doors fold shut. Jacob becomes part of the bus, part of the world that's hidden behind its steamy windows. He's swept away like a leaf on wind, carried without recall down the valley and into the long day.

Shadow Child

As I clean the kitchen in the strengthening sun, I feel his absence. He won't be home until the sun is lowering on the other side of the sky, the shadows are stretching in the opposite direction and the day is beginning to expire, glowing from within like coals. Someone else spends the day attending to his needs, answering or ignoring his surprising questions, deciding what he should learn, in what sequence and with what emphasis; someone else does or does not hold him when his heart aches. I will not be there to admonish or comfort him if he fights or is ignored or is cruel in the playground; he lives the largest part of his life with other people, in another rhythm, and I comfort myself with thinking that its astringent demands are as necessary and nourishing as the home pool whose waters spawned him. I think, too, that our bond is unbreakable, our closeness something that I need never question, like the rising of the sun.

His absence is like an accusation or a question that I have to answer every day, until it becomes part of me, like all the other barbs that are snagged on the walls of my soul. He never talks about school when he comes home. Perhaps he senses, and resents, the way my questions are posed to confirm my own vision of his life. "Did you have fun? Did you learn new words in French? Do you have friends?" Peter is more anxious about what he's learning. He wants him to do well, and wants to know if he's learning his math, if he can read in French. He worries, and his worry sounds to me like pressure. "Are you doing addition and subtraction? Do you have any homework?" I want him to be happy so I can be free. I take the long day, when I have no idea what he's doing at any moment, and imagine it as a box where I store him: in the box is a sunny room, with a red geranium, a kind teacher and nice children.

I have another imaginary box, a place where I put moments I don't have time to appreciate right away. I'm saving them up, deluding myself into thinking that they are retrievable.

Jacob is sitting in the tub one Saturday morning when I hear him say softly, "Her six-year-old son sat in the tub, staring intently." Just then, the phone rings and I vault down the stairs to answer it. I'm organizing a speaking tour for a veteran of the Second World War who has started a disarmament group; the living-room floor is covered with piles of paper I'm stapling together for a peace group meeting. Peter is out in the woodshop gathering tools to take to a friend's place, where we're going after lunch to help build a giant cruise missile for a protest march. I'm writing press releases; I'm waiting for a call-back from the president of the Kiwanis Club.

Upstairs, my child moves his hands through the warm, soapy water, musingly writing himself a role in the drama. I hurry through my phone conversation with the intention of catching the rest of Jacob's story, yet I'm aware I'm never going to know why he was staring intently, or what came next, because he will be doing something else when I finally get back upstairs. One thing displaces another without noticeable transition, the way seasons pursue one another, fluidly. His childhood and his boyhood are destined to pass with me vowing to watch more closely, to pay better attention, to distil time—just as we say, every year, that *this* summer we will go to the beach, or canoe the Saint John River, or hike to the coast, or go whale-watching off Grand Manan, and we seldom do.

Our lives are moving in directions we did not anticipate. Time becomes increasingly compressed, like a closet with too many clothes in it. We try to maintain all our original goals while setting new ones; we accept the opportunities that spread like fissures from every step we take. I am so busy that I write down every single thing I have to do in a week; I find a time-slot in which to

Shadow Child

make a cake for Saturday's party, schedule a meeting with Jacob's teacher to coincide with my trip to pick up an irrigation system that's been donated for a Tools for Peace Nicaraguan project, decide on a time to exercise my new horse, write down which days I'm working at our store in town and when I'm making my own pots or packing orders or getting ready for the Toronto show. Someone tells me I should be able to take three deep breaths, one after the other; I try it, but can't. I'm flying, racing, always behind or beside myself, engaged. I feel as if I'm endlessly arranging one thing, counting on it to stay as I put it, moving on to something else that needs organizing, finding the first thing in a shambles, racing back to fix it.

The more I do, the more valuable I feel. Yet I'm in endless competition with myself. Nothing I do is enough; everything could have been done better. I make myself think that this driven, anxious, intense, worried, motivated person is who I am; I believe I'm happy to be this person. Parts of my self are hidden, as if I scraped them into garbage bags along with my stories and the contents of my desk. I keep myself too busy to reach into my own darkness and sort through whatever's there. Peter, too, is busy. We feel that busyness is a kind of vindication or justification. It proves our worth. It furthers our goals. Gradually, it becomes a way of life.

I keep having dreams about people searching for meaning in their lives. My dreams tell me that I'm missing the heart of life, but I don't listen to them. I sense that there is something I should do when I get a chance, but I don't know what it is. It's a feeling that spurs my busyness, makes me hurry even faster, as if in my haste I'll finally arrive somewhere and then I can stop, or find out what it is I'm running to catch.

We have to leave Jacob for three weeks every November, when Peter and I take his pottery to a Christmas craft show in Toronto.

Sometimes I go for the whole show; sometimes I fly back after the first half. Every year we make different arrangements for Jacob: usually someone comes and stays at our house; sometimes he stays partly with neighbours, partly at home. But always, we leave him and go to a place he's never seen. We are the ones who go away, and he is the one who stays.

He accepts this situation as part of his life, trustingly. As a small child, he rolled forward within time, relaxing into events like a fish in a wave; he'd cling to us briefly when he went away to visit his grandparents, and then he'd release us, chattering interestedly to whoever buckled him into his car seat for the long drive south, patiently settling his thumb in his mouth and his head against the padded seat, teddy bear clutched to his chest. He always made it easy for me to put him inside whatever box, within my own mind, let me believe in his happiness.

As he gets older, is eight and nine, he begins to lose his trust. Memory darkens his eyes, obscures their clarity. Doubt makes him tense. He asks why he can't go to Toronto with us. He worries about himself. He begins to wonder how we can leave him, and why.

One year, we decide that Peter will drive to Toronto with a friend, pulling the heavy trailer behind the truck, and I will fly there the next day. The weatherman is calling for sleet, snow, winds. We are all—me, Jacob, Peter—encased in our separate dreams and fears, and too rushed to share them with each other. Jacob wakes up with a memory of Peter kissing him goodbye; when he comes down for breakfast, there's only a black place on the snow from the truck's exhaust pipe and tire treads on the snow-packed driveway.

That night, my suitcase is packed and standing in the hall; the house is orderly and clean, all my lists and projects put away. The furnace rumbles steadily, like a ship's engine. I tiptoe into Jacob's room. The hall light slants across the floorboards. The little yellow room is like a cave, a burrow, a den; its books and clothes and posters and toys mounded like soil, sticks and leaves, a frail bulwark against intrusion, predators, unspecific danger. He's in the heart of his burrow, deeply sleeping, and in his hand is a small cloth mouse. He's wrapped it in a handkerchief. It's safe in his sturdy hand, pressed against his flannel pyjama shirt. He's taken special care of his little mouse tonight. He's made sure it's warm. Made sure it's safe. He comforts it so it won't be afraid or alone.

I stand in his bedroom, gazing down at him. I see how he's tenderly wrapped what he loves in a soft cloth, how he holds it close to his heart. I realize that this solicitous care of a fragile thing is what I've been meaning to do but have been postponing. I suddenly understand what it is that my dreams are trying to tell me.

The year Jacob is nine and in Grade Four, he begins to move so slowly that Peter and I are frequently driven to despairing rage. It is as though his limbs are weighted, his mind disassembled, so he can't find his underwear in the morning or his socks, and he frequently goes down the driveway so slowly that he misses the bus. Sometimes, at the end of the day, he's stranded at school because he couldn't find his lunchbox or his backpack, and so missed the bus home. He's increasingly argumentative. Anger makes him distant, edgy. He's like a part of a complex engine that's slipped out of sequence and doesn't work any more, even though it's surrounded by other pieces that do.

We begin to notice how irritated he is when we question him about school; he's finally succeeded in forgetting his day by the time he gets home and he refuses even to visualize it. He seems at loose ends; he draws less, broods, is tired. He can't resume his easy, flickering swim through the light-shafted waters of life. Finally, he follows the only feeling that's clear to him; he stops. He refuses to participate. Since his teacher values speed, and grades tests according to how many words can be correctly spelled or how many sums calculated in one minute, he writes nothing on his paper. He won't do his homework, refuses to do a "creative" assignment about home, and will not keep a journal of his life or bring in drawings, as all the other kids do, of parents, brothers, sisters and pets.

One day, he and I have a terrible fight about neatness. I am frustrated by what seems to me his pathological disinclination to impose order on any aspect of his life: outdoor clothing, lunchbox, school notebooks, toys, books. I ask him to do things so many times that I feel a blackness before my eyes as I gather the will to repeat my request.

"Please put your stuff where it belongs."

"I did."

"Yeah, well, your coat's on the floor, your boots are still on your feet and tracking mud, and your bookbag is . . . "

He's not as adept at arguing as he will be when he's fifteen. The rage that he's been containing for weeks roars down the gully of his throat. I'm the boulder in the river and his waters bury me in white froth. He hurls his backpack onto the floor, kicks his boots off his feet and across the room, runs upstairs. Peter, at this minute, comes in from the pottery. I'm sitting at the table massaging my scalp; he pauses, kicks off his own boots and goes upstairs, following the trail of pain that coils through the house like cold air.

Jacob tells him, sobbing, that he spends all day long doing the same things over and over again, that he spends hours sitting at a desk when he could be at home doing interesting things. He says he hates to wake up in the morning because he has to leave his dreams; he has no time any more to play. He says he's losing his imagination. I come quietly up the stairs and lean in his doorway.

With his anger, he's letting me and Peter know that he wants parents who remember, and see, the child who came winging like a swallow into our world; parents who do more than slant into him, bright and hard as knives, pricking him with reminders, badgering him with recommendations, praising him for things he himself doesn't care about.

He arrests us, as he will over and over again; our job as parents never ends. He wants us to open our eyes and see what is in front of them. He wants us to stop pushing him into a mould that he will never fit. He refuses to lose himself.

We decide to take him out of school. For the rest of Grade Four, all of Grade Five and most of Grade Six, I set aside every morning to teach him. I learn to make a plan and then abandon it, or allow it to be pulled and stretched like taffy. We sit at the kitchen table and read *The Children's History of Civilization*, looking at pictures of bronze swords, cuneiform writing, knives made from hippopotamus tusks; in the garden, we find red insect larvae in the manure pile and sit cross-legged on the path looking them up in our Audubon field guide to insects. Later, I read out loud Kafka's story "The Metamorphosis" and try to explain the concept of metaphor, and then we crouch over the table, scratching with pencils, writing haiku that we read to one another. On two afternoons, I drive him to town to be tutored in French; every Tuesday morning, he visits our neighbour for geology lessons, learning how to read a compass, skin a mink.

Our lives change. We have time to watch the sun rise, to see the kindling of morning light in snow crystals; my son can help me knock ice from the water spigot in the barn; he can see the horse's whiskers speared with white frost, like Japanese dragons, and see the prisms that spark in the snow that explodes beneath their hoofs when they gallop and buck in the morning air, snaking their necks as if shedding the night. We can feel the passage of the sun, the shifting of shadows from east to west, the ripening of the day. Jacob begins to grow like wild grass, fluidly, shaped by weather, by the rippling continuity of light and darkness, rain and wind. He no longer leaves parts of himself behind when he steps onto the bus, no longer builds walls of self-deprecation or anger around himself that he sheds painfully every night, and then reluctantly puts back on again the next morning. There's no alarm clock any more; there are no weekends, no days off, no vacations. We're separated from the community of school, but we've begun to reshape and strengthen our own community. And I realize that it was as much for myself that I wanted my child in school as it was for him, that he might be someone who never fits easily into any place but the one inside himself.

We begin, in country-fashion, to mark time not by dates, but by events. One year we close our store in town, and I walk through its emptiness, remembering the excitement with which we opened it. Bob and Kathy and their four children move and sell the log cabin. I have my ear operations and my hearing is restored. The winter of Jacob's ninth year, the snow reaches the roof of the studio and we can no longer dig out the door. The next summer, our pony gets so enormously fat we have to exile her to the riding ring, and Jacob sleeps in the long-stemmed timothy grass under the stars to keep her company. There's the Christmas that Jacob and I surprise Peter by cutting a tree that is eight feet tall; we haul it down from the woods, lashed to the aluminum toboggan with baling twine, and collapse in the snow by the house, laughing, exhausted, exhilarated. Horses come and go; chickens die and are buried in the manure pile; a puppy arrives like a newborn child. Neighbours die from illness, old age, hunting accidents. One night everyone in the valley spends hours driving the back roads calling for a teenage girl who has run away, and she's found at daybreak walking in the woods; another day, our neighbour's children spend the afternoon in our house with Jacob while Peter and I are at their house, helping arbitrate their parents' separation. One friend's barn burns, another friend's house burns; there are barn bees, foundation-pouring bees, collections, pot-luck suppers. One night we drive home to find the covered bridge buckled, its roof broken like a snapped branch, its severed timbers plunged in the icy river, a pulp truck in its midst and logs strewn like spilled stick-matches. There are birthday parties when the wild blueberries are ripe and frogs hang, golden-eyed, in sharp-edged reeds at the pond's bank; bonfires in winter darkness; skating on black ice and tobogganing down the orchard hill on inner tubes. Jacob and his friends climb trees, make forts, throw hens out of barn windows to see if they can fly; and our farrier stands in the hazy sunlight after shoeing the horses, his leather apron wide as a table, and sings to Jacob in Gaelic, wide-eyed, red lips pursed over his beard, his legs straddling the hay-strewn concrete.

In these swift years of Jacob's childhood, when he learns about life while living it, unprogrammed and at his own pace, I abandon my lists, my schedules, my expectations. I'm embraced, cherished and transformed by mystery, barely realizing it, but as I longed to be, once, when I knelt in my garden and dreamt of becoming pregnant.

For a few years, when Jacob is nine and ten and eleven, our life as a family is restful, steady, calm at its centre. Peter and I begin to understand who Jacob is, not who we think he is going to be; we begin to see what he can do, rather than what he can't. He starts to see us as friends as well as parents. When we are all three engrossed in Frodo and Sam's final parched voyage across the Plains of Gorgoroth, or are listening to Sherlock Holmes stories on tape; when we travel to Cape Breton and see silver surf threading wild coasts, or find lady's slippers on trails, or see villages where boats and fish sheds are doubled at dawn in dead-calm harbours; when he works in the woodshop with Peter, making a tiny airplane with a metal propeller, or participates in a discussion about South Africa at a dinner party, or listens to artists discussing paintings, sculptures, movies, etchings, he is, as we are, a thread in a tapestry, a flower in a field. He bends or is stretched, just as we are. Time, no longer measured by the school year, stretches as luxuriously as a cat. Jacob's anger evaporates, and in equal proportion, so too does my unacknowledged guilt. I know, instinctively, that I'm answering his call, fulfilling his needs. He returns to himself, and becomes whole and strong, once he's sure that he's loved.

I learn that a child's soul is as fragile as a wild bird's egg.

I have only one child. It never occurs to me, during these years, that I'm the mother of two sons. Our lost baby is as insubstantial as a shadow, casting a vague, disturbing chill across the sunny places of my heart. I have buried everything about him, as if the real name he would have borne, and the year, the month and the day of the month he died and was born, are memories that bear nothing but raw grief, and so have no function beyond pain. I dread February thirteenth so much that after many years, the date passes without my remembering; and then a deep fissure sheers through my soul, jagged, unseen. It will spawn others, the way a glaze that does not adhere to clay makes tiny tinkling cracks, and then shivers and crazes.

The fissure allows a recurrent dream to rise from the dark places of my soul. I dream that I am weeping, weeping as I have never wept in waking life. I become the shape and texture and sound of grief; Peter is awakened by my strange strangled cries, which are the expiring remainders of dream-screams, breaking like bubbles at the surface. I wake up with my cheeks wet with tears. I am obsessed with the feeling that someone is missing. I stare at the white plaster ceiling, trying to figure out who it is. I make a list of the people in my life and mentally tick off their whereabouts. Jacob is safely sleeping in the next room; Peter lies next to me. I know where my parents are, my brother, all my extended family, my friends. I can't find anyone missing, and yet my heart is rimmed with weight, like a banner with lead sewn into its hem. I never realize that it's our lost son, Jacob's unacknowledged brother, who is alone and lost.

One afternoon, I trudge out to the orchard hill with Jacob in the cold stillness of sunset. I am angry. I've been irritable all day. Grievances surface like dead fish, bloated from long immersion. They wallow inside me, stinking. I feel like a servant, an adjunct. I feel thwarted, denied. I feel rejected and without worth. Home school did not go well today. Jacob, too, was irritable, seemed disengaged, as if part of him was beginning to question his situation. Later, I crouched mutely over my desk in the pottery studio and paid bills; then I went into the house and scrubbed potatoes. Now Jacob wants me to toboggan with him. I don't want to go, but feel I should and so crossly yank on my felt-lined boots, shrug into my parka. Something he says breaks my brittle control as we're stumping knee-deep through the snow, and I snap at him. He yells back at me instantly, welcoming the chance to acknowledge my mood and lance it, but I gather all my feelings together before I roar back with such viciousness that for the first time in his life, Jacob runs from me in fear.

We eat supper in mute misery. I go out that night to a meeting of my peace group, and as I'm driving home, I hear a program on the radio about a mother whose daughter died. I suddenly realize that it is February thirteenth.

The car's headlights bore the darkness, exposing two narrow ribbons of asphalt where the road is not snow-packed. I feel the weight of my unhappiness lighten as it suddenly defines itself. *I knew.* I am amazed, the same way I was filled with wonder when I realized, after our baby died, that Peter and I were parents. My wonder comes from somewhere outside myself. It's not something I created or desired or sought. I realize that all day long I knew it was the day our first son was born; it was a thought seeking form, a feeling trying to come unknotted. Hot tears surge into my eyes, and I turn off the radio; the snow-streaked road blurs beyond the salt tears that I lick from the corners of my mouth. I feel stripped, strangely relieved of the loneliness of my rage and its cumbersome shape that didn't fit, was difficult to bear. I knew. I'm grazed with the edge of a new thought, so unfamiliar that it's as barely formed as was my grief all day: the baby is not inside me, is not in my mind, was never only a dream. His spirit exists, formless but nascent, its emergence as inevitable as change.

I feel empty when I get home, and simple. I walk into the house to find Peter and Jacob asleep on the living-room floor with the cats sprawled next to them. I curl on the floor next to Jacob and put my arm around him.

"I'm sorry I yelled at you," I whisper.

He says, "That's okay, Mum," and his forgiveness is entirely without reluctance, coming as strongly and easily as a mechanism unworn by time or use.

The next month, Jacob's friend Gregory comes for a Saturday. He and Jacob sit in the kitchen when he arrives, and Greg describes an epic playground snowball war, naming boys Jacob doesn't know, describing feats of daring, bloody noses, visits to the principal's office. Greg's face is alive with remembered excitement. I watch Jacob's face. Fear and desire chase one another, like shadow and sun recasting the mood of a field.

I ask him, the following Monday morning, if he wants to go back to school, and he admits that he misses other kids; he's become aware of his isolation, the fact that he can relate better to adults than to people his own age. He picks at the spiral of his notebook. I watch him with my chin in my hands. I'm amazed at the way he's seen all sides of his choice; he's reluctant to give up

Shadow Child

his freedom, but he knows that he's free now to face the things he needs. And he sees clearly what he needs, just as he knew, but couldn't articulate, what he needed three years ago, when he wanted to reknit himself, when he needed to know he was loved. He's secured his place in our hearts and he knows it; the bond between parents and child is forged. Now other parts of himself need honing, forging. It's not history or French or math that he wants; he needs to be part of a group, to see himself reflected in other faces.

That afternoon, I pore through my home-school books. I find plenty of support for the parents who decide to withdraw their child from school, but nothing about the child who decides to return. Then I realize it's me who needs support, not him. Over the last few years, I've given up making pots, I've resigned from the peace group, I've stopped riding my horse. I've come close to the shape of my son's soul. It's as strong as the wind, as fierce as fire. It's wild, savage and doesn't belong to me, but is part of everything knowable: rain on cobblestones, the sound of singing, a woman's caress, neon in puddles and loneliness. Its shape makes me remember my own soul and how soft it is, how malleable, how like sand or wind or fire it, too, will always be. I know that I am lonely for myself. As Jacob and I sat at the kitchen table bent over our poems, my feet on the chair's rung and my mind playing with words like water-slicked pebbles, I caught the edge of myself between two fingers. I feel this tenuous hold and know how slight it is. I'm afraid that when Jacob goes, I'll slide back into days that were like a barrel, filled and rattling with the empty cans of recurrent tasks.

I've been in a child's world with Jacob, a place of marvels where words lead to music, archeology illuminates history, myth reveals fact. Now we've come to a fork in the road, and he's going on alone. I have to continue without him, hoping that I will remember the spirit of adventure, hoping that I won't forget how to allow, adapt, watch, see. Lately, I've begun to dream of white spaces—white walls, white ceilings, white curtains—of plaster houses whitewashed and dappled by limpid sea light; of emptiness filled with sweet wind. Like him, I'm ready to start something new. Inside myself I'm poised, like a butterfly with raised wings. I want, like him, to believe in myself enough to be brave, to do what I believe possible.

A week later, he goes off on the bus. His excitement is restrained; he's slightly stern, doesn't want to acknowledge our anxious and quivering expectation as we wave him out the door. There's a new set to his shoulders, a new way he holds his mouth. He's discovered the slant of his eyebrows; he slings his bookbag over one shoulder, equivocally.

Peter and I hug each other once he's gone. Peter goes out the back door, on his way to the studio, and I turn back to the empty kitchen. I catch my breath in amazement and stand stock still, one hand at my throat. Last September, Jacob brought in a green chrysalis dusted with gold dots. He held it in the palm of his hand reverently, and then carefully put it in a Mason jar on a bed of grass and leaves. It has become part of the changeless pattern of the shelves, like the dusty dried scarlet runner beans in a porcelain bowl, or the warbly shelled, triple-yolked egg that we blew, years ago, and perched in an egg cup, or the dead dragonfly in a sherry glass. This morning, of all mornings, the chrysalis hatched. Inside the glass jar, a fully formed butterfly spreads its wings. The jar is entirely filled with the butterfly. It's a monarch; its tissuey orange wings are black-veined, bordered with black velvet that glistens with silvery, opalescent dots. Its antennae stir, bowed against the glass, and its wings quiver as they rise and fall and rise again, stretching, constrained, bound by the transparent walls of its prison.

Shadow Child

My first thought is anguished. Jacob is the butterfly, and although he's stretching his wings, he's going to be trapped again within the walls of school. Then I cross the kitchen floor and carefully pick up the jar. I look closely at the butterfly. It can only flex its wings a tiny bit before they are bent by the glass. It continues to flex them. They tremble, beating upwards, seeking their function, seeking release.

Then I imagine Jacob running down the driveway with his bookbag bouncing on one shoulder; how the step up into the schoolbus is an easy bound for him now; how his friends will circle him, delighted, clapping him on the back, drawing him back into their world.

I stare at the butterfly. It's meant to be trembling like flickering light, probing the heart of tiger lilies. It's meant to be ascending the sky in papery bursts, improbably strong.

I wonder if this is me in the jar. Or if it's all the things I hold inside myself, trapped away from the light of day and the lilt of the wind.

Chapter Fifteen

Jacob finishes Grade Six. Another summer of crickets and swallows, swimming and hay-making reels past; then ends the same way it arrived, ebbing away as steadily as a tide. Hot-weather clothes and games are shoaled, like the Fundy fishing boats that lie keeled and lifeless on mud flats. In the boot hall, the croquet set lies on its side, untouched since the last visitors. Under the fly-specked window, there's a cardboard box whose arrangements of odds and ends seems permanent, like a forgotten vase of flowers: the Frisbee with its dog-chewed rim, a baseball glove, flip-flops with pancake-thin heels, grass-stained sneakers. Out at the bottom of the lawn, long-handled forks spear the tall grass next to the barbecue pit, and the wooden chair sits under the hawthorne bush; a beer glass, beneath it, shelters beetles and turns algae-green. In the flower garden, the delphiniums are broken-necked and the orange lilies have stiffened into hollow spears sprouting leathery seed chalices that rattle. The faded canvas chairs are stacked on the porch, ready for unfolding, but there's a new wind. It's insistent; it smells of the dry leaves it has loosened, of pumpkin skins, of frosted cabbage. The soft, early apples thud from their branches and nest in the rain-swept grass where the deer step, delicately, after dark.

The house feels larger, the summer visitors—cousins, grandparents, friends—like shore birds who have flown away. Its rooms are vacant, as abandoned as a winter beach. When I left this afternoon to go out with my camera, I could hear Jacob making thumping sounds in his room. He was getting ready for school, which starts tomorrow. There were no other sounds save the pulse of crickets in the straw-dry grasses, which rustled like furtive skirts just beyond the open windows. I felt the lovely freedom of autumn, its decadent peace, its glide towards stillness.

I walk down the valley road with my camera bag slung over one shoulder, tripod balanced on the other. It's late afternoon, and when I pass the church, its long shadow gathers the gravestones. On the hills that rise on either side of me, trees break into colour like sudden bonfires. Midway down the valley, a woman is standing on her back stoop in a print cotton dress. She's reeling in her laundry as her two granddaughters play at her feet, their hair shining. I can smell the clean sheets that she's looping over her arm. We wave and call to one another. Across the road, I notice the rich, musty light seeping into a small shed door; its layers of paint have faded unevenly, blue patched over red paled by green, one era glimpsed through another. I peer through my camera, sharpen the focus, catch my breath at what I see. I press the shutter, reel the film, change the focus, snap the shutter again.

I've discovered over the past year how photography is like music, with its ability to contain and preserve the essence of a moment; how a camera is a tool that I can use to keep life from slipping through my fingers. When I look through the lens of my camera, I'm like a child again, lying on my stomach gazing at bluets, or being assaulted by the texture of rotting pears, or sliding my fingers through the springy mane of my pony. I realize that I'm still in love with the world, and that I want to gather its beauty like a harvest, pick its fruits before they spoil. I begin to appreciate things I never noticed: how the fields are banded with colour, yellow buttercups rippling into beds of soft pink clover dusted with pools of daisies; how the woods are like a diamond, faceted and shimmering with small beauties, pools of white bunchberry flowers, ferns echoing one another's sweep, the skin-soft texture of dead wood. This beauty is outside me. I don't sit at my desk with closed eyes trying to find it, trying to make it; I walk in the wind, in the dawn, in the wet grass, and wait for the moment when my eyes begin to see, when I become part of what is outside me, when what is outside becomes part of me. I feel freed from myself. I open the plastic boxes of slides as if I'm un-wrapping a Christmas present or unbricking the kiln. Unlike my writing, I can share my pictures easily. They are not about me. I feel that I'm recording the cold, pure beauty of nature; they are my vision of divinity.

When I get home, I go upstairs to the large bedroom over the kitchen, which I've recently claimed as my study. It has two nar-row windows facing east, on either side of the chimney, and a skylight in one of its low, slanting ceilings. I've taken away the bed. There's nothing here now but a table made from a door, a chair, a filing cabinet and some shelves. I always wondered what a room of my own would look like. This room echoes with empti-ness, is lambent with afternoon light. Yet its air is sweetened by the past, like the dry-room in the shed where my grandfather stored his apples. The place where I'm going to put my light table, by the window, is shaped by my memory of the sultry summer nights when I was pregnant with Jacob and sat there, in my grandmother's rocking chair, watching the moon rise over the hill. It's thickened by another memory: me, sitting in the same chair, leaning forward graceful as a flower, rapt with absorption, running the back of my finger over the cheek of my tiny baby. And like an umbra, shadowing both these memories, my grandmother sits in the same chair, in another room and another time, with my mother in her arms. But I've taken away the rocking chair. There is nothing soft in the room, nothing rounded or forgiving; no bed, no quilt or pillow, no cushioned chair, no rug. The place is hard, spare and rectilinear. I love its clean, shadow-sharpened angles—the two slopes of the plaster ceiling, the little door under the eaves that leads to the attic, the narrow floorboards with their square-headed nails, each nail islanded on the golden spruce by brown paint that the sander could not remove. I want to move into this room slowly. I want everything that comes here to earn its place.

I put away my gear. I have begun to have dreams of losing my camera bag, losing my film, searching for them in anguished desperation. I stand clutching a roll of film in my hand. It's solid, real. I begin to write in my journal again; I haven't opened it for three years. I'm like a mole, tunnelling blindly but steadily as if there's something I'm seeking, some place that I know I need to find.

Jacob is still banging around in his room. He's busily tearing the cellophane covers from notebooks, digging through his clothes, perusing last year's folders, dumping the summer's gatherings from his bookbag onto the floor—shells, baling twine, half-eaten mouldy sandwiches. I stop in his door to talk to him, but he looks up only briefly, says, "Hi, Mum." His shoulders are hunched dismissively, but I'm not sure whether he wants me to go away or to stay; I'm not sure whether he wants comfort or freedom.

Tomorrow Jacob starts Grade Seven. He's wearing the new glasses he got yesterday, his first pair. They are black metal, round, with gold temples. He's stunned by the world. "It's sharp enough to eat," he keeps exclaiming. He seems much older to me, as if his improved eyesight makes him more aware, and thus wary and prescient.

He is hanging like an apple on a fragile stem. He's about to fall, spinning, into a new epoch—junior high. He knows it. All morning, we gathered apples together from the tree that Peter and I planted seventeen years ago on the west side of the house. Jacob straddled the tree, one foot on its trunk, the other on a branch, leaning dangerously forward to shake a branch while I dodged and ran, hearing the apples pattering down like muted hoofs; but I sense that he's not really here, as he used to be. He doesn't care what I do with these apples, isn't thinking about pies or applesauce, doesn't want to help me cut thin slices with star-shaped centres through which we pull string. His mind unfurls on the September wind and he sings snatches of Sting songs in his breaking voice, needing to be somewhere else, in some other world that's obscurely imagined and deeply felt.

Over the next five years, he becomes less and less a part of our lives. Peter and I feel farther from him, wonder what he's doing, who he is. His teenage years are stormy and tortured, just as we expected they would be, but nothing prepares us for the pain of rejection, even when we know it's necessary. And Jacob will never be able to understand how we see, behind his face, the soft-skinned infant he once was, the boy who lay in our sunny kitchen, gazing at his open palms, as if he could hold the light. He is our only child, and bears all our hopes, and fears, and expectations. These wrap around him in the guise of care and love, and he twists within them, trying to free himself from their complex web, trying to separate who he is from who we hope he will become. Peter and I are as bewildered as we are frustrated; Jacob's instinct seems to be to do the opposite of what we ask, to fail if we want him to succeed, to hide himself from us so that we'll have no purchase, no leverage, no insight. He wants his friends, possessions, dreams and decisions to be entirely his own, free from our attention or examination. We become a family at cross-purposes. Jacob's hackles rise when Peter makes suggestions; he's intensely defensive and takes them as accusations. No discussion avoids becoming an argument. I find myself trying to explain Peter to Jacob, or else defending Jacob from Peter. I feel caught between them, and frequently alienated from both.

Jacob is like the seabird he once said he wanted to be; he spends his adolescence strengthening himself for his long solo flight. He does this in ways that clarify only in retrospect, that make sense only when the sediment of outrage no longer roils in turbulent waters.

I can barely endure watching his procrastination. The book he has not yet started to read, whose report is due tomorrow, lies face down on the bed like an abandoned tent. I think about how I would have approached this alarming situation. I think of my fear of being chastised or receiving a bad grade. "Get it over with," I rage. "Just do it." Two hours later, he's lying on his floor making a complex chart for Dungeons and Dragons. He does things his own way, in his own time. He won't be hurried.

I wistfully imagine he'll continue to participate in my projects the way he did when he was younger. Once, we dug flower-beds together, talking excitedly about how our place was like a castle and these were its grounds. Now, on an autumn Sunday, I ask him all day long to mow the lawn and am met with exaggerated patience. "I am *going* to, Mum. I just have to finish this song," and as I'm spreading hay on the perennial beds, I hear the piano, out of tune after its summer spent next to the open porch door, and his raspy voice, singing portentously. Then, at four o'clock, I hear the lawn mower running until it dies suddenly, out of gas, and I find that he's blasted all the sticks under the maple trees into powder and mown, for reasons I can't fathom and am too exasperated to examine, the number five on the lawn.

Peter worries about him obsessively. He checks to make sure he's wearing gloves on cold days, whether he's got all his books, if he remembers what time his dentist appointment is and has the money to pay for it. As a consequence, our contrary son both ceases to remember these things himself and then insists on their lack of importance. He exercises his mind with dexterous feats of imaginative manoeuvring around what seem to us to be simple facts. Once, when he and I are driving home from town, we spend twenty minutes arguing about why he should wash his face before going to the dentist. Ten-foot angle irons are bungee-corded to the car roof; I'm driven to such fury by this argument that I stamp on the brake, and the heavy bars career forward and smash the car's hood.

We try to outmanoeuvre him, but never win. I hear Peter and Jacob doing dishes together. Jacob aggressively denounces a teacher, and Peter calmly sympathizes. "Uh huh. Hummm." I hear Jacob pause and then ask Peter caustically where he picked up this technique.

He's the product of a generation that flaunted Question Authority bumper stickers until its children became teenagers. We become accustomed to calls from school; he refuses to take his hat off, or is insulted by a teacher's tone of voice, or revolts against a teaching method. He takes stands against injustice and fiercely protects what he considers to be his personal rights. Like any teenager, he's consumed by his own needs and has difficulty seeing anyone else's. I'm sitting peacefully in the rocking chair by the kitchen window. It's spring, rain runnels down the windowpanes and pulls the greening lawn into sinuous curves; a pink geranium holds white light in the cup of each shell-shaped petal. The fire hisses and ticks in the woodstove and I'm writing in my journal, my pen unravelling a long thought, when Jacob bursts in. "Hi, Mum!" The quiet shatters like a dropped egg. He dumps his rain-drenched coat and bookbag on the floor, forgets to remove his muddy boots, takes out orange juice and leaves the carton on the kitchen table, goes straight to the piano and begins playing at top volume. I want to say, "Hi, I missed you. How was your day?" but instead I'm yelling over the piano's volume "Hey! Hey!" knowing that he doesn't want to hear about mud, boots, coat, bookbag, orange juice, the stain his glass leaves on the piano's varnish; doesn't want to tell me whether or not he has much homework; doesn't want to hear that he has to do the barn chores early because we're going out to supper. None of these things is important to him. He's like an emerging creature whose skin is irritated by everything that touches it. He sees the home we've made— flowers, paintings, books—but seems to receive no message from them, no impression. Our authority has no basis in fact; we're like people for whom the same words have suddenly acquired different meanings. He explodes at us for our arbitrary requirements: why shouldn't he watch whatever television show he wants, at whatever time? What's our problem with his playing the piano when we're in the same room trying to talk? Why should he keep his room picked up? It's *his* room. It's *his* life.

He emerges from phone conversations either elated or silent. Once, after he has his driver's licence, he comes storming into the house at two a.m. when we think he's spending the night at a friend's house. We call out sleepily and receive a curt response; the house shakes with the force of his door slamming. We will never know why. He drives to town and never looks back to see me waving at the kitchen window; he's as intent as a hunter, his hand rising from the stick shift to the tape deck.

Yet to all of this there's a familiar pattern, a vital tension, as vibrant as a calyx pressed by its unfolding flower or the moan of autumn wind roaming the fields, collecting leaves, seeds, sticks in its invisible sheet. I grope blindly through the storm of my son's adolescence, seeking footing, solace, a lifeline; but I'm as helpless and as overwhelmed as when I watched, with astonishment, my own pregnant body or felt my child's heels thud against the walls of my uterus. I'm like the leaves of autumn, tossed and rearranged by an irresistible power. I think I'm strong, I believe that I'm making choices, I try to be wise and rational. But I'm a mother, and the force of my child's growing sweeps me up in its rhythm, one I've been caught in ever since I lifted my baby's head in my hand, or hung six bright clowns over his crib, or pushed him on a swing, or ran alongside his first bicycle and then let go. My love for him tells me what to do, even though its messages are complex and paradoxical. He needs to hear the passion of my fury when he comes in at four a.m. and I have been lying awake, dread rising in my heart, fear thickening my blood. He needs to hear my despair when he makes poor choices, and my disproportionate joy when he succeeds. I'm his measure. Because I love him without reservation, he will use me to find out how cruel he can be and how deeply he can love.

My anger and despair at the ways in which I see that he's not getting on with his life are balanced by my relief when he does. He begins to solve his own problems in his own ways. Peter and I are relieved when he turns to the guidance counsellor for advice. We see him, obliquely and yet more clearly, through the eyes of people who view him not as he was or may become, but only as he is now, at this moment. He goes hunting with Bear, the blacksmith who sang Celtic songs to him long ago, and who now serves as his mentor and guide. They drive off into the autumn hills, wearing their long hair in ponytails. Hounds pant eagerly in the back seat of Bear's battered car, squeezed in with bagpipes, bodhran, axe, blankets, bow and arrows. Jacob returns, filthy, his voice deep and brusque, bearing a hunting horn and a brace of partridge wings. His group of friends forms and reforms; there are alliances and feuds, brokered romances, bitter rivalries, trusts, kindnesses and dogged loyalties. It changes patterns as subtly as watercolours until the last years of high school, when certain combinations meld and are fixed for life.

He gets larger, stronger, more remote. He begins the perilous quest of self-revelation, opening himself to other people for quick glimpses, like a boy who brings some precious discovery to the playground, trusting that no one will snatch it away. I watch him on his sixteenth birthday, drifting across the fields, going out to the pond with his best friend and two girls. They walk in couples, holding hands, their heads bent towards one another. It's a warm August evening; swallows cut over the ground mist that holds both the red haze of the setting sun and the dusty pollen of the uncut timothy. A harvest moon, heart-red, is rising over the eastern hills. The young couples are like grazing horses, moving purposefully yet seemingly without direction, lured by one mouthful of grass and then another. Jacob's eyes, when he says goodnight to us and thanks us, sweetly, for his birthday presents, are seeing a landscape that I will never see, that is not mine, that I cannot expect to share. His hand, brushing the bannister as he goes upstairs, is tender against the buttery wood, as it will be on the face of his lover, the cheeks of his children; and I realize how children never see their parents' love as the gift that it is, but absorb it like air, and understand only once they've left home what it is that they've been given.

One day he returns from school in an unusual state of excitement, one that's tinged with awe. He describes a red horse that he drew in charcoal, says he spent the entire lunch hour working on it. As he talks, I realize that he's bypassed a strata of communication that includes grievances, defenses, false assumptions; he pays no attention to his words or how he says them. He's speaking from the power of the red horse, which came from nowhere, unexpectedly. He seems slightly askew, as if he's seen something new about himself. But it's not here, it's not with him any more; it's in the smell of charcoal, the texture of paper, the sure black-and-red strokes that came from his hand and became a horse's neck, rushing like wildfire from darkness.

In the high school play, *Oliver*, he acts the part of Fagin. He channels his energy into this project as he does not when it comes to homework or chores or anything else that seems to him, at the time, irrelevant. He creates a memorable Fagin whose dark obsessions are made fascinating by hints of loneliness.

I watch as my son, on opening night, reveals himself behind the self-obsessed character he plays, and I remember how, when I held Jacob in my arms on the first night of his life, I felt the presence of a wise spirit. I wonder if we are all born with souls that are whole and complete, like songs; if the song of ourselves becomes lost and we spend our lives trying to recover it, remembering fragments, hearing phrases unexpectedly. I watch my son with awe as he dances in his boots, the skirts of his long black coat whirling behind him as he crosses the stage. I'm hearing a passage from his own song, one that no one else will ever sing.

As Jacob begins the long, lonely trudge to adulthood, the struggle between father and son intensifies; moments of tenderness between me and my son are less frequent. Time spins faster, as if nearing the end of a cycle, and Peter and I feel increasingly helpless and can't articulate our feelings, either to ourselves or to each other.

The years of Jacob's childhood seem so unbelievably brief. We're nearing the end of something that will happen only once in our lives. I'll never again be the light of a child's life. There's no other child I will ever hold in my arms and comfort so completely; whose sobs I will be able to sing away, whose cuts I can bind and kiss, whose fears I can dispel with whispered words. No one will ever need me as entirely. No one will ever make me feel so sure and swift. My baby, sleeping in sunlit blankets, kindled a fire that might have remained unlit, gave my footsteps grace and my hands sweetness, taught me that tenderness was part of strength. I long for this woman as if I've lost her, as if she'll go away when Jacob leaves.

Peter, making pots, listens to a song on the radio about a father who regrets the things he didn't do with his son; his eyes fill with tears.

One afternoon, I stand on the threshold of Jacob's door and gather my courage, knowing what I'm about to unleash. He's propped on his pillows, lost in fantasy, reading *The Dark Is Rising*. I ask him if he has started his term paper for history. As if he's been waiting for me to ask, so he'll have a reason to defend his decision, he tells me coldly to stop badgering him, and when I continue to probe, he raises his voice and begins a familiar defensive argument. I go downstairs, leaving him behind the closed door of his room. Peter's in the kitchen and I tell him about the latest confrontation. It sets off his worries, which simmer within him, waiting for the slightest augmentation of heat to come to a boil. He begins his litany of all that Jacob hasn't learned or doesn't do, as if these are things that he, as a father, is responsible for. I listen, staring out the window sightlessly, and wonder if I've been too selfish, too wrapped up in my own concerns, too remote. I wonder if my son has suffered from the same faults that I've been certain, all these years, made my first baby decide not to be born.

Jacob's impending departure is like something we've been through once before, only we can't see it. We are parents who lost a child. As Jacob grows, and approaches the independence that we've spent all our parenting years preparing him for, we are terrified that once again, we will have failed; that if we haven't prepared him well enough, he won't survive; that his success or failure is our burden, not his.

He fights the coils of this mesh with increasing passion as his time to fly approaches. And since we've been left behind by a child once before, his rejection of us is devastating.

I feel a terrible emptiness in my heart, a dawning sense of futility.

We're frantically busy again. I'm photographing gardening books now and writing magazine articles, as well as growing my huge gardens and continuing to work in the studio. I take off my watch so I won't be made sick by realizing how few hours in a day I have to accomplish everything. Peter is in a frenzy. He builds a new studio, hires workers, increases his production, commits us to wholesale and retail shows. We load our truck and trailer, drive to Toronto, Boston, Philadelphia, even San Francisco. We ship his raku pottery to exhibitions in New Zealand and Japan, supply galleries across Canada. I spend hours of every week taping bubble wrap around pots, stuffing them in boxes layered with shredded paper, phoning shipping companies, filling out forms, ordering supplies. Now we have an office in the new studio, which gradually accumulates machines to duplicate information and keep us in touch with the world: telephones, fax, photo-copier, computers. Peter talks worriedly about how he and Jake should have a father-son trip, go camping, canoeing, bike riding. I imagine the pilgrimage to see Welsh castles that I wanted to take when Jacob was still quickened by his romantic vision of the Middle Ages. But none of these things happens, and time tumbles with increasing disunity and acceleration, like spreading froth at the base of a waterfall. I feel a creeping sense of hollowness; I fear that the lack of peace in our lives is the uneasy accompaniment to a mad, veering trajectory away from what is real.

One summer night, Peter and I swim in the warm waters of the pond and then walk back to the house through the daisied fields. The moon is almost full, silvering the ground mist that rises over the wildflowers like the earth's breath. I'm holding Peter's hand; my hair is damp and smells of pond water. Our house looms like a ship, its lights chopping the darkness for short distances before being broadened and diffused. I feel the equivalence of pain and beauty, how each precipitates the other. I realize that it's this paradox that makes me love the world; it's this that makes me want to pinion my own tiny scrap of time or to hold my life in my arms, as much of it as I can gather, like daisies. I realize, suddenly, that I want to write again; my own writing, not articles. I remember the manuscript that I finally removed from the car's trunk and put on a shelf. It seems like part of another epoch and unconnected with the writing I want to do now. I walk over the clots of newly mown grass on the lawn, drape my towel over the clothesline, walk barefoot up the stairs and flick on my light table. I pick up my loupe and bend over a slide of pears. The black lines between their curving yellow skins make me remember the pear tree of my childhood.

I go to my desk. My window is open, and across the driveway, the leaves of the poplar tree rustle and sigh. Farther out, in the fields, the crickets chirp dispassionately, like the night's heartbeat. I'm in the pool of light of a small desk lamp, but my mind is reaching out into its own rich darkness, catching hold of a vision that shines like a trout.

It's beauty that I want to write about and photograph; it's the stirring of the wild heart of life that's made me dare to tread this path again. I want to let words take me to the same place I go to when I'm kneeling in cold mud, photographing blue-flag iris, and the dew on their bearded faces begins a molten dance as the sun rises over the hills. I don't know how this pure, wild feeling can be expressed with words. I don't know what I will say, or in what form, or how the photographs and words will relate to one another, but I am compelled, nonetheless, to begin.

I scrabble from our schedule what mornings I can find, in the winter to write, and in the milder seasons to roam the fields, photographing leaves, lichen, pebbles, bird-tracks, mushrooms. As I write, I search my memory. I try to hear the sound of the wind, to remember the smell of leaves after snow-melt, to picture the lift and fall of raven's wings. I reach for these things as if, should I gather them into myself, I will become part of them, and so whole. I imagine a boundary that separates humans from the natural world. I remember moments that have carried me closest to this boundary, and put me in a place where I could feel the world's spirit. I remember the strange birdlike fluting of a doe's warning cry when I walked thigh-deep in drenched daisies. I remember the moon floating at sunrise like a jellyfish in shoals of gold-bellied clouds. I remember wishbones of geese scratching a white sky, birch trees on a winter hillside, hawk bones beneath red bunchberry leaves. I write as an outsider looking in, and yet the briefest glimpse makes me feel closer to the heart of life.

During the two years I spend writing about and photographing the world around me, a book shapes itself in my mind. When it's finished, I feel as if I've emerged from a dream. The book has become something separate from me, and perhaps was all along; I followed rather than led, walking the long path of its creation. Writing it has been an act of love. I've been held by its spirit, and now I feel as if the fierce beauty that I've been celebrating is inside myself.

I put the finished manuscript on a shelf. It's still lovely and secret. It's like being pregnant and not telling anyone.

Shadow Child

In Grade Eleven Jacob states that he hates school so much, he is going to drop out. He has taken all the art courses the school has to offer, has little interest in any of the courses he still has to take. Unwilling to let him end his education, Peter and I find a private school in Vermont that emphasizes art, music and theatre; he can go for two more years of high school. We make this decision in spring, and Peter and I begin to face the fact that our son has only a few more months left of the continuum of his childhood.

Jacob has a friend named Aaron who's a year and a half older, one grade ahead of him. Together, they are energetic, exuberant, funny, intense. Jacob tells me that Aaron's the kindest person he knows; he can tell Aaron things he never tells anyone else. He and Jake wear tweed caps backwards and huge trenchcoats they found at the Salvation Army. Both boys are wiry, with shoulder-length hair; Jacob's is blond, as was Aaron's before he dyed it jet-black. Aaron swings between two extremes. He's either twitchy with unfocused energy, his brown eyes opened wide as he spills forth hyperbolic fantasies, which he believes, at that moment, to be true; or else he's without propulsion, like a vehicle whose engine has failed, shambled in a chair with blue bags under his eyes, staring and hopeless. His face is gentle.

I love Jacob's friends. It's a complex mother instinct; I'm glad to know that my son has other people in his life who care about him, and who will help him if he needs them. But even more, I love seeing him caring for them: listening, giving advice, throwing his arms around a girl's shoulders, giving her a friendly hug. Jacob's face is changing; it's becoming raw-boned, strong, his jaw outlined with whiskers. He's less contentious, slightly less defensive. He's beginning to think before he acts, to consider how his responses affect others. He's very serious when he tells me one day that Aaron wants to come live with us because he has irreconcilable differences with his parents. Sometimes, after fights, he won't go home for days. He wanders around town, spends nights outside or stays with friends.

One day, as a group of kids are leaving our driveway, piled into a car, I bend down to the window and smile at Aaron. "You can come anytime you want, you know," I say. "You're always welcome here." His eyes lock onto mine with such intensity that I wonder, after the car has left, who he was seeing. He wants to be with us. He needs us. He makes me want to save him, comfort him. Jacob, too, is an advocate of having him come live with us. He wants Aaron to become part of our family. Peter is concerned by our uncharacteristically impulsive generosity. He's uneasy, wants time to think it over.

One rainy day in May, after we've discussed with both Aaron and Jacob some of our concerns—how long will he stay? what about his parents? to what extent will we support him?—the phone rings and Jacob answers it. Aaron's in a phone booth; he's had a huge fight with his parents. Jacob hangs up, scoops the car keys from the table, drives straight to town and brings Aaron back to our house.

The next day, I meet with Aaron's father and we discuss, at length, having his son stay with us. We agree that he will be a member of our family for as long as he needs space and renewal, and that he will be welcomed back into his own home whenever he decides to return. His visit will probably be brief, but it seems, for the moment, to be a sensible decision.

And so he comes to live with us, crossing paths with Jacob during the last months that we're still living together as a family.

Aaron and I spend hours talking. He helps me in the garden, drives me to town. He tells me about his childhood. He tries to figure himself out. He tells me that living with us is like having a second childhood, another chance. I, too, am getting a second chance, at mothering. Peter has a harder time. Now he has two teenage boys to challenge him; the boys disappear in the family car, and he has far less knowledge of, and no control over, what Jacob is up to. He has little time alone with me, since my attention is frequently absorbed by Aaron's intense talk. The house is chaotic; there's no privacy. Peter has no place to quietly wind down after his day in the studio.

But I don't mind any of it. The kitchen table is never clean—there's always a jammy spoon, or a drift of crumbs, or a pool of coffee—and the hall is tumbled with huge sneakers and jean jackets that have slipped off their hooks. In the living-room, there are chip bags by the couch and a guitar plugged into its amplifier. Cars come racing down the long dirt lane. Kids bounce across the lawn wearing nose rings and tiny braids; they're like baby goats frisking in a spring pasture, too high-spirited to notice the fence beyond the green grass. I imagine that I'm in the centre of a whirlpool. The waters of these kids' childhoods are circling faster and faster, and we're all at the vortex; soon they'll all spin away, merging into the great sea.

I lean in the window of my study and watch Jacob and Aaron pulling up the fenceposts of my riding ring, which I haven't used in years. They knock off the railings and pile them on the farm wagon, which is hitched to the tractor. I can't hear what they're saying, but I see their hammers glinting in the early summer light, I hear unhinged laughter, derisive whoops. I watch with interest, seeing that Aaron is a better worker than Jacob, with more experience and better skills; I notice that Jacob, like a younger brother, is willing to let Aaron take the lead as they dismantle the fence. But I see how Aaron defers to Jacob, subtly, as if he's aware of Jacob's veiled and emergent inner strength.

I realize, at this moment, the intensity of my longing for Jacob to have a brother. Aaron fills a place that seems to have been waiting for him. I tell myself, clearly, that he is neither our son nor

Jacob's brother, and that I must never confuse my longing with this young man's needs.

But his presence makes another fissure crack open in my soul.

I'm at my desk in the studio when the phone rings. It's our friend Karl. My heart leaps with eagerness. He and his wife, Cathy, have been trying to have a child for more than twelve years. At the age of forty, after an ectopic pregnancy, numerous miscarriages, two adoptions that fell through at the last minute and many unsuccessful attempts at in vitro fertilization, she has finally become pregnant and their baby is due this week.

I realize instantly that he is not calling to tell us the baby has arrived. His voice is dim, shocked. He tells me that at Cathy's appointment today, there was no heartbeat. Their baby is dead. He is completely bewildered and wants to know what they should do. He asks me what we did when our baby died. He has not absorbed, yet, the truth of what has happened.

Peter picks up the extension. I feel as if I've been struck by a wave. I'm standing, but I feel as if I'm falling backwards. Then I slide into my chair, drop the phone onto the desk and cover my face with my hands. Grief fills my chest, heavy and full, like overripe purple grapes whose skin will soon split. It's fully formed and violently present, and I'm suddenly swept with enormous rage at this injustice, so profound. I pick up the phone again. "Rage, Karl," I say brokenly. I hardly know what I'm saying. "*Rage.*" He doesn't know what I mean and numbly asks me to repeat what I've said, but I put down the phone again and sit on the concrete floor with my back against the wall and my head buried in my knees, crying until I can get myself together enough to rejoin Peter and Karl on the phone. "Karl," I say. "Have a name ready." Cathy's labour will be induced tomorrow, just as mine was. We tell them all the things we now realize we should have done.

Shadow Child

"Hold the baby. Name the baby and hold him. Hold him."
"Have a funeral. Grieve with your family."

Our voices seem to come from somewhere far away. We are saying things that we have held hidden in our hearts for so long that it seems strange to give them shape with simple and familiar words.

Peter stays on the phone for another half-hour, while I stand staring out the window at the fields that are gathering the shadows of dusk. He finds the name and phone number of a Unitarian minister and a funeral home; he calls them and then calls Karl back. He hangs up the phone, finally. I turn from the window. Peter's face is wet with tears. We hold each other and weep. Then we wash our faces with the studio towel and go out into the dusk, where the swallows make high, wild cries in the darkening sky and bats, darker than darkness, flick like erratic shadows past our heads.

I live through my friends' grief. I imagine every event. They live far away, so we can't attend the funeral, can't see the beautiful tiny coffin that someone made for them, can't hold them or cry with them as we want to. I picture them sitting in their living-room with their families, driving through cruel sunshine to the church, watching as the coffin is lowered into the ground. I imagine Karl placing his guitar strings into the coffin before it is closed on the tiny baby. I imagine Cathy's face, gaunt with longing. I picture the baby's perfect fingers, and wonder how they dressed him.

Chapter Sixteen

I want to tell people about the book I've made. It's like wanting to show my vegetable garden to friends; I feel neither pride nor modesty when I take them down the path past the peas whose green vines are interlaced with scarlet runner beans, between the purple cabbages whose dew-beaded leaves are trailed with golden nasturtiums. The flowers and vegetables and their exquisite, fecund patterns are neither mine, nor me, but are like a treasure that I've discovered and want to share. I feel the same way about my book. I wove the words, made the pictures, just as I planted the seeds for my garden; but the book's source, and impetus, came from outside me. I tried to make a place within which it could flourish.

I'm hoeing my garden in early summer. I lift a weed with the corner of my hoe. The sun bakes into my shoulders. High overhead, the swallows are like circus performers, swooping in dangerous trajectories over the garden, as if the sky is the Big Top. I think about my manuscript. It's sitting on a shelf in my study, along with all the others. But unlike the other bulky piles of paper, this one reproaches me. I think about it constantly, as if the spirit that I wrote about is an unquiet ghost, haunting me, asking for deliverance, wanting to be named.

I know I have to send it into the world. If I leave it on its shelf, I sense that I'm repeating a pattern that feels familiar: I make something that I think is good and then decide that it's not good enough; I won't let myself try to succeed because I'm so afraid of failure; I'm afraid to expose my secret self, as if, should I never try to give birth to it, there will be no risk of its death. But I know that if I leave the manuscript on the shelf, I'll be the one who destroyed it. I feel a familiar triad of feelings—fear, despair and loss—and the familiar impulse to hide. I'm sick of listening, I'm tired of entertaining. I interview people about themselves and then listen, with increasing resentment, to everyone else's story and never tell mine. I begin to detest myself.

The next morning, I phone a publishing company in California that specializes in nature books. My heart pounds so I can barely breathe and my hands are shaking as I draw tight squares with a pencil. I ask to speak to an editor and am amazed to be put through to someone. The young man to whom I speak tells me to send him the work, and promises that I will have his response in three weeks.

Three weeks later, on my birthday, I find a thick manila envelope in the mailbox. A form letter tells me this is not the kind of work that this company needs. They wish me the best of luck placing it elsewhere. I toss the envelope on my desk, scribble a note to myself in my journal recording its return, tell myself that I'll try it somewhere else. I'm surprised at my own calm.

We spend the day preparing for a party: mowing lawns, setting up tents, stacking wood for the barbecue fire, stringing outdoor lights. But disappointment breeds in me, maggot-like, throughout the day, and by evening has become a teeming mass. The presents my friends bring me are like accusations; my false self receives them with a stretched smile while my heart aches. I feel numb. Peter reads me a rude poem, and instead of laughing, I hurl white wine at him.

The next day, I go downstairs before Peter, Jacob and Aaron are up. The sink is filled with cake-smeared plates. There are beer bottles on the table, bits of shrivelled sausage on paper plates, wine glasses on the woodstove and grass clippings on the floor.

I begin to clean up. I pick up two beer bottles by their necks and then I stop. I can't begin to clean this kitchen unless I am motivated by the memory of its potential, unless I can envision its pine floorboards swept clean, steam rising from the wheezing kettle, hazy in sunshine, and the smell of apples on morning air. But I can't. I can't imagine serenity in the midst of this chaos. I want to smash everything in this room rather than restore it to its place. I find myself squeezing the necks of the bottles. I make myself lift them to the table and set them down. I'm behind the salty, swimming veil of grief. I make myself go into the hall and slide a denim jacket from a hook.

I walk past the barn, and head out into the fields that sweep up against the sky like dunes, now that their grass has been cut. My sneakered feet feel the sun-baked soil beneath the stubble; every step I take quickens the crickets, whose rasping song is the sound of endings, of dissolution.

I don't know where I'm going, how far I'll walk. I know only that I want to get as far away as I can from my life, and that I'll never be able to walk far enough. I stop, in fact, at the orchard, where six old trees crouch like arthritic hands; in the long timothy grass beneath them, apples slide together and gather in nests. The trees are in a hollow at the bottom of the big field; the hill sweeps up from them on one side, and behind them the woods begin, beech leaves rippling like light-faceted water.

I lean against the rough bark of the yellow transparent apple

Shadow Child

tree, remembering the dream that I awoke from this morning, and that seems so real I can hardly believe it didn't actually happen. I dreamt that a group of women editors sat together in a semi-circle staring at me. They asked me what I was doing and I told them, nervously, that I was writing a book. They raised their eyebrows, bored. They told me they were surprised that I would be doing this, since they'd read my previous book in manuscript and thought it was terrible. Suddenly I'm in a chair. I'm bound from head to foot in white surgical gauze. It's wrapped around me so tightly that I'm mummified and bound to the chair. I can neither move nor speak.

When I picture this, it hurts so much that I'm bent forward by the pain in my heart. Alone in the orchard, I wrap my arms around my knees and bury my face in my lap. My heart spills what it can no longer contain. I'm consumed with a sense of failure. I try, and I fail. I fail and fail. I reach and can't grasp. My hands clasp one another like a hinged trap that snares only emptiness. I'm curled over the centre of myself, which I feel shattering into shards; I can't stop it from breaking, and in my bewildered rage I don't want to.

The summer's juices are sapped, transformed; fruits hang on woody stems, the lettuces sprout tough stalks hung with seeds. The land is emptying, seems larger; from my study window, I see a V of geese rising from the hills, their necks outstretched, and I hear the rustling flap of their wings as they pass over the house.

I force myself to send my manuscript out again. I harvest the garden, finish photographing the gardening book I'm working on, edit and label slides. I listen to Aaron, who talks to me constantly, and worry about Jacob, who doesn't. I don't know what he's thinking about. It's late August and he's putting off packing. He's increasingly remote, as if he's already gone.

I feel an enormous pressure building inside myself. I look at slides from last week's shoot and feel sick to my stomach because they don't measure up to my own standards. My family comes to visit, and I find myself standing in the field, struggling anxiously with whether I should go for a walk with my father, talk to my sister-in-law on the porch or visit with my mother. I feel torn into shreds, tortured with a sense that I am failing all of them. I feel responsible for everyone else's happiness. I can't leave a room to tend to my own needs without wondering whether I should leave my guests unattended.

I begin to have vivid dreams that I remember clearly.

I am two people, and I kill one of them. Once I stab my double with scissors; another time I push her from a boat, watch her body sinking through water and then see her lying on the sea bottom, shadow-dappled, hair stirring like a lobster's antennae. Once I am in a great hall standing before an Aztec king. He has killed my son. I seize the king by the shoulders and repeatedly smash him against the stone floor until he, too, is dead.

I dream of being killed. I'm standing on a rock in the Bay of Fundy. A shadowy shape swimming underwater circles my rock and then vanishes beneath it. It is a cougar. I see its face emerging from the water. It rushes up towards me, its neck shedding water, and I say to myself, in my dream, "Let it come; see what happens." I hear bones crunch as the cougar bites my hand, and then, just before I wake up, his teeth are on either side of my head. He appears again in a dream of trees. Jacob has gone into the forest, and I've said to someone, "It's okay for my son to go there, there's no danger." Yet I begin to sense a finality about his disappearance, as if the space he left is drained of his essence. The cougar appears from the trees. It stares directly at me. I know that it's the same great beast, and that it knows me; and then it leaps to kill me. Another night, I dream that three otters are lying in a shallow brook. Their heads are buried, and I think they are dead. Suddenly, the largest one pulls its head from the mud and lunges at me with its teeth bared. Its face is huge and horrible and we sink our teeth in each other's faces, locked in deadly combat.

I dream that I am in a coffin. I step out of it, then realize that there are coffins as far as I can see, and every one of them contains a duplicate of me.

I dream that Jacob is singing a beautiful song to me and I am weeping.

Finally, at the last minute, Jacob begins to pack for school. Peter and I can't dissuade him from taking far more than we think he should. He's stubborn, resolute. He takes his talismans, selecting them with care. He stuffs clothes without thought into boxes. He takes all his books. He doesn't want me to help. His blue eyes are no longer receptive, wondering, lively, but are bitter with concealment, haunted with pain. He carries his fear like a shielded flame. He knows this departure is his own decision.

He gives me a poem that he has written. He writes of his destiny, his aloneness; how he feels torn apart, his body one place and his heart another. I'm sitting on the back steps when I read it. The swallows are scribing the sky with their remote and urgent wheelings; there are crickets in the woodpile and the bitter smell of phlox. My face is tear-swollen as I read my son's words. I don't realize that my heart is breaking, as it has broken once before. He's sitting next to me quietly. We've lost easy words. He puts his arm around me, kisses my head. "I love you, Mum," he says. He speaks these words steadily, as if he has just realized that they are true.

I watch clouds surging swiftly over clouds as another summer fades away, and I feel space opening inside myself, a chasm, a pit that I may fall into headlong.

I make an appointment to see Dr. Kay because I think I'm getting an ulcer. When I arrive, the waiting room is empty. The receptionist stares at me blankly. "Oh, your appointment was yesterday. You missed it." My hand goes to the ledge of the office window, and I try to speak, but I begin to cry. The receptionist tells me hurriedly to wait, and returns with Dr. Kay. He takes me to his office and holds my hand. "Talk to me," he says almost fiercely. "Talk to me." I crouch forward with my face in my hands. I hear my voice, twisted and high, like a river swollen by flood waters. I find a long list of grievances unwinding from me, spilling, pouring out. I tell him that I've taken over the bookkeeping in the studio, on top of packing and shipping; that I've been working to a deadline, trying to get images photographed for a book; that we've had a lot of company and I've been trying to be sure everyone is having a good time, as well as getting the garden harvested before we take Jacob to Vermont; that I'm having to deal with the fact of his leaving and that our friends' baby died. But when I reach the baby, I can't speak any longer. I try, twice, to say the word "baby." I begin to sob again. Dr. Kay holds my hand tightly and stares intently, and worriedly, into my eyes, as if trying to bring me back from the place I've gone. He tells me that as usual, I'm doing too much. He asks me if we're going away, taking a vacation. We'll be having a break in the fall, I say. He tells me that if I still feel this way after our vacation, I should consider "talking to someone." He gives me medicine for the pain in my gut.

As I resume my errands, tears spill from my eyes as if there's no end to them. There's no way to stop them. I feel bewildered and strangely released. I don't care if anyone sees me crying. I keep wiping my cheeks with the backs of my hands. I have a hard time seeing as I drive; the world is distorted.

Shadow Child

Early one morning in September, we leave for Vermont. Aaron's looking after the place for us while we're gone. He's sitting on the side of his bed in the little front room, stupefied with sleep. Jacob goes in to say goodbye. I hear their young-man voices, sternly repelling emotion; "See you, man." "Yeah, take care, man." I hear the slap of arm against back. Then Jacob's leaping down the stairs with his pack on one shoulder; the truck's in the driveway, Peter's making adjustments to the load. I poke my head in Aaron's door; he's sitting on the side of the bed, scratching. I give him last-minute instructions, glance at the door to Jacob's room, which is closed. The moment of departure rises and folds in pink dawn streaks, dark hills, windless grass bent under dew, the sound of a suitcase zipper and the truck's engine running, the smell of sleep through half-closed doors, and coffee, and toast. The rising sun glares red in a puddle. I think, "Here we are for the last time, me and Peter and Jacob, together in this kitchen," and then Jacob goes out the door. The first ray of sun flashes on the rim of a glass, trembles there like time-present.

As we start down the driveway, I lean forward as I always do when we leave, looking back, wondering about what I might have left undone; but Jacob puts the score from *The Piano* in the tape deck and doesn't look back, not even once. He's looking straight ahead with his lips tight, listening to the urgent, passionate voice of the piano.

It's hazy, hot New England fall when we arrive the next day. We walk through a horse pasture to get to Jacob's dormitory; his room overlooks the distant Green Mountains. He unpacks immediately, defines his space with great intensity. His thick blond hair is shoulder-length. He wears a pinstriped shirt, a wool sports jacket with a silver Celtic pin, brown jeans, black army boots. His face is closed, expressionless, yet I see the effort he is making to neither fear the future nor regret the past, but keep himself in the moment, without emotion.

There's already such a distance between us, parents and son, that when the time comes to say goodbye it feels as if we've already said it. We leave him scuffing through leaves on the path he will walk every day between his dorm and the school buildings. He's with his roommate. I say lightly, "Would you like to get rid of us now?" and he says yes. We laugh, hug and say goodbye. I look back and see him walking up across the pasture, going back to the dormitory with his new friend, and I know that he won't look back; he's walking into his own life. I feel a burden lifting from my shoulders. I'm surprised at how calm I feel. We get into the truck and start down the road and suddenly I am sure that I've left something essential in his room: my wallet, or my contact-lens case, or my chequebook. I twist, scrabble, look on the floor, find my purse, dig urgently through its contents. Then I stop, let my hands and my head fall back. My lips tighten. It is Jacob I've left behind. Jacob and his snakes in alcohol; his staffs carved with runes; his books, his skulls, his raven feathers; the sword, Daryn-wye, that Bear made for him, propped now against a new wall.

Two days after we get home, I go with Aaron to the train station. He's moving to Halifax, where he's found a job and an apartment. He takes a backpack, a duffel bag. Like Jacob, he too is intently focused on the unknown, staring straight ahead as he drives while I look out my side window at the fields whose oats have been harvested, whose dry straw is stacked in yellow bales.

I go into the station and wait while he buys his ticket at the grill. I look across the street and see the building where we once had our shop. I feel time, like wind, blowing the sand of my life into new shapes. I think of all the friends and young people I've stood with here, speaking final, futile words, then watching as the train carries them away.

Shadow Child

I give Aaron a hug and he hugs me back, tells me he'll come to visit again soon. I nod and can't speak, and then I walk to the car swiftly, with determination. I don't look at the train station. I drive around the block, then I drive around the same block again. I can't do my errands.

I drive home. I turn off the engine and sit in the car with my head back and my eyes closed. I roll down the window and listen. It's as quiet as it was the day we first found this farm, twenty-five years ago. Wispy grasses by the woodpile bend their feathery heads, brush the air. Sturdy shoots of wild roses sprout from the lawn. A loose piece of metal roofing taps slightly, the way the house settles at night, like water grooving rock or dead trees creaking against their roots.

I climb out of the car slowly, feeling exhausted, as if I've carried something heavy for a long time and have finally set it down. I feel as if I'll never be able to carry anything again. I drop the strap of my leather purse over the back of a chair. The house feels like a summer place whose owners have left it empty for many seasons. Nothing is animated; dream, the substance of life, has been drained from every object. I walk up the stairs and go into Jacob's room. It's the first time I've opened its door since we returned from Vermont.

It's as messy as ever. There are shirts and socks on the floor, lids of shoe boxes holding disparate objects: shells, a broken wrist-watch strap, a Jack Daniels belt buckle, dice, candle stubs. On his desk are crumpled letters in a girl's handwriting, a broken-nibbed calligraphy pen, aborted school-books whose biology notes evolve into drawings of swords. The bedclothes are tossed back, describing his final morning. His stuffed bear is propped against the pillow, as if at the last minute Jacob remembered to make him comfortable.

I pick up a shirt and hold it to my nose.

The things in this room seem abandoned. They are things he did not want or need. They are things left behind, and so they become empty, without purpose, unconnected to his life.

Across the hall, the little room where his friend stayed is completely empty; only a poster is still taped to the sloped ceiling. Much as I wish that Aaron, like Jacob, was coming home someday, I know that he never will. It's only a guest-room once again.

I lie on my bed. The sky is white. Cloud passes over cloud. I roll my head sideways and watch their slow evolution while tears trickle into my ears. I think of how Jacob has been withdrawing, preparing himself to leave home. My heart feels as empty as the house. I lie without moving, knowing no one will come, the phone will not ring. The boys are gone.

I remember the time I found a sparrow hawk beating its wings frantically against the window in the barn. I trapped it against the glass with both hands, then carefully lifted it. For a brief moment, it folded its wings within the sheltering darkness of my cupped hands. I felt its quivering stillness, its profound pause. Then I carried it to the barn door and opened my hands. Just for an instant, it sat, exhausted, free to go but hesitating; and then, with a flash of all its wild energy, it became a speck in the sky.

V

1993–1997

Chapter Seventeen

I'm breaking down. My soul is like a northern river during the spring thaw. The little cracks in the ice have been forming for a long time, hidden, unperceived, until they become deep seams which groan and crack under pressure. One block breaks away and pushes up another. Once it's started, there's no return; the ice turns opaque, gathers dirt on warm days, crumples into a chaotic tumult.

I'm pondering the times between seasons, when it's no longer winter but not quite spring; or no longer spring, but not yet summer. These are odd, perilous slices of time, when the present shifts into memory, even as I watch. I feel caught between my son's youth and my parents' old age. I'm poised on the edge of being no longer a parent, no longer a child, and I grieve for both—the lost childhood, the inevitable absences.

Meanwhile, we're getting ready for the Toronto craft show. It occurs in late November, but by the end of September we're already feeling pressured. I spend every afternoon assembling pots by category, cutting multiple strips of bubble wrap, then rolling each pot in its strip, taping it, labelling the bubblewrap with a marking pen. I assemble cartons, fill them with dunnage. I wear a face mask as I rip apart dusty handfuls of shredded paper, scatter them into the bottoms of boxes. I feel as if the pots are like eggs that hatch money. Peter, in the next room, is throwing pots at the wheel, or pushing clay into his pug mill, or carrying trays of vases to the damp closet. Our two assistants sit at the sink and table, bent over pots which they glaze or scrub clean. We listen to CBC radio. I hear interviews with women who are university professors, authors, psychologists, biologists. I compare myself with them. I think about what I am not, what I didn't do, how I didn't continue my education.

The dreams that began in the summer, dreams of killing and of being killed, dreams of rage and violence, of stabbing and biting, were like signposts warning me of what was ahead. Now I don't leave these dreams behind when I wake up. Their feelings accompany me through the day, like a residue that won't wash off. In October, I begin to awake filled with something that has no name. It's like a nightmare that doesn't go away once I've woken up, but stands in broad daylight. It makes me curl around myself and seek oblivion. It saps my energy. I go into battle with it as I swing my legs over the side of the bed. I fight it as I stare at the bureau trying to decide what to wear. I push against it as I go down the curved stairs, holding the bannister, refusing to be defeated by its derisive spirit, which mocks my decision to start another day, which mocks my desire to create. I visualize a brick wall in my mind. On one side is a place where anything is possible: wind and dancing leaves, a hayfield at dawn, breakfast in a courtyard by the sea. On the other side is black sludge. It's heavy, creeping. It obliterates light. It seems unstoppable. Sometimes I press the edge of my hand against my forehead in a vertical salute, like the wall that I imagine; I close my eyes, try to hold back the welling darkness.

Shadow Child

I begin to realize that there are two of me. As the last wrinkled leaves hang from the maple trees, motionless in the predatory air which broods over the frozen fields, these two people become more distinct. One of me is charming, attentive, authoritative and friendly, capable of unleashing life stories from strangers; I'm made unexpectedly ecstatic by the sight of sun on clapboards or the face of a friend; sometimes I feel too much energy, too much potential, and am fuelled with a potent mixture of power and grace that keeps me from sleep, makes me dart and hover, extracting nourishment from beauty like a hummingbird. The other me has no centre. She's like a dandelion gone to seed, a collection of fragile parts, once connected and now so tenuously attached that the slightest breeze will blow them away. This person has no power of attraction, can neither smile nor speak, wants only to crouch somewhere safe, holding herself together, and cannot summon the will to imagine anything beyond the present, which is without hope.

My thoughts run over and over the same material, like a chant that has no meaning and yet never stops. When I'm doing repetitive jobs—wrapping pots in bubble wrap, slicing onions, vacuuming the house, driving the car, shovelling manure from the horse stalls—the voice drones on and on. It's my voice, whispering angrily. It's hissing about all the things I resent: the fact that I didn't go to England but got married instead, Peter's success, my subservient role, the ways I've been slighted because I'm a woman, the time I sat at a dinner party with three career women and never spoke. It says that I'm a bad friend, a bad daughter; that if the people who think I'm a nice person really knew me, they would feel betrayed. It goads me, says that if they could only read what I have written, *then* they would know who I am, *then* they would respect me, as they respect Peter for these beautiful pots he makes. It tells me that I'm not good enough to do what I want to do, and derides my attempts. It reminds me of the beauty of the world and says if I were a real photographer I'd be out there at every sunrise, I'd catch every shimmering cobweb, every nuance of cloud, every flower in its prime. It says that I'll never be published, that I shouldn't bother to try. Then it begins choosing new careers for me. I could teach. I could counsel teenagers. Another part of my mind protests, tries to protect me. It's a brave little girl standing up against a bully. She whispers softly, reminding me of the light that shines inside me. But her voice is hesitant, timid.

All the while, cleaning the barn, my eyes watch the shining tines of the pitchfork sliding into matted slices of manurey hay. I'm in the steam of the horse stall; I'm rugged and strong, wearing wool socks and rubber boots, my hands in leather mitts. The hens croon, the sunlight flashes in frost crystals on the barn window, and frozen grass steams as it thaws. But I'm not hearing, seeing, smelling. I'm not aware of anything but the cage I'm in. My mind turns and turns, even as I walk out into the sun, pushing the wheelbarrow, and it's another glorious day.

The visions in my mind begin to be the reallest thing that I see.

When the snow starts, I begin to lose the battle with the nameless dread. The second of my two personalities seems to be the real person I am, and I'm sickened by the first when I'm called upon to use her. One night, I awake feeling a sensation of dropping, like being in an airplane that falls into an air pocket. I roll my head on the pillow and feel it again. When I get up the next morning, I take one step and then I fall. I am so dizzy, I have to clutch the walls to walk. I close my eyes, shut out the world, which jiggles endlessly, which has come unhinged.

Some part of me is desperate for my attention. I can hear it calling, but don't understand its messages. It's what is making me break apart. It tries, in different ways, to make me listen.

Shadow Child

The dizziness comes and goes. Sometimes it lasts for a week; once, for seventeen days. Inexplicably, I'll wake and it will be gone.

My life becomes an endless battle. I go to bed at night dreading the way I'm going to wake up several hours later, and then lie awake for hours, unable to sleep. In the morning, I sit up slowly, waiting for the moment when the room falls away and begins to reel. I make my way from bed to bureau holding onto walls and chair backs. I walk outside and look at the hills, but they no longer stand against the horizon with reassuring permanence; like everything else, they've lost their solidity. They slant and shift and slant back again. I shield my eyes, walk out to the barn looking only at my feet. My actual field of vision, like my mental one, becomes ever narrower.

Dr. Kay examines me. He tells me briskly about several things that could cause the dizziness; it could be a tumour in the inner ear, or a disease of the ear, or a harmless condition that's chronic and has no known cure. He's trying to sound matter-of-fact to indicate that these are improbable, but even so must be eliminated as possibilities. I know that I'm not immune from the worst thing that could happen. I'm instantly certain that I have a tumour. I grip my cheekbones with my fingertips as he considers me.

"Do you want to talk to someone?"

I pause for a long time. The thought of articulating my sense of dread terrifies me. I feel that if I say yes, I am knocking an escape ladder away; the only way down will be the hard route.

"Yes. I think so. I feel as if I can't live with myself any more."

He muses over several psychiatrists he might send me to. "No, you wouldn't like him . . . .", then makes a decision. Dr. Coates.

"Is he a kindly man?"

He looks at me over his glasses. "He wears bow ties," he says, and smiles briefly to himself.

At first he seems like an ordinary person. He's about fifty, medium height, has a salt-and-pepper beard, intelligent brown eyes behind glasses. He wears a white lab coat that says Psychiatry over the left breast pocket. He wears a brown-and-yellow plaid bow tie, and sneakers with velcro fastenings. He's lifting a file folder from his desk when I make my own first rapid assessment of him, but then his eyes dart up and hold me. Only my peripheral vision registers the desk, the two chairs, the cluttered bookshelves. His eyes are keenly focused, bemused, acute. He's studying me with intense interest, as if I'm a puzzle someone has handed him.

He greets me calmly, and reads the letter Dr. Kay has sent him. He says that it seems I'm suffering from dyspepsia. I instantly ask him what that means. He begins to answer and then checks himself. "Why," he says, putting aside the file, "do you want to know?"

I'm confused, on guard, my pattern interrupted. I say I suppose I want to know what things mean. He asks me why I want to know what things mean. I feel my heart begin to hammer. I sense his dispassionate patience and his relentlessness. We begin to unravel the knot of my need to know. I feel like a cornered rabbit facing a ferret. I'm carrying a file folder of my own under my arm. It makes me feel important. He asks me what's in it, and I say I've brought some sections from my journal for him to read. He says he doesn't want to read them. I begin to cry. He asks me what I'm feeling. I say I'm ashamed, that I will go home and torture myself for having brought the file folder. He asks me why I wanted to come see him. The size and shape of the room changes; the walls seem to be very close and high, like the coffins of my dream, and Dr. Coates himself is huge and malevolent, the embodiment of my dread. I am terrified of his judgement. The habit of concealment wraps around me like a shawl that I clutch. I am an asker, not a teller. I hide behind my questions, I draw out other people not only from my interest in them but in order to deflect them from me. But he cleverly finds untucked bits to pull. I begin to talk about myself. I find words coming in a torrent. I tell him things I have told no one else. He listens calmly, without sympathy, without comfort. I lose all sense of myself as a single entity. I feel as if there are pieces of me flying up into the corners of the room. I say to him that life is meaningless; I state this as a given, something he will not question since it is true, a simple fact—and yet it's one of the pieces that lodge up by the ceiling, where it will hang, waiting for my next visit. I tell him briefly about the baby. His face registers concern, a heartbeat of compassion. I tell him about my Aunt Bernice and how I have failed her, how I have failed my family. I feel selfish and spoiled telling him these things, but I can't stop myself. I tell him about my recurrent dream, where I am on a stage being forced to play a part that I don't know; I've never seen the script, and the spotlights are on the audience so I can see them watching me fail. Unexpected things drift to the surface in this turbulence that stirs my soul's sediment. Unexpected things make me weep until I can't talk. I feel as if I've almost disappeared. I'm the wet tissue in my hand. I think of the expressions "fall apart," "break down," "crack up," and I sense that I desperately want to be goaded, I want this person to help me break. I hate the pieces of myself as they are presently configured. I need to rearrange them, but I don't know how. I need to fall into the emptiness that makes a pattern of its own between the broken pieces.

I expect to feel ashamed when Dr. Coates glances at his watch and I know my time is up; but he looks straight at me, and without a word, acknowledges me as a person whose pain is important and whose value is unquestioned. He says in his light, reasonable voice, "I'll be happy to see you. If you want to work with me, give me a call and we'll set up a series of appointments."

I realize that nothing I have said makes him think less of me. I stumble over the rocky passage between therapy and my return to the outer office. He's used to this. He listens patiently, but he's still assessing what I say, and I hear myself thanking him, as if I'm still seeking forgiveness.

I push open the heavy door and go out into the sunny corridor of the psychiatric ward. I'm on the fourth floor of the huge new regional hospital. I'm drained, exhausted, but it's like coming up out of icy water. I feel shocked, empty, cleared. For the first time in months, I'm calm. I carry away no residual guilt, no ache of what I didn't say or shouldn't have said. Honesty is like clear water, drunk cold.

I hear a piano. It's odd, because there is no other sound or movement in this part of the hospital; there are no nurses at the nursing station, which is at the apex of two long corridors. All the doors are closed. I slip around the corner and go past the desk. Beyond the shining gloom of polished floors, there's a lounge whose door is open. I go to the threshold and look in.

A woman sits in a rocking chair, facing the windows. She's wearing pink phentex slippers and a turquoise terry-cloth bathrobe. She's thin; her face is like a house whose paint has worn away. She seems neglected and defeated. She holds her ankles close together and squints her eyes almost shut when she brings her cigarette to her mouth. She resumes rocking once she's inhaled deeply, and looks up at the windows, listening. The piano's in the corner. All I can see of the man who is playing it is his back and his hands. He's tall, broad. He looks like a man who can lift heavy weights, wrestle stubborn objects into place. He wears a ball cap. He's playing "Good King Wenceslaus." He's improvising, makes it as complex as a Bach prelude. He doesn't stop or turn to see if anyone else is in the room. The woman seems unaware of my presence.

I lean against the door frame, let my head rest against its cool edge. The man never sees me, never knows I am listening. I don't know if he is playing for the thin woman in the rocking chair, but

I don't think so. He's playing his own song, for himself, with such a passion of need that it becomes her song, and mine.

Peter looks at me frequently, the day after I see Dr. Coates.

"You look younger," he says wonderingly. I laugh. He laughs back, delighted. I've told him everything I could remember about the appointment. Even though so much of my anger has been directed at him over the years, he never fails to support me, his love never falters. I remember when I realized that he loved me the way Granny loved me. He listens, with unfeigned interest and caring, as I reveal to him my own discovery of myself.

My inability to sleep intensifies. I fall asleep when I go to bed, but later in the night slide up into wakefulness the same way one drifts down into sleep. I usually wake in the middle of a dream, and I lie staring into the dark, considering the strange stories that my mind has been spinning.

The next day I write my dreams in my journal. I try to remember every detail. I scribble them without reflection, keeping them as loose and wildly disjointed on paper as they were in my mind. Their details seem to have no apparent relationship to one another, and yet when I squint sideways at them, mentally blurring them so I can see them whole, I understand what they tell me. They are like another language which I learn to understand.

After I see Dr. Coates, I dream of houses.

In the first dream, our house burns down and someone builds us a new one. It's ugly, looks like a chicken barn. Yet inside, it's clean, new; it is filled with clear light from windows that don't show on the outside, but that, from within, admit both sunshine and long views over wooded hillsides. It has a laundry room and all sorts of appliances that in my real life I don't have; it's easy to live in. All my aunts, uncles, and cousins descend to help me prepare for Peter's birthday; they seem to feel this is their place. I say to them: "I just need some space." Someone comes rushing in and says Jacob is in the woods and should come back, and I begin passively to agree and then say, angrily: "No. It is okay for him to be in the woods."

I think about this dream and decide that the house is me; I don't care what it looks like on the outside, or what other people think of it. Inside, I'm clear, new, lovely. Someone helped me build this house, just as I'm needing help right now, but eventually I'll go on rebuilding. I won't be smothered by other people. I'll set my own agenda. I'll take my space and have the strength to do what I want to do within it.

In the second dream, I'm swimming across a bay and Dr. Coates is swimming near me, giving me encouragement. It's hard work; I can't use one arm because of an injured shoulder. I scramble up a hill and stumble across a scree slope. I come to a stone wall. Beyond it, I see dark, forbidding country with deep chasms and steep cliffs. Far away, a tiny black square against the stormy sky, like the alpine hut that we hiked to in Switzerland, is my parents' house. I think, "Oh yes, I could go there, I have been there before. I have parents in this alien place." But I decide to turn back, and I recross the scree slope. I come to a place that is like the Golden Books of my childhood: geometric, immaculate. There's a white house with blue trim. It's lit by blazing California sunshine. It's empty. I think, "How strange, this place has been abandoned, but it's still perfectly all right." I walk up a swept path that is lined with cactus and jade plants, which are twice as big as when I last saw them. They are thriving, healthy, glossy.

I can see, as I approach the house, that it's as shiny inside as it is out. Dr. Coates helps me reach the shore upon which are both the forbidding territories of my buried memories and the clean, pure place that is me now. I need to visit both places. I need to appreciate my real self, whom I've abandoned for so long.

Shadow Child

We go to our show in Toronto, and Jacob takes the train up from Vermont to meet us there, since it's American Thanksgiving. He's still very involved in rejecting us, as he is supposed to be, I tell myself; but I miss him, even when he's walking down Queen Street beside me. I no longer know what to point out to him, knowing that whatever I think will excite him will only elicit cool dismissal.

It's not a good Christmas and I crash into January, dizzy again.

At the beginning of February, my agent forwards me a letter from a publisher. If I were someone more important, it says, better known, then they could take a chance on the book. But I need a name. I need to make myself a name.

My eyes skim the words on the paper. I try to delay the moment when their meaning hits my brain. Then the frustration of years pours out. Peter is appalled by my incoherent rage. He tries to take the letter from me. Part of me sees that I'm frightening him; the rest of me is caught in the flood of despair. It's the moment when I know that I'm locked in the cage I feel I've been in my entire life, and realize that I will never get out.

The extent of my rage reveals to me the depth of my hope, which I've been carrying like an unborn child.

The next day I have an appointment with Dr. Kay to discuss my dizziness. As soon as he comes into the examining room I know that I'm going to let go. It's as if I've been holding my own hand, squeezing hard, as I drove through the snowy morning, as I sat in the waiting-room. Now I let go. I don't want to be here. I don't want to be anywhere. I don't know if I want, even, to exist.

I try to explain how I feel, but I find myself twisting my mouth to control my tears, knowing that the moment I begin to speak I will find no words, only the torrent of grief that is all that seems real and has no apparent cause. I open my mouth and begin to cry.

"I want . . . I want . . . " I'm tightening my lips and staring at the floor through my tears. I twist my tissue. "Sometimes I feel that I want to . . . " I fling my hand up as if I'm holding a vase.

"Don't say it," he says, swiftly, warningly. "Don't say it."

Then he explains to me that I'm suffering from depression. He says that the dizziness is probably caused by depression; yet, since I'm depressed, I can't cope with the dizziness and that makes me more depressed, and so I become more dizzy. I'm on a downward spiral. He names the symptoms of depression: insomnia, inability to concentrate, feelings of low self-esteem, loss of perspective, appetite, appreciation, hope. He tells me it's not my fault, and that I can't "get a grip," "cheer up." It's physically impossible. I'm sick. I'm actually sick.

I become still inside as I absorb his words. I've been walking in a dark place that has been getting steadily darker and more confusing. I've been standing in one place, turning and turning, not knowing any more which direction to take. I've almost decided to sink to the floor with my hands over my eyes. His words are like a light, very far away.

He stoops and picks up my sodden Kleenex, which I haven't noticed has fallen to the floor. I'm touched, suddenly, by how much he cares about me. I notice this as if for the first time I have no energy left to make things appear as I wish them to, but have to see, simply, what is real.

My seed catalogues arrive. Geraniums bloom in the sunroom, while on the other side of the glass, chickadees hop on the snow's crust, bodies perfectly balanced over twiggy legs. I sit in a rocking chair with my eyes closed and head back to control dizziness. My chest aches as if just beneath the surface a fist takes my heart and wrings it. I'm suffocating. I breathe through my nose and can't fill my lungs no matter how deeply I inhale. I want to go outside to get more air, but it makes me queasy to stand.

Shadow Child

Inside my head I'm continuing the mental battle that began as soon as I woke up and had to face another day. I resist, now, the desire to stumble to the couch and pull a quilt over my head. I make my way to the kitchen table and sit down. I open a catalogue and stare at the page with twelve different kinds of green beans. I hold my head in my hands. I not only have to decide which of these bean seeds to choose, but also I have to go on through beets, broccoli, cauliflower, corn. I can't do it. I can't imagine how anyone could do it.

The phone rings but I can't answer it. I can't pretend that I'm a normal human being on a normal Saturday morning.

I decide to stop everything I'm doing. I write my agent in shaky handwriting and ask him not to contact me for a while; I feel too fragile to withstand any news. I abandon the chapter I'm writing; it's about Christmas and a lunar eclipse, and I've reached the point where darkness is shrouding the moon. I resign from a committee that I've been on for several years. The only book I can absorb is *War and Peace*, because I've read it so many times before. Otherwise, I can't read; the long strings of words won't stay connected to one another and I forget the beginning of a sentence by the time I've reached the end. I turn down all invitations. All I want to do is to sit in a soft chair. I want not to be distracted from the deep listening that I feel I have to do. I'm consumed with my own deconstruction. The house of my self is falling down around me and I want to watch the slow-motion descent of its pieces.

I spend the rest of the winter renovating the living-room. It's a room that we seldom use, even though it's in the southwest corner of the house, and in winter is both clarified by the sun's rising and burnished by its setting. Its white walls and high ceiling make it cold and repellant. It has no side tables with lamps, no cozy chairs, no rug, no pictures on the walls. Its cheap pine bookshelves are sagging, and dust rises from books when their pages are riffled. Its plaster walls are fissured with meandering cracks, like rivers seen from the sky. The couch smells of dog. We've never taken the time to make a true living-room, a room in which to live, to rest, come to a stop, and reflect. Living, to us, has meant movement, and so we gather on winter evenings in the kitchen, where all the activity of the day has been centred, as if we don't know how to separate ourselves from the day's rhythmn.

I shove all the furniture to the middle of the room and cover the pile with old sheets. All day long, I plaster, sand and paint. I don't want to hear anyone else's words. I don't want to talk or be talked to. I'm listening to myself. The thought-hamsters in my head have been replaced by my dreams, which I examine as if I'm looking at pictures in a museum, and by fragments of my last session with Dr. Coates, which come floating to the surface of my mind without sequence or logical connection, each thought like a path that takes me a long way from where I started and yet sometimes ends at the place where another pathway begins. In the absence of everything, I begin to realize what has been clamouring for my attention. I feel as if I'm holding something special and rare in my cupped hands. I'm looking at it wonderingly. I've discovered some beautiful, delicate part of myself and am amazed by it.

The bristles of my brush spread like a fan as I work them into a scar in the woodwork. I paint steadily, without seeing; my real work is going on in my mind, which has become a place of riches, a place I could roam forever without discovering everything that's there. I set my brush on the paint can and sit on the floor with my back against the wall. I'm wearing baggy overalls; the backs of my hands have puckery places where paint has dropped and dried. The sunlight is dusty, and the room smells of fresh lumber, plaster, latex paint. I listen to sweet women's voices singing in Gaelic, and, although I don't understand the words, tears well from my closed eyes. I feel like an onion whose layers of protective skin are being peeled away. The outer layers are sun-dried, feather-light, and crumble into dust as they fall. The inner layers will need to be cut with a knife. I'm finding my way back to my spirit, which has been there all along, like the sun-dazzled blue-and-white house of my dream.

In the meantime, I have no sense of purpose, no drive, no will. I'm sick of striving. I remember the summer I was so busy that I was afraid to look at my watch. Every few days I would write in my diary, "Now I have everything under control." I made sure everything was in perfect shape: gardens weeded, lawns mowed, wildflowers photographed before they faded, studio books up to date, friends invited to dinner, bread baked, pots shipped, chapter written. But every time I finished one thing on the list, I added another. Only when winter came, and I slowed my pace, could I see how I had been poisoned by obsession; how the desperate need to create, and the fear that nothing was good enough, made me unable to stop.

One evening, I'm sitting on a new, dark green leather couch. I've finished painting the room; it's the colour of blueberries, ceiling and walls. We've hired a cabinet-maker to build and install maple shelving and cupboards, which will cover the north wall. Peter is making raku tiles to set around the fireplace. He's set track lighting on the ceiling. Now I'm working on the curved bannister, stripping away its layers of paint, revealing the blonde birch. I wake up now, most mornings, knowing what I'm going to do, knowing what I'm going to wear, knowing what I'm going to accomplish, knowing that no one cares. I set myself no challenges, take no risks. I do small, specific tasks whose completion satisfies me. Obscurely, I know that my strongest need is to prove to myself that I am not a person who fails; I am not someone whose dreams always die.

There's a floor lamp next to me, and I'm sitting in the pool of its light, looking at the reborn room, when suddenly a vision comes like a waking dream. I imagine a river running beside me, just next to the couch's padded armrest. I actually turn my head and look at the place where I imagine this river, and see in my mind how it is composed of hundreds of shining bubbles, all the same size, all leaping in the current. I realize that every one of these bubbles represents the things I do, the roles I play, the people I love. One is mothering, another is writing; there's gardening and working in the studio; there's reader, thinker, lover, friend; there are the facets of my personality, the person who is silly, sensitive, brash, hesitant. All the pieces of myself run in the same river and are the same size. There's not one that is larger or more important. Without all of the shining fragments, the river doesn't exist.

I lean back against the soft couch and nod, fist to mouth, narrowing my eyes as I think. I'm always the river, no matter whether the river is leaping with snow-melt or sun-baked into stagnant pools. I'm the sum of all my parts, and no part is more important than any other.

I begin to talk to people from a new part of myself. It's the part of me that noticed Dr. Kay picking up the Kleenex. It's the part of me that cuddled Jacob, the part that curls in Peter's arms. It's the part of me that responds to music with tears. It's tentative, unused. I begin to sense that there's a well of laughter as deep as the sorrow, but I haven't reached it yet. I'm still shedding my onion-like skins. When people ask how I'm doing, I tell the truth. I say that I'm having a hard time. People respond with surprise, and then they seem relieved, as if my honesty releases theirs. They are concerned, and ask me about myself. I love their concern. I let them give it to me and I take it gratefully, as if they're giving me back myself. I have never let anyone take care of me, not even when my baby died.

One day, I go to our small town to do the weekly errands. It is a bleak day in March. Parking lots are like craters, rimmed by diminishing banks of gravel-studded snow. Cars are salt-streaked. Christmas and Valentine's Day are long past; the stores are languishing

Shadow Child

between commercial holidays. The sky is grey, without promise of snow.

I talk to people everywhere. In the post office, the clerk tells me how her daughter in Alberta may move back east. She tells me how much she misses her grandchildren. At the co-op, the young manager and I talk about birds. I discover that he raises exotic chickens for a hobby. The bag-boy at Sobey's rescued a stray cat. He tells me in detail about how he took it to the vet for shots, how glossy it is now, how it sits on the windowsill waiting for him to come home. In the feed mill, I get a half-bag of horse feed and the man who sews it for me shows me how to work the sewing machine that's suspended from the rafters. His eyelashes are thick with grain dust. He tells me about the man who sewed his arm into a bag. I lean against the car in the parking lot by the liquor store and talk with the father of one of Jacob's friends. His wife has just left him. We talk about loneliness and dark nights. We discuss music, and how it helps us. It takes me all day to do what I usually would do in two hours.

Late that afternoon, I drive home on the familiar valley road. It snakes past grey barns and steel-roofed houses. Fields rise on either side, dead-brown grass quilting the swell of land. Spruce trees claw the white sky, whose monotony is broken by one black raven flying low. The landscape doesn't look bleak to me. It's stripped and pure. I can see its sinuous lines, clean as driftwood, scoured as bone.

Nothing seems more important than what I have done today. I am carrying my encounters the way an archeologist hoards findings. Each one is rich and, if examined, leads me to its connection with something else, so the boy's love for his cat and the man who rescued his friend from the sewing machine and the longing of a mother for her daughter and a man's naked pain come together like the hay and horsehair and pale grasses and appleblossom petals that birds weave into nests. I feel myself settling within the nest of these stories, as if I can trust the spirit that I've felt in all of them. It's still here. It's with me in the car, it stands stern in the silent fields. It's love, the rare and delicate thing that's been germinating in my own soul.

My centre has shifted from my head to my heart. It's like discovering a new source of life, a nourishment I never before tasted.

Therapy is a meandering road. Dr. Coates never chooses the path, but waits to see where I decide to go, and then helps me follow it. I have to make my own discoveries. I have to understand that I have the power to heal myself. I have to figure out where I'm injured, find the wound, probe it, clean it.

He's patient. He may have seen the wound all along, but he waits for me to find it.

I'm terrified, at every appointment. My heart begins to race in the elevator; I have tunnel vision as soon as I enter the outer office and my palms are sweaty as soon as I go into his consulting room. We usually begin our discussions with an examination of my fear. I am so afraid that I will fail. I write what I want to talk about on scraps of paper and hide them in my pocket. I thought they would make me safer, but gradually I realize that they do not. What I hide makes me vulnerable.

My terror of Dr. Coates makes me see how I approach life like an exam. I believe I've failed some essential and central examination. I try to succeed, to make up for this failure, but I never can. There is some judge who has condemned me, who watches me continue to fail, and is pleased. I'm being endlessly punished. I have committed a crime for which there is no redemption. Meanwhile, I'm desperate to create. I create gardens, cakes, events. I create photographs, articles, essays, prose. Afterwards, I never see what I've done, but only what I might have done. I see only potential that did not resolve itself into perfection.

Shadow Child

I can't talk about the baby for many sessions, and Dr. Coates doesn't ask me to. The baby still has no name, no shape, no soul, no sex. I use the expression "the baby" as a euphemism for our child's death. We're talking about things that make me guilty. He points at the waste basket and tells me that that is where guilt belongs. I am only just now beginning to realize that I'm haunted by guilt.

Dr. Coates keeps his expression without judgement, although his face registers surprise, acceptance, pleasure, interest. He watches me, puffing air into his cheeks. He leans forward. His eyes are suddenly more intent. He says to me, "You killed your baby, didn't you?"

I am deeply shocked. "No," I say, confused, outraged. "No!" I say again, my voice breaking. I begin to shake.

He says nothing.

I stare at him with my hands pressed against my mouth. I feel violated. I can't believe he has said this to me. I can't believe anyone could even think such a thing.

He says quietly, "You've been in prison for twenty years for a crime you didn't commit." He raises his eyebrows and waits. I have a vision of a huge bird cage. I see its bars bending around me and coming to an arch over my head. I've seen this cage before. I see the bars and how they are evenly spaced in front of my face. He watches me seeing this. He watches me understand that I am the one who has accused, and imprisoned, myself.

"That's a long time to be behind bars," he says. There's a questioning sound in his voice, as if he's wondering if I'm going to accept this hypothesis.

For the first time, I have rejected the idea that I'm responsible for my baby's death. For the first time, I've defended myself against my own hate.

"Do you think you killed your baby?" he asks.

I think about this for a long time. The words are so sharp,

knife-like. They imply intent; I see a hand rising and stabbing. Kill. Only an evil, terrible, deeply cruel human being would kill a baby.

"Yes," I say. I wonder if Peter, too, feels responsible; if this is why we can't talk together about the lost child. This child is our failure. The idea of this child stands between us, mother and father, and stares accusingly. We are the parents who could not protect our child from death. We are the parents who let our child die.

"Why did you think you killed your baby?" he asks. He uses the words deliberately. He wants me to begin to name things. Baby. Die. Stillbirth.

"I cross-country skiied right up until the birth. One afternoon Peter and I came down a steep run and I fell forward at the bottom. I couldn't get up for quite a while, and the next day I couldn't feel . . . him . . . kicking."

"The baby was a boy?"

I glance at him. I register that he's pointing out to me that I've never told him this. I take a long breath. "Yes. It was a boy. I don't know if it was that; it could have been some strong homeopathic vitamin pills that I didn't tell Dr. Kay I was taking. It never even occurred to me. They were just vitamins."

He nods. Now he cradles one arm with the other, his chin rests in his hand. He curls his fingers over his lower lip.

I look at the floor. My eyes slant towards the leg of his desk. My voice drops so he leans forward. "I was ambivalent. I wasn't sure, at first, if I wanted to be pregnant." I can hardly bear to say this. "I always thought he knew that, and so he decided not to be born." My mouth twists as I recognize a feeling I've repressed for so long that I've forgotten that I've been carrying it. I put the thought into words. The words are like pus pressed from a festering wound. They are alien and come in a rush. I can hardly believe I am saying them. "He didn't want me to be his mother. He thought that I wasn't ready to have children."

I think about this accusing, rejecting figure that has drifted within me. I wonder if I would have felt this way, all these years, if I had touched the perfect skin of my baby. If I had lifted his fingers, one by one. If I had seen what colour his hair was. If I had kissed him and known how real he was.

Dr. Coates watches me as I grip my mouth with my hand, staring at his wall.

I wonder if I would have understood, then, that nothing in my own mind could have had any effect on such a miracle, or that this tiny baby had no more control over his fate than killdeer eggs in the pasture, killed by spring snow.

I dream of horses. I have two horses in the dream; the one I've chosen to ride is small and scrawny. I keep looking at the other one, Minnie, and seeing how beautiful she is, how she moves with unconscious grace, how she fills her skin with healthy muscle and fat, how her mane shines, how big she is.

I catch this dream, just as I'm waking, and I reel it into my conscious mind and examine it as I lie in bed, my eyes not yet opened. It tells me that what I'm striving to achieve is thin and insubstantial compared with what I already have; that Minnie, the horse I've always had and am not riding, is who I already am and who I have always been.

One morning, I hear the red-winged blackbirds as I'm coming downstairs. My hand slides over the bannister, which is the colour of honey; the sun has come back from its exile behind the southern hill, and touches the blue walls of the new living-room. The room is both dark and light, balanced between delicacy and weight. The dark blue walls are strong, and support Jacob's red horse, whose vivid energy is free to rush from the dark background and emerge. The golden wood floor is like a field of oats standing against a storm sky. The big windows are painted cream white, and they frame the lucid spring morning as if the gleam of spruce needles and the glint of the rushing brook are part of this room.

The blackbirds are warbling so loudly, and there are so many of them, that I can hear the cacophonous blend of caws and cackles and fluting trills even before I slide back the glass door. There are hundreds of birds in the maples and their jubilant, juicy chatter claims the day, pulls everything into it, becomes the sound of granular snow, of limp grass and soggy goldenrod, of wet bark and mud. Of me.

That morning, I take the hay off my gardens and find a whole new season emerging, yellow-green daffodil spears, red tulip shoots. I stand with my hands loose at my sides. I put back my head and sniff the air. I feel as if I, too, am spearing up out of darkness. I feel a new, strange, unsmiling intensity. I know my own capacity for joy and sorrow, for deep feeling, but feel no necessity to mask my face. I'm no longer trying to fool anyone. Least of all myself. I'm beginning to understand that what I thought needed to be hidden is not what threatens me, but is rather the source of my strength.

I dream I'm on a wild beach. The sky is stormy. Behind me, windblown sand forms a dune whose root-bound lip is undercut. Straw-coloured grasses stream in the onshore wind, which carries foam from the cresting waves. I'm running anxiously along the beach with a man who looks like Dr. Coates. He's short and bearded. He doesn't interfere, but he keeps up with me. I'm watching the progress of a woman in a coracle. It's a frail craft, and she has my baby with her. She's a large, capable, attractive woman with dark hair. She wears flowery silk scarves, bangles, billowing skirts; she's direct, self-contained. I have trusted her with my baby. As I watch, I feel that what she's trying to do, taking my baby in this frail craft on a rough sea, is impossible, and yet I see that she will not give up. Suddenly the baby, who has been batting its fists, is underwater. I plunge into the water, snatch the baby. I'm not angry with the woman. I know that what she was trying to do was impossible. I hold the baby close against my chest. The instant I forgive the woman, the baby becomes distinct. Its face is red, and wrinkly. It is wise, stern. It is a boy.

My study, the room over the kitchen, is gradually becoming like my own reliquary, a box within which I keep my sacred objects, one of which is myself. I feel calm now when I duck through the low, warped wooden door and come into my attic-like room. Its shelves hold poetry whose words have become like familiar music. Oblique sunlight touches snakeskin, a dessicated spider, ferns taped to the attic door, beach stones, gourds, deer antlers, a bull's horn filled with feathers; folders and manila envelopes contain slide sheets, letters, sections of chapters. I lean over my light table examining slides of lilies and lilacs. A stamen thrusts from a day-lily's red-orange heart, culminating in a club-shaped knob, its anther; in the close-up photograph, I can see golden pollen. I move my loupe to a slide of blue lilacs; a monarch butterfly perches on them. Its black claws are like tiny hinges, clasping the clustered petals. Last summer I viewed these same slides and was sickened by them, seeing them through the distorting lens of perfectionism. Now I realize how scrawny is the horse of my desire, and how full and lustrous is the body of the horse I've always owned. I slowly dismount from the chosen horse and turn to embrace the one I've neglected, the one who has been patiently waiting for me to see her. I've been confusing myself, with my work. The source of my strength is not my work but myself, is not other people's belief in me but my own belief in myself and the knowlege that nothing I have found, so far, in the long process of uncovering my own detritus, has been as frightening as what I imagined.

On my work table are scissors, glue, photocopied manuscript pages, colour Xeroxes of photographs. I'm making dummy books to send out to publishers. My conviction is like a line that I'm casting out as I stand thigh-deep in my own determination. The line loops, tautens as it encounters the shock of weighted water whose depths it seeks. I'm prepared to reel it in empty and cast it out again.

I realize that I have to believe in my book, to fight for it. I'm not fighting for myself, for if the book isn't published, only it will die, not me. I am learning to see myself, as the green river that I imagined, to retain my vision of the equality of all the shining bubbles that make me who I am. I tell myself sternly that if the book isn't published, it won't be me who destroyed this particular bubble. It's simply the nature of the current, a compression of the banks, an errant fish rising; and I'll continue, unabated, leaping and twisting to the sea. But I have to believe in its beauty, the music which sang in me while I wrote it and that came from the rivers, the sky, and the earth. I have to fight with absolute conviction to make it live in the world, apart from me, to let it be part of other people, something that came from me but is not me.

I sense that I musn't do to my book what I did to our baby. Because I hid him, I lost sight of the fact that he was not me, not even a part of me, but was a separate soul, a precious and unique boy. Because I hid him, he has been lost within the twisted shapes of shame and guilt, has been extinguished by the cold breath of my belief that I caused his death.

If my book never resolves itself into the lovely thing I imagine, then when it dies, it will still be itself, whole, separate. I will

Shadow Child

remember its beauty with love; I won't bear the guilt of having destroyed it.

I'm coming to the skins of the onion that don't come off easily, the thick brown ones that protect the sweet and glistening inner layers; that are almost inseparable; that cling so tightly that the knife must slice, the thumb must peel.

I'm sitting next to Dr. Kay's desk looking at the pictures of his children. Now they all wear gowns and caps. There's even a grandchild. He's writing in my file and murmers to me to go ahead and talk, tell him what's wrong. I watch the curved nib of his black fountain pen scribbling across the paper. I've cancelled this appointment twice. "Go on," he says easily, in his amused, guarded British voice, still writing, and I feel anger rising in me like clouds racing from the southwest. "No," I say, "I'll wait for you to finish." "I can do two things at once," he says. "I can't," I say. He looks up, smiling, and then looks uneasy. "Why don't you smile?" he says. "I don't feel like smiling." He puts down his pen. I see his broad impassive face drop its own mask, see his prominent eyes widen. "I'm angry," I say. "You made me angry." He stares at me, dismayed, and then he pulls his chair closer to me, renouncing his desk. "Why? Tell me. What did I do?" He is not defensive; he urgently wants to know. I tell him how insulted I felt at my last physical examination, when he made a flippant remark. I tell him how, on another occasion, he turned away from me and laughed with another doctor, dismissing my fears. I tell him that he has never known me. I look at the wall. My mouth feels ugly, twisted, and I say that I am sick of smiling, sick of hiding how I feel. I am sick of hiding who I am. His eyes are open so wide I can see their whites. He explains, apologizes. We both know there is something beneath this that we haven't reached. I feel my heart flooding with hot grief, as if it is twenty years ago and I am sitting in this office and am still beautifully pregnant. "I can't get over the baby," I say. "It gets worse." Tears spill. "I can't talk about it without crying." I feel emotion rising in him. He turns back to his desk, picks up his pen and flips it end for end as if he's wedging himself open, as if he's raising the lid of himself and letting out what he's wanted me to see. He looks at me. There are tears in his eyes. "Do you think," he says intensely, "I have forgotten what it felt like when I couldn't find that heartbeat?" We hold each other's eyes. "Do you think I haven't tortured myself for what I could have done to save that baby?"

I look at him and I see something that I have never known. I see how he, too, has carried this pain, how it has made him who he is, how my son changed this man's life as well as mine and Peter's and Jacob's. I absorb the strange realization that I am not carrying this guilt alone. I look at my doctor's tear-filled eyes, and it's like sunrise allowing the shadowed shapes of a room to become simply and strongly what they are: a blue-painted chest of drawers, a rocking chair whose wicker seat has been frayed by cat's claws. The dark corner of my soul is lit by the fact that Dr. Kay mourned the little boy he felt he had let slip through his fingers. The blood-grief heaviness inside me begins to spin like galaxies, like life's nexus, and I feel my unknown child begin to come alive inside me. I hear the name I have buried for so long it comes up from the darkness soil-clotted and rusty.

Tate.

I'm moving more slowly. I'm observing my behaviour, learning to be myself the same way I learned to use my camera, when I carried a little notebook and carefully wrote down every variable, and then compared my slides with the F-stops and shutter speeds that produced them. Another summer bursts and flourishes and expires, with its northern violence, its bewildering rush; and as I continue my own slow growth through its blowing daisies, its

Shadow Child

breezes that smell of cows and river mud, its elusive and persistent fireflies, I evaluate myself. I'm learning how to connect my heart to my head, swiftly. I'm finding my own feelings, translating them into words, gestures, actions. I'm still setting myself free.

I try to do one thing at a time, and so I photograph another gardening book and am not concerned with whether or not there are weeds in the wild tangle of delphiniums and nasturtiums along the east side of our house. Meanwhile, my own book hovers in a nether region of possible acceptance at Penguin, whose editors say that they love the project but are having trouble making the numbers work. I spend much of the next winter trying to obtain outside funding to offset the high costs of colour reproduction, convincing more people of the book's value in the process. A momentum of collective energy is building; it seems unstoppable, and yet at every instant I must remember that it could crash to a halt.

I bear this uncertainty with increasing anxiety. Despite what I try to make myself believe, I know that my personal stakes are as high as they can possibly be. I know that I am trying to give birth to a new self, that I fear the consequences of failure. I try to move ahead steadily, trying to visualize neither success nor failure; I doggedly continue to write letters, make phone calls, explain, convince.

It's late afternoon on June first and wind harasses the grass, blowing it into disarray like young girls arriving at their first dance. I'm squatting in the garden, setting out broccoli plants, separating the clinging fibres of their intertwined roots, when Peter calls me to the phone. I wipe my muddy hands on my jeans, run up the steps of the deck, pick up the phone, which is already wet with clay from Peter's hands. It is my agent, and he tells me that Penguin has finally agreed to publish my book. He is elated. I take the phone away from my mouth so I can lean back and whoop at the ceiling. I run out to the deck and call Peter. My arms rise over my head and I'm both pulling the sudden rush of limitless space into myself, and sending my joy out into it, like casting sacred sand into the wind.

I stand in the wind, the blowing grasses, the tipping leaves, my face turned to the sky as I let my arms drop back behind me like the strong rudders that they are. Just at this moment, I don't need them; I don't need anything. I know how strong I am. I know my joy and my grief. Like pain and beauty, they make me balanced and augment one another. I feel that I'm at an end and a beginning. I know that in the seeds of my soul, a flower has opened that has been seeking the light for forty-six years.

For the next three months, I work on the book, and it grows, it becomes real. We name the book *Seeds of Another Summer*. It is no longer a dream that haunts me with its potential. It comes alive. As I work through the stages of its growth, it is taken by one person after another and becomes theirs to nurture and encourage. It feels like the bird that I shelter in my hands, and then let go at the barn door. It's something else that I've held briefly and then set free.

By the end of summer, I've finished my work. The book goes away, now, to be printed. Next spring, it will be something that anyone can hold in their hands, can take to bed, can absorb and possess. Like a child, it becomes part of a community, and passes beyond my control.

I have had no time to think about anything else. In June, I see Dr. Coates for the last time. We shake hands. I cry quietly most of the way home, the way I cried when I lay in bed absorbing the fact of Jacob's leaving for Vermont, or when Peter and I immigrated to Canada and left my parents beneath the willow tree of my childhood home. I'm mourning not the loss of these people, but the passing of a time in which we're in the same flux, we're absorbed in the same light and rain, our stories are concurrent. I mourn divergence, the breaking of context. I say to Dr. Coates, "I'm going to miss you," and he tells me the truth back, simply. "I'm going to miss you, too."

But it's not Dr. Coates I miss so much as the opportunity to attend to the petals that continue to unfold inside me, so slowly, that require a certain balance of fecund darkness and merciless light, and might wither if untended.

In early September, the morning after I've sent the final, completed book to the publisher, I sit beneath the hawthorne bush cradling my mug of breakfast coffee in both hands. The sun strikes the flowers with a cool light that seems to lift them from beneath and does not simmer in their chalices but trembles in the dew that bends them forward. I can smell autumn in the cold soil at my feet, where the sun hasn't yet penetrated. The blackflies are gone. The air is clear and still, and the swallows are flying higher, like kites whose strings will soon break. For the first time this year, the sun illuminated the dusty Italian earthenware plate that hangs in the northwest corner of the kitchen; the sun is slipping down the horizon, rising over the pond rather than the hilltop. I sense the ocean that's beyond the forest. I imagine the glittering light of its wild beaches, and I want to be there, propped against a smooth rock, head back, ankles crossed, arms folded. I want to be doing nothing. I want to listen to the boom and hiss of breaking waves for hours and hours.

I'm forty-six years old and I've accomplished what I've wanted to do since I was a child. Jacob is at art college in Halifax; he comes home now only to visit, so my active mothering years are over. I have time to do anything I want, but the sky, which seemed limitless in June, now seems strangely darkened and inaccessible. Finally a day has come which stretches before me like a dirt road meandering to the sea, but I don't feel like stretching and wandering down it. I'm not released from pressure. I put my head back against the wooden chair and look up into the leaves of the hawthorne. I examine my surprising lack of relief or sense of fulfillment. And then I realize that I'm still harbouring grief. It hasn't yet found form or expression. It's the one flower that did not bloom, whose petals are not now sending condensed dew into the fresh earthy air.

In the vacant hours of my first day without work, I glimpse something that's like a dream that I've scribbled down but haven't yet pondered. The final stage of mourning, which I never finished twenty-one years ago, has to begin now. I wonder how long it will take, what form it will take, if it will ever be finished.

I've brought my book to life. But there are the two sides of life: shaping and being shaped. My postponed grief beckons me, and now it is time to heed its call. I have to bring my hidden baby out of the shadows. I have to spread my arms and embrace the truth of what happened to us so long ago.

Epilogue

The hardest thing that I have yet done is to make my mouth shape the sound of his name. It is like the name of any baby; it's meant to be grown into, to be infused with memories so that it becomes the name for a whole personal history. *Jacob* is the sound of bicycle tires on gravel, of boys swatting June bugs with badminton racquets. It is the dry scratching of pencil lead, the rubble of Lego in a cardboard box. It's the clink of beer bottles, the sight of bare-chested teenage boys in kilts balancing barefoot on a snowball the size of a car. It's the sound of Dad's closet door opening stealthily, it's peanut butter and jam, it's swords and skulls, Shakespeare, Celtic mythology. *Jacob* gets fuller with time, ages like wine. I roll it in my mouth and can taste its vintage. But *Tate* is the sound of pain, and my heart is wrung every time I say it.

No one other than Peter or Jacob speaks of him, or knows his name. I discover that my aunts and uncles either never heard of our first child or have forgotten. Tate was finished and did not begin, and it was our own misplaced shame that truly killed this child. I begin to understand that no one has asked about our lost child, or what this experience was like, because Peter and I have not allowed them to.

I am now at the beginning of his beginning. I am his mother and I seek him, asking his forgiveness for having abandoned him for so long. I want him to join us in our community. I want to celebrate him. I want to tell him that I understand what he has given us. I want to speak of this baby with love. If his name brings only tears, then I choke on his memory, and turn away from him endlessly.

Jacob draws a Celtic knotwork for a memorial stone. He draws the tree of life. It has no beginning and no end; its branches bend down and seamlessly connect to its roots, so its strong trunk is encircled by the endless cycle of birth and death. Jacob loves the fact that he has a brother, even if he is not here any more. I call our neighbour Russell to ask if we can put a stone in the church-yard, although we are not members. I hear his voice, made grav-elly by eighty-five years of life, yet still lilting with the energy of muscle and bone; he says, "I forgot you had another one. Yes, indeed," he muses. "A little boy?" And I hear how my lost child is gathered into the fabric of place and so begins to come alive.

I dream that I'm in the cab of a truck with a woman I've just met. She is permeated with grief. Her face carries sadness like a scar. She talks about the baby she and her husband lost. I am struck by how frequently and easily she talks about it. I realize that I recog-nize myself; that her colour is mine; that grief makes her who she is, just as it makes me who I am. As she's getting out of the cab, I finally say to her that I, too, had a stillborn baby, and that someday we should talk about it. There's a sense of chaos; of pages fluttering that I'm trying to gather; of some event that we're going to, and that I'm preparing for both of us. I see the houses of my past—my Granny's house, my uncle's house—and they have no substance. They are stage settings, and I scratch them with my fingernails, amazed.

I remember how in earlier dreams, there were two of me and I killed one. Now there are two of me, and I am taking us somewhere together. We are going to talk. We will become dear friends. We will become one person.

I have talked, once or twice, to other parents who have lost babies at birth. Once unleashed, their grief is like a flood. I recognize the sandbags that they keep stacked between it and the rest of life. It does not recede, this flood. It is on the other side, always and forever. It is a peculiar grief, a pregnancy that never ends.

If the grief never ends, then I will embrace it. I'll understand that grief and love are as inseparable as light and dark, and that one does not exist without the other. I'll gather grief into myself and name it with love. I'll call it Tate.

I go to see Dr. Kay about some minor medical problem, but what we end up discussing is how I am going to heal my heart. He points to my chest and says that I'm harbouring a lost spirit. He wonders if perhaps we could have a funeral with our family. I can't bear this idea. We've waited too long. He asks me if I would talk to a woman who has lost a baby. He thinks we might be able to help each other. I agree and one day she calls me. We talk together on the phone over a period of several months. She tells me how the hospital arranged for a counsellor to be at her bedside before the baby was even born; how she was given a lock of hair, an imprint of the baby's foot, and put in touch with a support group, which encouraged her to make a scrapbook for her baby. She speaks of her baby by name, as often as she can, as if the name is the sound of love. She asks me eagerly if I have a scrapbook for Tate. I say I have nothing to put in it. She tells me I would be surprised, that I have more than I think.

I begin to search. I find a picture of myself pregnant. It's a black-and-white photograph that Peter took of me standing by a kerosene lamp naked, one arm cradling my egg-white belly. I've come across it over the years, when digging through a box of old photographs; I've always shuffled it away quickly, confused, not wanting to explain to anyone that this is not Jacob. I can find nothing else. I can't find a birth certificate, a death certificate. I can't find the sympathy cards. There are no petals from the flowers that Dr. Kay and his wife sent to the hospital. There's no footprint, no lock of hair. Worst of all, I have no memory. All I saw of my baby were his ashes. I remember the texture of them on my fingertips; not soft, but hard, what was irreducible.

I begin to understand that although I can't make a real scrapbook, Tate is part of our lives in another way. My sons lived at different times in the same womb, and their lives spiral around one another, as flexed and fluid as the self-embracing curl of an embryo. Jacob was honed in the crucible of Tate's loss. He was made and born in the fire of my passionate longing for a baby, my understanding of life's precariousness. Because of Tate, I understood the delicacy of Jacob's passage, I felt the grace of his remaining. As he grows, Jacob pulls Tate like a kite; Jacob runs through the deep grasses of his life, wind-blown and laughing, and his hand is pulled back over one shoulder, holding the string of his attachment to the brother who flies high overhead, barely visible but following, so that I can see him grow along with Jacob, and I can love the child, the boy, the man, he becomes.

These are the gifts the brothers give one another. I understand how Tate prepared the way for Jacob; I realize that he has never ceased to grow, in our hearts. I begin to heal when I see that this is Tate's life.

I dream that I'm in a classroom. A teacher asks us to draw a picture of a window. He has drawn the window and put it on the wall for us to copy. I cut myself a piece of paper. I notice that the other students have cut their papers into odd shapes, but I cut a perfect, careful square. I'm conscious of being a good student. I copy the window exactly as the teacher drew it. Suddenly, he looms over me and sternly tells me to leave. Then I'm sitting outside on concrete with my arms around my knees. I'm sure I've done something wrong. Around me is nothing but whiteness, emptiness. There are no boundaries. Only myself. The teacher calls me back. The class is gone. I am suddenly extremely angry. I insist on my rights. I demand to know why he asked me to leave. He says that he wanted to tell the class about my stillborn child and he wanted to protect me. I realize that he knows what happened. He knows why the baby died. I demand to know. Reluctantly he shows me a diagram. He shows me how the death was connected with my brain. I'm hungry to know. I want every detail. I'm not afraid.

After all the other dreams that have mapped my inner journey, this one is like a map of the entire territory. I ponder it until its meaning clarifies. I've been trying to be a perfect person—conscientious, compliant, obedient—in order to hide my belief that I am the kind of mother a baby would abandon, or who would kill her child. I draw a perfect square because I'm afraid that unleashing my creativity will reveal my darkness, my destructive nature, my evil spirit. Yet I assume that I will be punished, no matter how perfectly I behave, no matter how hard I try to hide the truth. In the white space, when everything but me is gone, I realize that I

305

have no choice but to embrace myself for comfort and for strength. I hold myself and gradually I feel as pure as the whiteness within which I'm suspended. Once I've done this, I have the courage to seek the teacher, to face the inner judge who has condemned me; only then can I demand justice. I will not be expelled for something I didn't do. I will not accept his explanation that I'm not being punished, only protected. I want the truth. I will face the reason the baby died, no matter how terrible this truth may be. But the dream-teacher's answer is enigmatic, and when I write this dream in my journal, I realize that he can't tell me why the baby died. He's only telling me that as long as I choose to repress Tate's memory, I'm responsible for keeping him in the shadows.

I have to accept the fact that no one knows, or will ever know, why the baby really died.

When the cat, who has slept on Jacob's bed for his entire childhood, his white-and-yellow cat who walked beside him through the fields with his tail erect and twitching, who settled on Jacob's leg, happily kneading his knee with prickly claws; when this cat in the prime of his years gets cancer of the tongue, Jacob asks why with rage.

When I'm in the prime of my childbearing years, when I'm supple and full-breasted, strong and healthy, when my hair still falls to my waist and is blonde and silky, I carry a perfect baby boy in my womb and he lives to full-term and then, perhaps the day before he might have arrived, just before he might have emerged with stretching arms, batting fists, kicking his long feet in the boundless space, blinking his eyes at the wondrous light, he dies.

I am forever changed. No promise is sacred to me or unbreakable. Every departure bears the weight of permanency. My soul is furrowed by the claws of rejection. No divine hands will ever

Shadow Child

hold me protectingly. No justice prevails. No one listens, and no one answers.

I've held death in my body. I've given birth to death. Death has stood by my bedside; he's filled my mind. He has walked with me, carrying his scythe. He's put his dark arms around me and held me close. I learn that he is present, always, everywhere, and so I reach deeper into the folds of life. I hold beauty like a butterfly on the back of my finger. I lean into the shadow-leaping moment of shared words, whisper at nighttime into my child's shining eyes. I see a new-born baby and I weep. My soul is wrung by the cruel and beautiful mystery, and I am both scarred and graced by the touch of deepest darkness.

This, too, I will call Tate.

I'm still on this leg of my journey. I can't yet look back and see the remembered landmarks that, when recollected in sequence, reveal the truth. I still cry when I speak my baby's name; perhaps I always will. The wound may never heal. Perhaps this is the nature of loss, and I must let my tears run like a river. Perhaps the empty place that this child might have inhabited is the shape of sorrow, is the sadness on my dream-friend's face. Perhaps I will bear my grief forever, thick and full as a pony's mane. No one ever *gets over* a child's loss. There's nothing to get over *to*. For the rest of my life, the birthday will come that reminds me of the years he did not live.

One morning, after I begin writing a book I call *Shadow Child*, I wake feeling a familiar emptiness; someone is missing. I go through the process of locating my family: my parents are still there, in my childhood home; Jake's at art college in Halifax; Peter's right next to me in bed. Then my mind flies to my desk and with it goes my heart, singing. Tate is there. That's where he is. Soon he'll be other places, too.

February 13, 1997.

It's Tate's twenty-second birthday. When darkness falls, I light a candle. I tell Peter that this is Tate's candle. The name still comes from my mouth awkwardly, my lips still warp slightly. The candle burns between us as we eat supper in our quiet farmhouse. In the snow-covered fields, coyotes trot steadily down into the swale by the brook, where the ice is swirled with blue whirlpools. Partridges hole up beneath the snow. Ice-covered branches creak as the poplar trees in the hedgerow shift like sleeping horses.

I leave the candle burning until it's time to go to bed. Peter goes upstairs first, and I lean on the table, cradling my chin in my elbows. I've turned off all the other lights, and shadows make the walls rock, as if I'm in a cradle, or held in cupped hands. I look into the candle's flame, and I feel the presence of the child whose soul lived within mine, for nine months. I'm not crying, but I'm smiling. I'm smiling the way I smiled at Jacob, when I tiptoed into his room just to watch him sleep.